IMAGES
of America

CENTREVILLE AND CHANTILLY

On the Cover: The Grigsby House, also known as Four Chimney House, in Centreville, was the headquarters of Confederate general Joseph Johnston during the winter of 1861 until March 1862. (Courtesy of the Library of Congress.)

IMAGES
of America

CENTREVILLE AND CHANTILLY

Mary Stachyra Lopez
Foreword by Eric Cox and Gina Richard

ARCADIA
PUBLISHING

ISBN 978-1-4671-2023-4

Published by Arcadia Publishing
Charleston, South Carolina

Printed in the United States of America

Library of Congress Control Number: 2013932832

For all general information, please contact Arcadia Publishing:
Telephone 843-853-2070
Fax 843-853-0044
E-mail sales@arcadiapublishing.com
For customer service and orders:
Toll-Free 1-888-313-2665

Visit us on the Internet at www.arcadiapublishing.com

*To the people of Centreville and Chantilly
and all who treasure this area's rich history*

Contents

FOREWORD

We met and started dating when we were 16-year-old students at Herndon High School. When we were 18, we got married and started Cox Farms with Eric's brother in 1972.

We bought our Centreville farm and moved here in March 1979. Of course, Centreville's history goes back centuries, but in 1979, it was still a small, quiet spot in what folks from more established areas like Herndon, Reston, and Vienna considered "the boonies." At that time, the bankers and business advisors all told us that "nobody will ever travel that far out . . . you'll never get any customers way out there."

That fall, a few local teachers brought their classes out to the farm to pick pumpkins and go for a hayride. From there, the school business started to grow, and on one weekend in 1983, we had our first "Fall Festival." And the rest, as they say, is history! Over the next 20 years, we went from a few hundred visitors per season to 10,000 visitors per season to more than 10,000 visitors in a single day during the peak of our season.

We purchased the farm from the Lintons, whose parents moved here in 1922. When the oldest, Alva, was married, his bride insisted they move out of his childhood home and move into a new trailer home, parked only yards from the old house. They lived there until they sold us the farm, and that trailer—eventually modified with several additions over the past 30-plus years—is where we moved in, raised our three children, and still live today.

Now, four of our grandchildren are growing up here on the farm. As our business and our family have grown over the decades, so has our community; we have marveled at the changes taking place around us. We have so enjoyed being part of it.

It is a pleasure to revisit the "olden days," to reminisce about what used to be and to appreciate the transformation. Mary Stachyra Lopez's work takes us on a beautiful and fascinating adventure, one that is well worth taking for curious locals (natives and transplants alike), history buffs, and anyone interested in witnessing the remarkable evolution of our town. We're sure you'll enjoy the ride.

In community,

Eric Cox and Gina Richard
Owners and founders, Cox Farms

ACKNOWLEDGMENTS

I am deeply grateful for all who took the time to assist me. I would like to thank the staff at the Virginia Room at the Fairfax County Public Library, particularly Elaine McHale, who scanned many photographs. Without the photographs and resources in the Virginia Room, this book would not have been possible. The Library of Congress digital photograph collection and work by local historians were also key in making this book a reality. A thank-you goes to the Cox family for graciously agreeing to write the foreword to my book. Thanks to the many people who spoke with me about their memories of the area, suggested resources, or shared photographs, including, but not limited to: Cheryl Repetti and the Historic Centreville Society, Lee Hubbard, Ralph Duke, Andy Bittner, Aaron Cox, and the staff at Centreville Elementary School. I wish that I could have included every photograph and memory that was shared with me. My gratitude also goes to my editors at Arcadia Publishing, Lissie Cain and Rebekah Collinsworth, for their patience and assistance as the scope of this work expanded. Last but not least, a thank-you is owed to my husband, Mauricio Lopez, for getting me through this project.

INTRODUCTION

Centreville's roots go back to a tiny village known as Newgate. After purchasing land over a number of years, by the early 1740s, Willoughby Newton had acquired about 6,400 acres, which he leased to farmers. Around that time, a man named William Carr Lane operated a store and built a tavern. Lane was possibly involved in selling convict labor, and the convicts may have come from Newgate Prison in England, and the tavern became known as "the Newgate Tavern." In turn, the surrounding village then took on the name "Newgate." Hoping for more settlers, the villagers sought to have the Virginia General Assembly charter a town in 1792, and, hoping to rid themselves of the connotations surrounding the name Newgate, they renamed the area "Centreville."

Chantilly's name has roots that are, perhaps, a bit more elegant. The community was named after the home of Charles and Cornelia Stuart. Cornelia was the granddaughter of Richard Henry Lee, who signed the Declaration of Independence, and she decided to name her home after Lee's plantation, Chantilly, in Westmoreland County. The land was situated on property originally owned by Cornelia's parents, Henrietta and George Richard Lee Turberville. Chantilly was one of several beautiful colonial plantations in the area, including Leeton, the property owned by Cornelia's parents that was demolished in 1960 to make way for Dulles International Airport; and Sully, a home built by Northern Virginia's first congressman, Richard Bland Lee, which is a historic park today.

Today, much of the farmland is gone, and both Centreville and Chantilly are sprawling communities filled with town houses, condos, and industrial buildings. Yet, they retain their rich history, which was shaped in so many ways by the Civil War.

Take, for instance, the tiny Ox Hill Battlefield Park near Chantilly, across from the Fairfax Towne Center shopping plaza; 1,500 soldiers died or were wounded as they fought over terrain of about 500 acres in August 1862. Only 4.8 acres have been set aside to remember the fighting that day, which the Union army called the Battle of Chantilly. Union general Isaac Stevens and major general Phillip Kearny met their deaths as they fought through a tumultuous storm.

In Centreville, the Mount Gilead Home is a reminder of how Centreville was once occupied by about 40,000 Confederate troops. A local tradition maintains that Gen. Joseph E. Johnston set up his personal headquarters at Mount Gilead, and his army headquarters was just a short walk away, at the Four Chimney House. Down the road from the Mount Gilead Home is the Old Stone Church that housed a Methodist Episcopal congregation at the time of the war. After the First and Second Battles of Manassas, the church became a makeshift hospital to treat wounded soldiers.

The battles of Manassas had attracted both armies to the village of Centreville and the surrounding area due to its high terrain and easy access to roads leading to Washington. The once-sleepy rural village—whose main attraction was Newgate Tavern, which was visited by George Washington during his travels—turned into a scene of destruction and devastation. Even half a century later, the impact was still visible.

"Centreville is not a stirring place. It does not feel a single busy throb," a correspondent from the *Washington Star* wrote in 1914. "It is stagnant and drowsy. Some men will say 'it's dead.' If ever a village was killed in war it was Centreville. Perhaps it was choked by smoke of burning powder or smothered by the sulphurous gas from guns; perhaps it was blighted by the rain of shell or overcome by the horrors it saw. Today, it bears wounds and scars. Its wounds are bullet-pitted walls and shot-riven trees. Its scars are sunken graves and vine-veiled redoubts."

New life would come back to Centreville and Chantilly with a new century. New families, in time, replaced the ones that had fled after the Civil War, lured by the prospect of a country home with access to the metropolitan area, thanks to the invention of the automobile. Enterprising men and women put up gas stations, restaurants, and lodging for tourists along Route 50 and Lee Highway.

With the improved roads, came more commuters and the trappings of suburbia, such as the home of Roger Spindle, who purchased a Sears catalog kit home in 1934 and also built a garage and driveway. The home is a rare example of a popular kit house preserved in almost the same condition since it was built. Subdivisions popped up near Lee Highway in Centreville as early as 1938, including the Katherine T. Moore subdivision, which was later demolished and replaced with Little Rocky Run, and Ratcliffe subdivision.

The area even attracted Ellanor C. Lawrence, the wife of *US News & World Report* publisher and columnist David Lawrence. She purchased a country estate at a historic farm called Walney and also bought land including Cabell's Mill and Middlegate House. The couple had many notable visitors, including Franklin and Eleanor Roosevelt. David Lawrence donated the land to Fairfax County as a park upon Ellanor's death.

Chantilly was further transformed by the addition of Dulles International Airport. Workers poured into the area to build the airport, which opened after four years of construction, in 1962, on 10,000 acres of land. Tens of thousands of people used the airport in its first year, a symbol of the many changes to come in this area, which had once been filled with verdant farmland.

One

Civil War

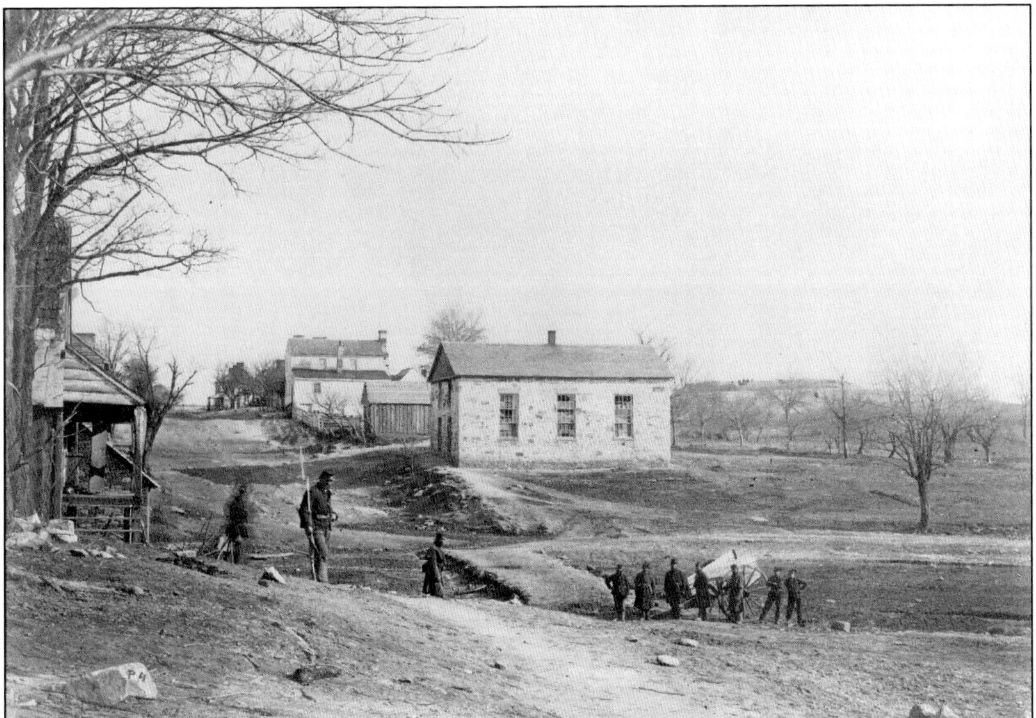

Centreville, like most precincts in Fairfax County, voted overwhelmingly for secession from the United States on May 23, 1861. The local vote was 105-0; it was taken in public after Virginia had already seceded from the Union. President Lincoln had already called for volunteers to put down the rebellion that had begun the month before with Confederate troops bombarding Fort Sumter. In the ensuing years, the Civil War would devastate Centreville, as both armies occupied the village. (Courtesy of the Library of Congress.)

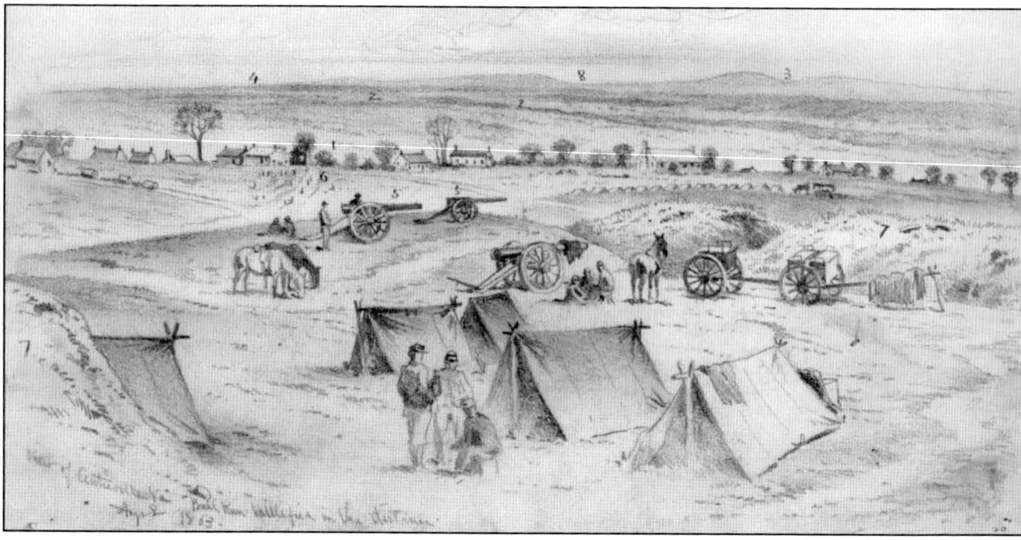

Civilians traveled to Centreville on foot and in carriages to watch in expectation of the fighting that would unfold on July 21, 1861. *London Times* correspondent William Howard Russell wrote, "The spectators were all excited, and a lady with an opera glass who was near me was quite beside herself when an unusually heavy discharge roused the current of her blood—'That is splendid, Oh my! Is that not first rate? I guess we will be in Richmond to-morrow.'" Instead, the civilians—who included Rhode Island governor William Sprague, Sens. Jim Lane of Kansas, Ben Wade of Ohio, Henry Wilson of Massachusetts, and Lafayette Foster of Connecticut; and Congressmen Elihu Washburne of Illinois and Alfred Ely of New York—had to beat a hasty retreat as the Union troops fell back. (Both, courtesy of the Library of Congress.)

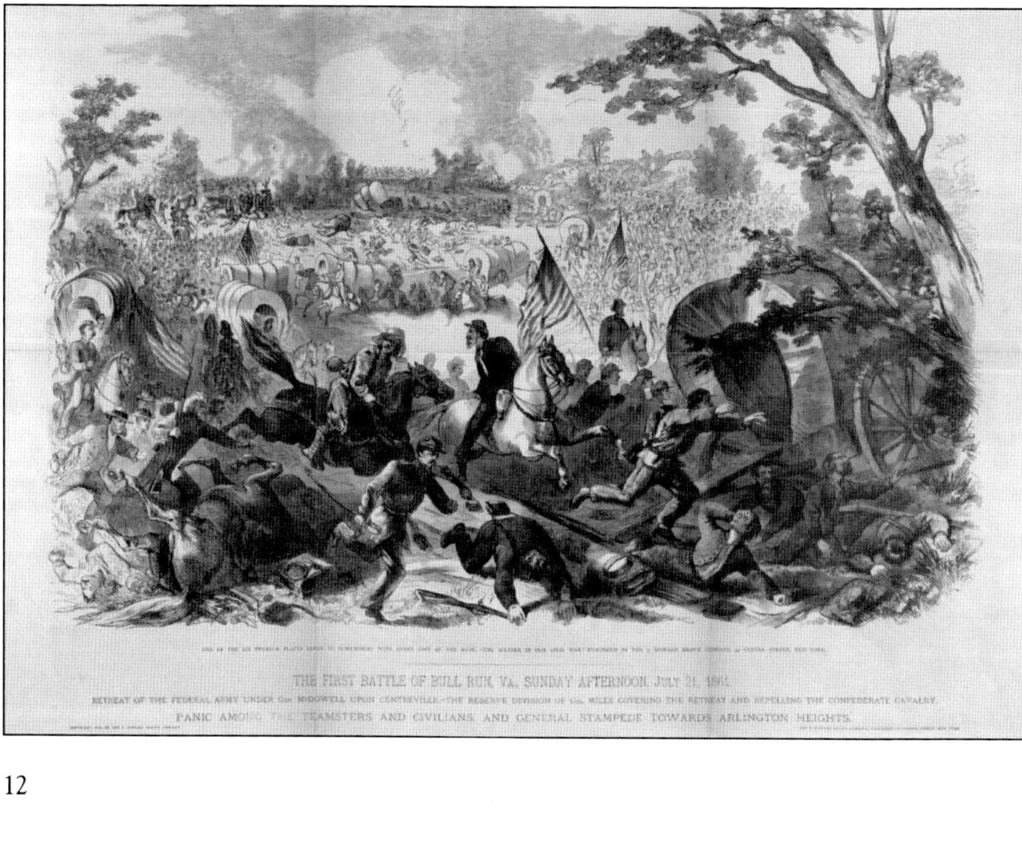

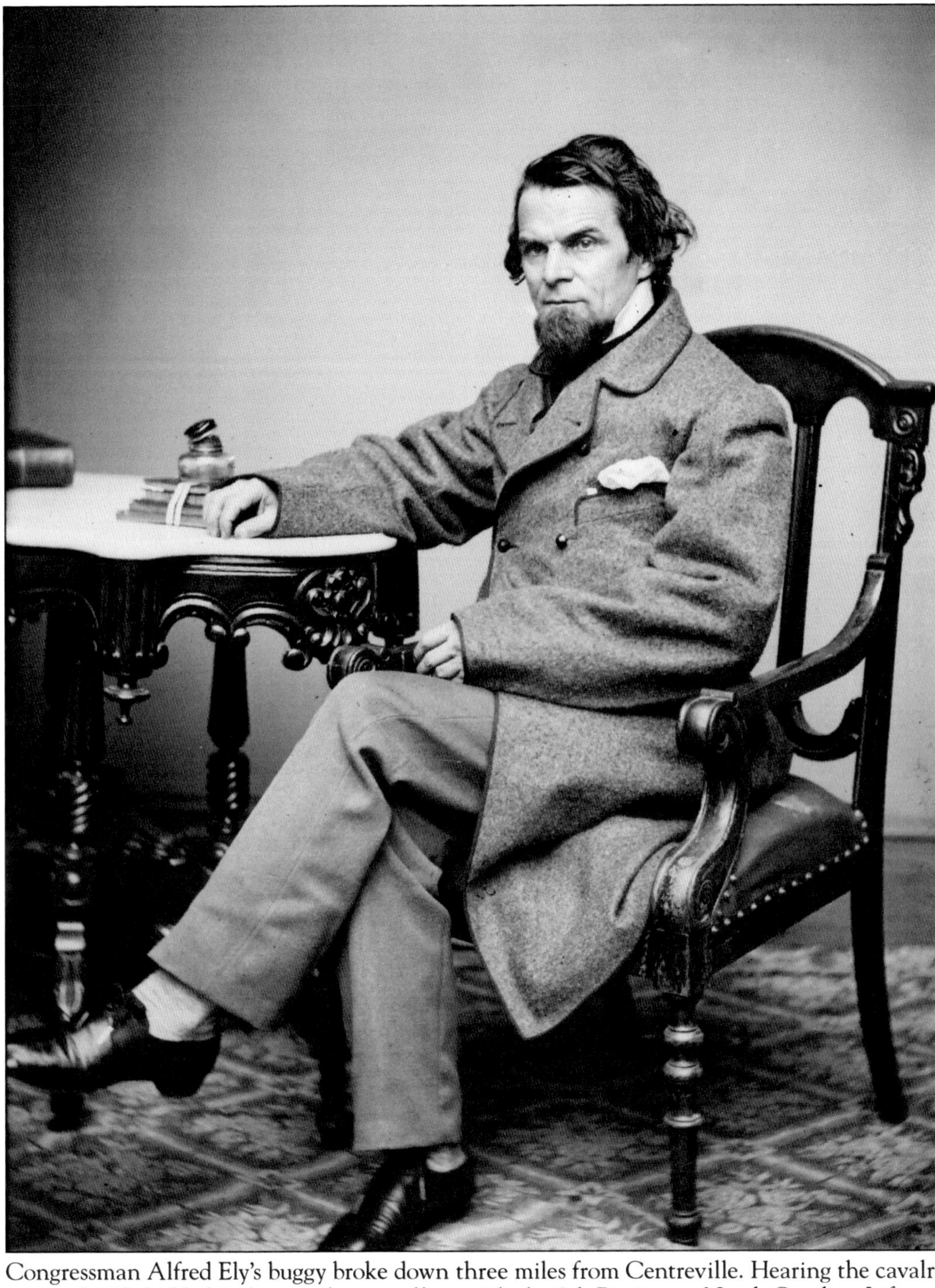

Congressman Alfred Ely's buggy broke down three miles from Centreville. Hearing the cavalry approach, Ely hid behind a tree, but an officer with the 8th Regiment, North Carolina Infantry spotted him and demanded identification, according to an account that appeared in the *New York Times*. After Ely explained who he was, the soldier said, "Mr. Ely, put your foot in my stirrup and get up behind me—I am going to take you to Richmond." Ely was imprisoned for five months. (Courtesy of the Library of Congress.)

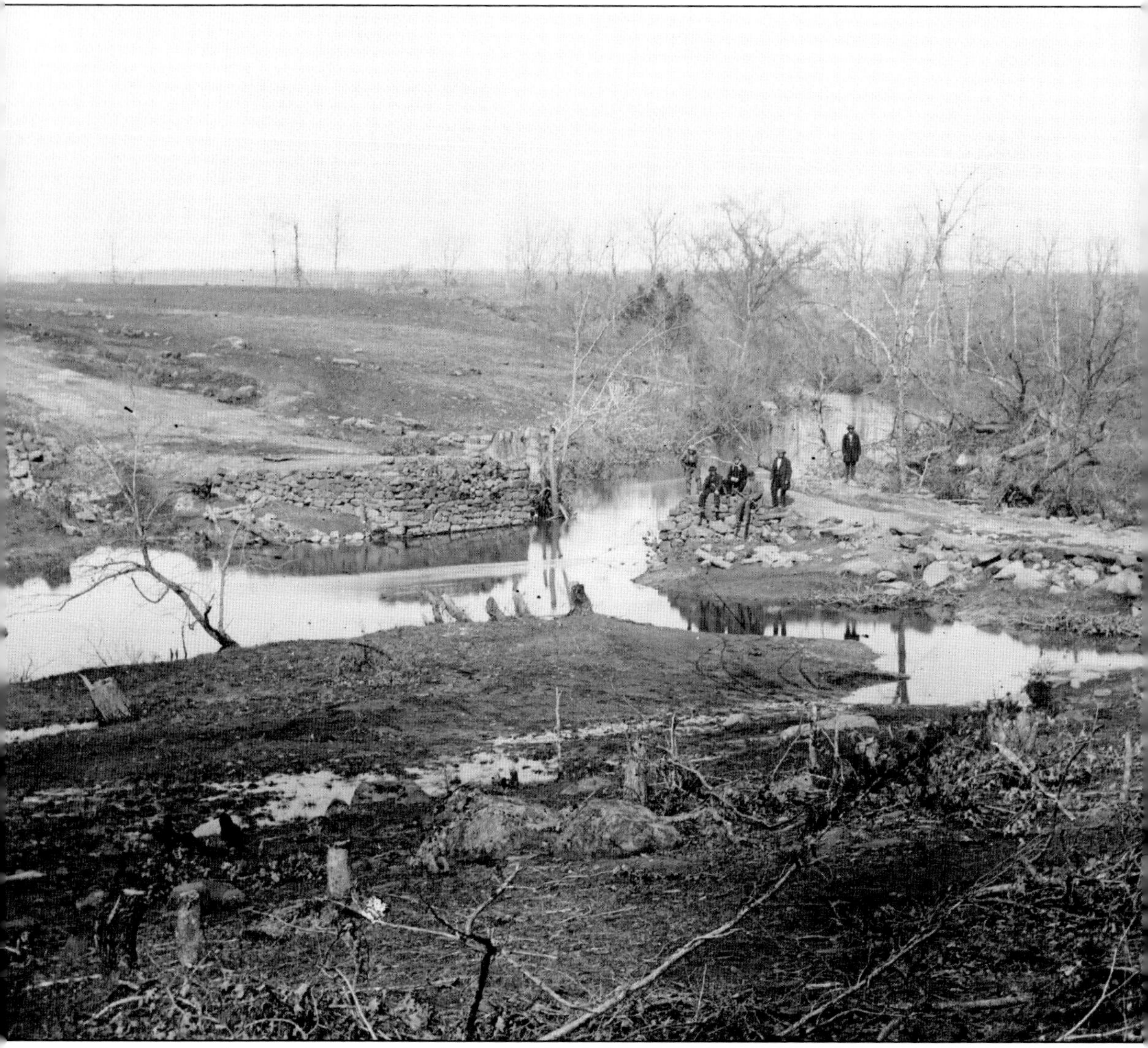

This picture shows a destroyed bridge at Cub Run. Panic broke out at Cub Run on July 21 after a wagon overturned and blocked the soldiers from passing. Men left their wagons and let their horses free; wounded men were left unassisted. (Courtesy of the Library of Congress.)

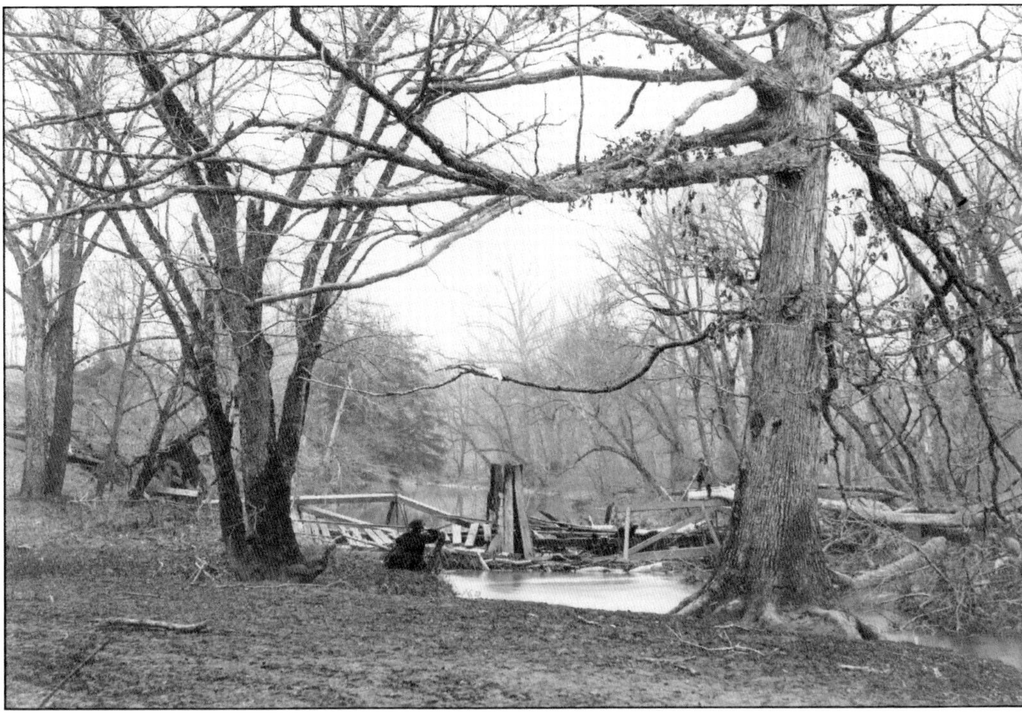

The skirmish at Blackburn's Ford was in some ways a prelude to the Union defeat at First Manassas. On July 18, 1861, the outnumbered Confederates managed to repulse thousands of troops led by Brig. Gen. Irvin McDowell. The ruins of the bridge built for the military railroad in the winter after First Manassas are pictured here. After the battle, the Union army returned to Centreville and set up hospitals for the wounded. The two armies met a few days later at First Manassas. Route 28 in Centreville, pictured below in 1968, is looking toward the Prince William County border. It is near the historic site of Blackburn's Ford. (Above, courtesy of the Library of Congress; below, courtesy of the Fairfax County Public Library Photographic Archive.)

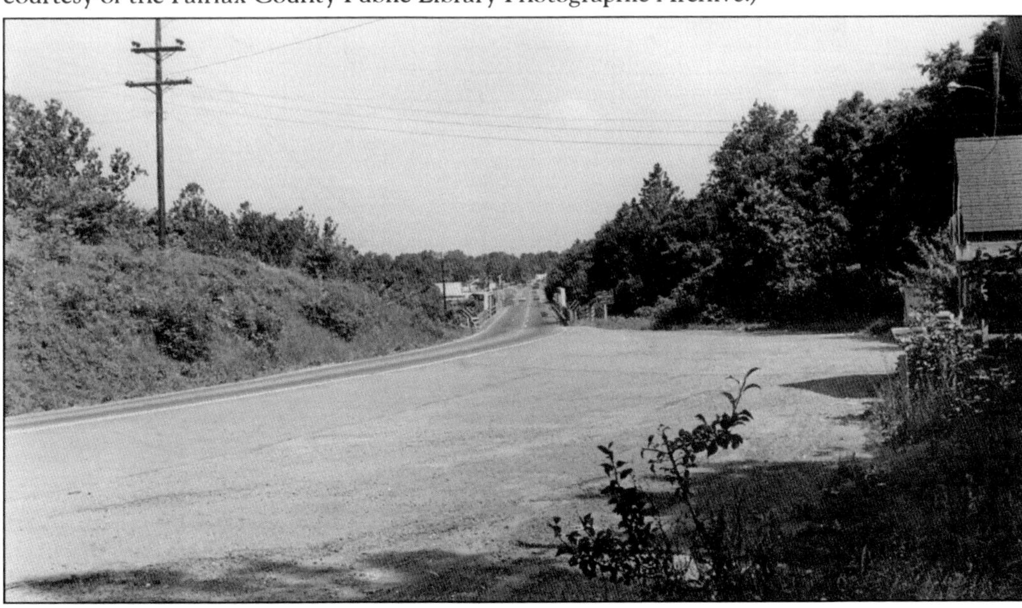

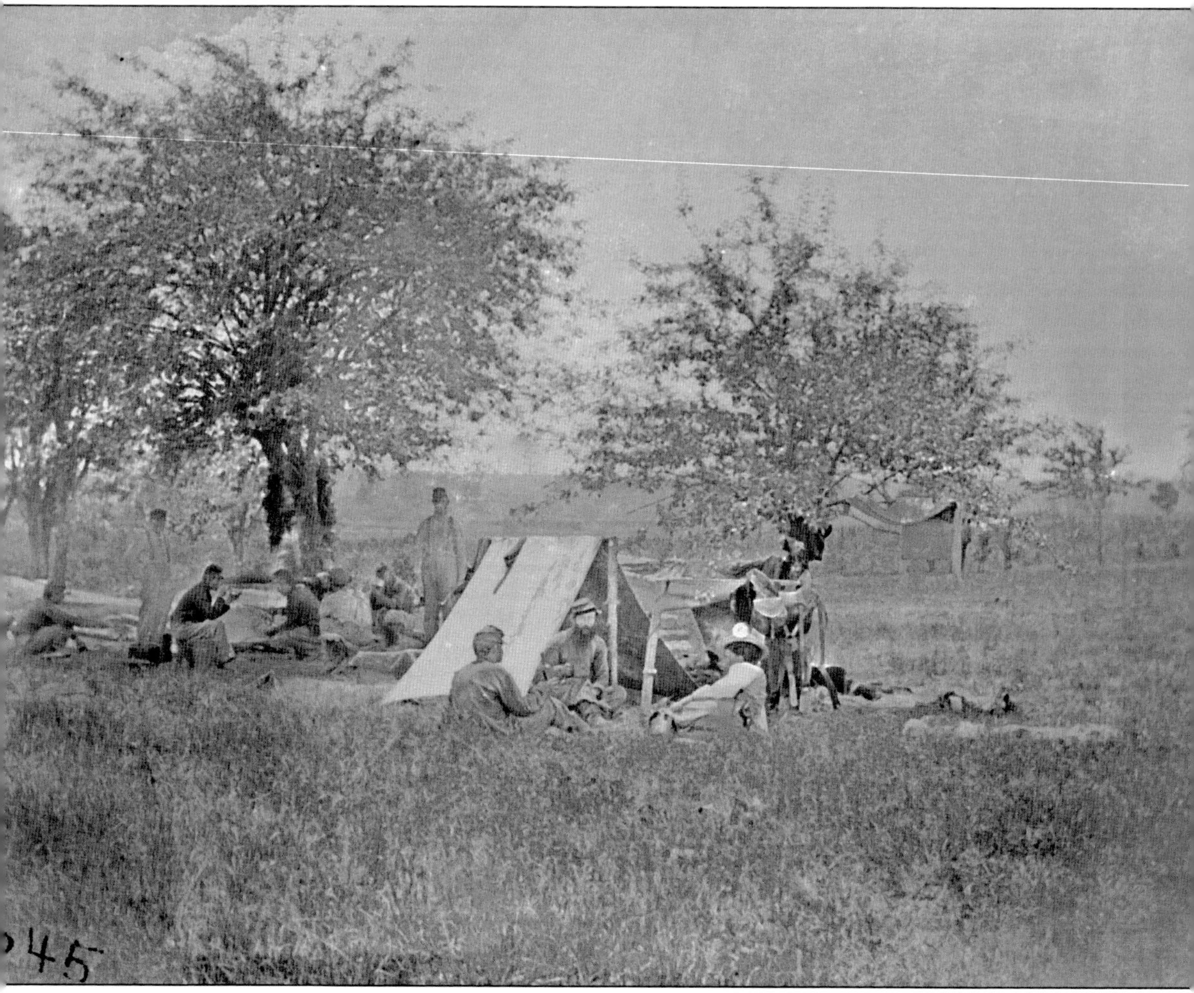

Pictured is the Federal encampment at Blackburn's Ford on Bull Run on July 4, 1862. The site of fighting at Blackburn's Ford occurred by the present-day border of Centreville and Prince William County. (Courtesy of the Library of Congress.)

Union general Irvin McDowell marched to Centreville on July 18, 1861, under pressure from President Lincoln to put a quick end to the war. He set up his headquarters in the Grigsby House. McDowell spent two days in the home, preparing his strategy for the coming battle at Manassas. His troops were soundly defeated by the Confederates and retreated to Washington. (Courtesy of the Library of Congress.)

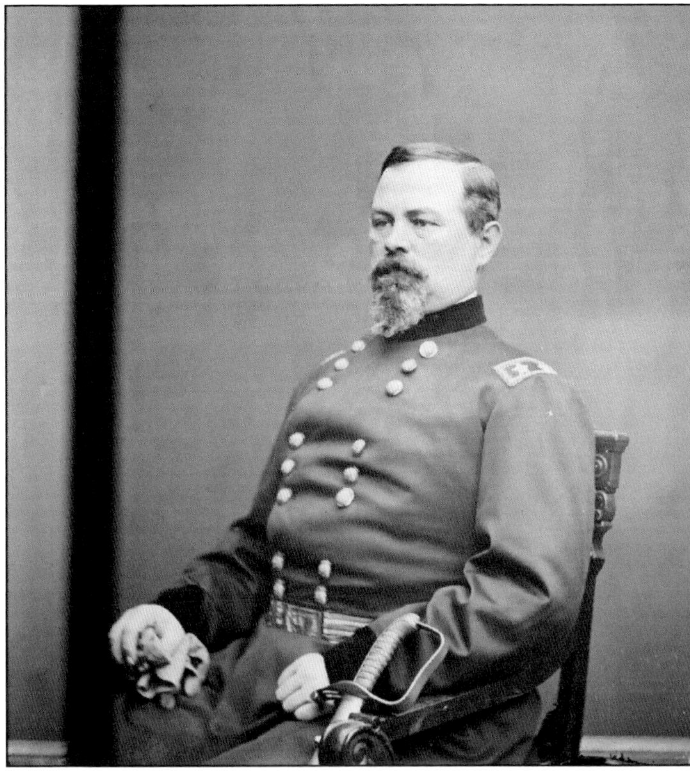

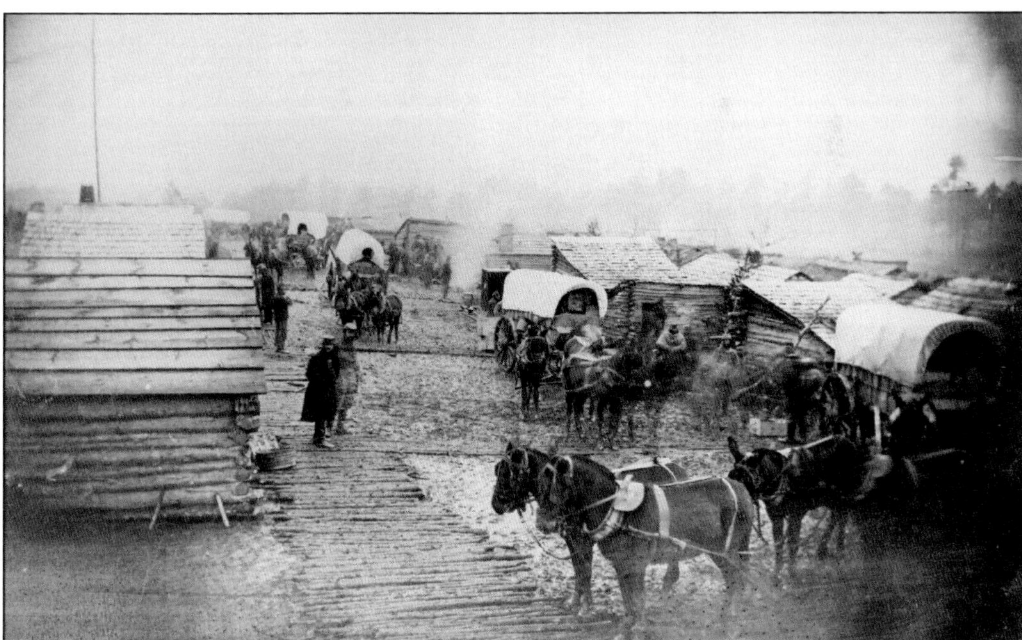

This picture shows the Union camp at Centreville, including horses, wagons, and log cabins. The village was valuable for the military due to its high ground and easy access to road networks and nearby military railroads. (Courtesy of the Library of Congress.)

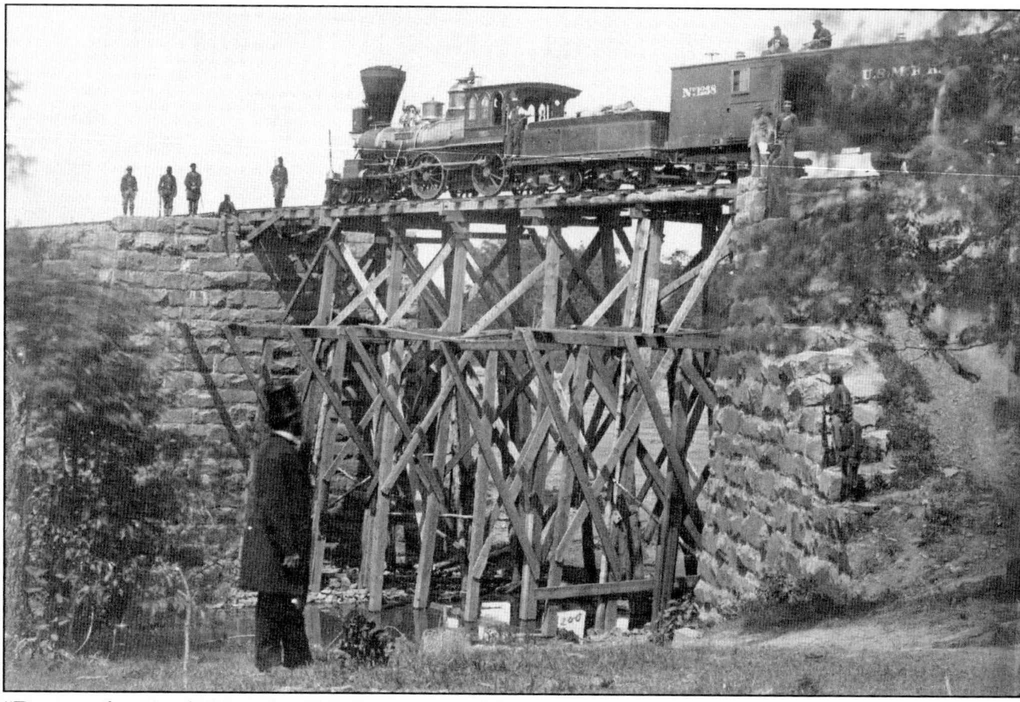

"During the Civil War, the O&A was arguably the most fought over railroad in Virginia. The railroad provided the most direct all rail route from Washington to Richmond and the Orange and Alexandria would serve as a main highway for the troops to march on and be supplied," according to historian Chuck Siegel (nvcc.edu/home/csiegel/). "In moving down the O&A to the Virginia Central at Gordonsville, the Union army would be taking the quickest land route to Richmond as well as cutting Southern communications with the Shenandoah Valley. The North almost relentlessly pursued this course of action for the first three years of the War." Pictured below is wreckage in Manassas caused by retreating Confederates in March 1862. (Both, courtesy of the Library of Congress.)

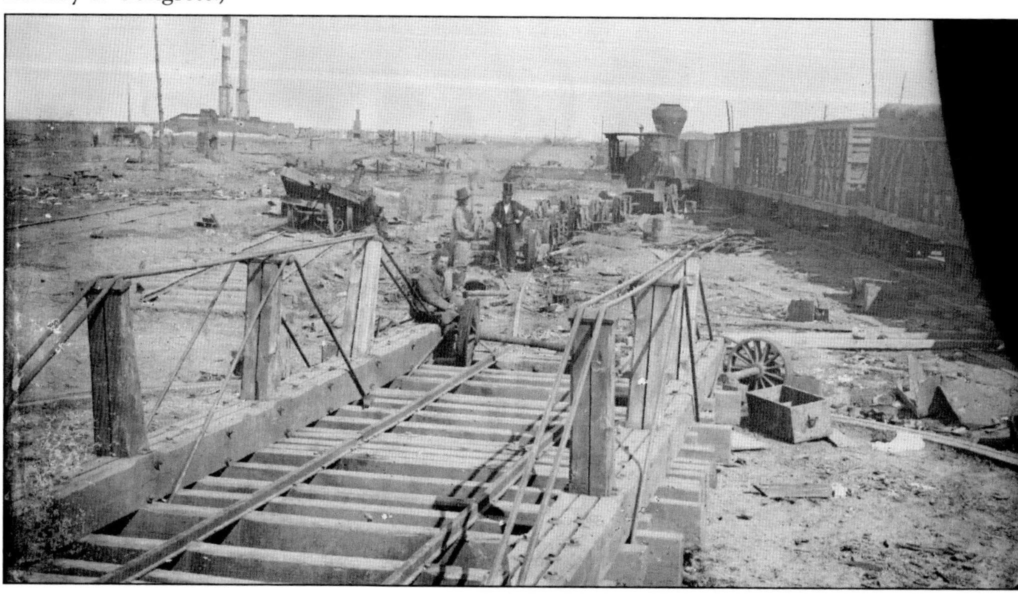

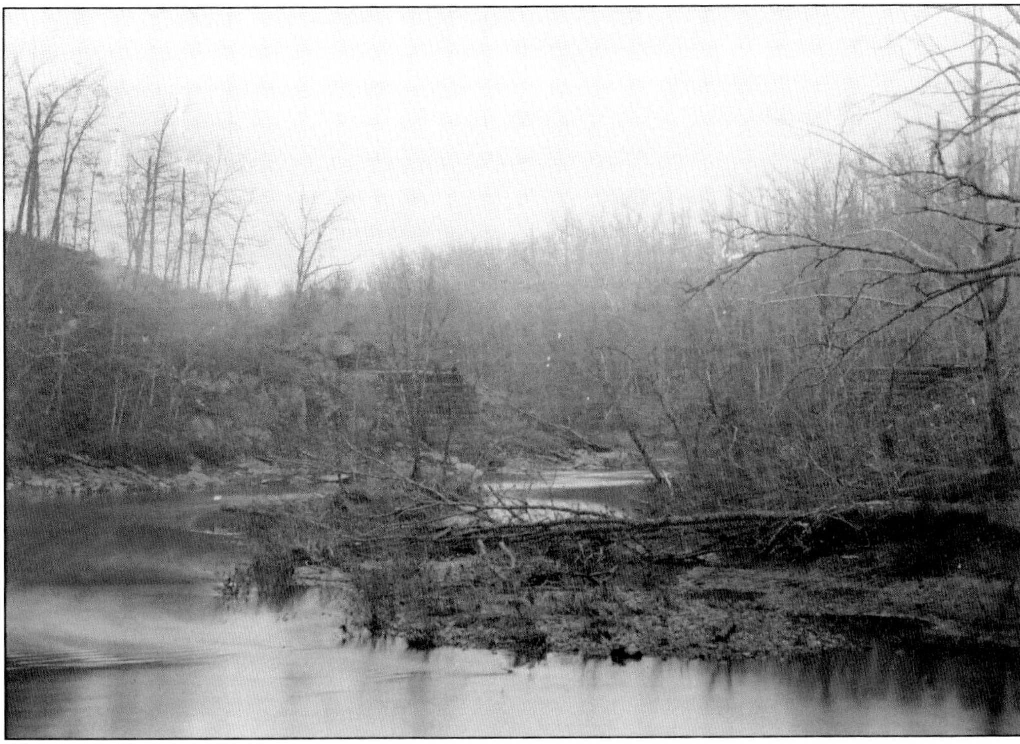

The crossing of the Orange & Alexandria Railroad is shown here at Bull Run. The stones were cut no less than 10 inches thick, many surviving despite the Confederate army and nature repeatedly destroying the bridges here. (Both, courtesy of the Library of Congress.)

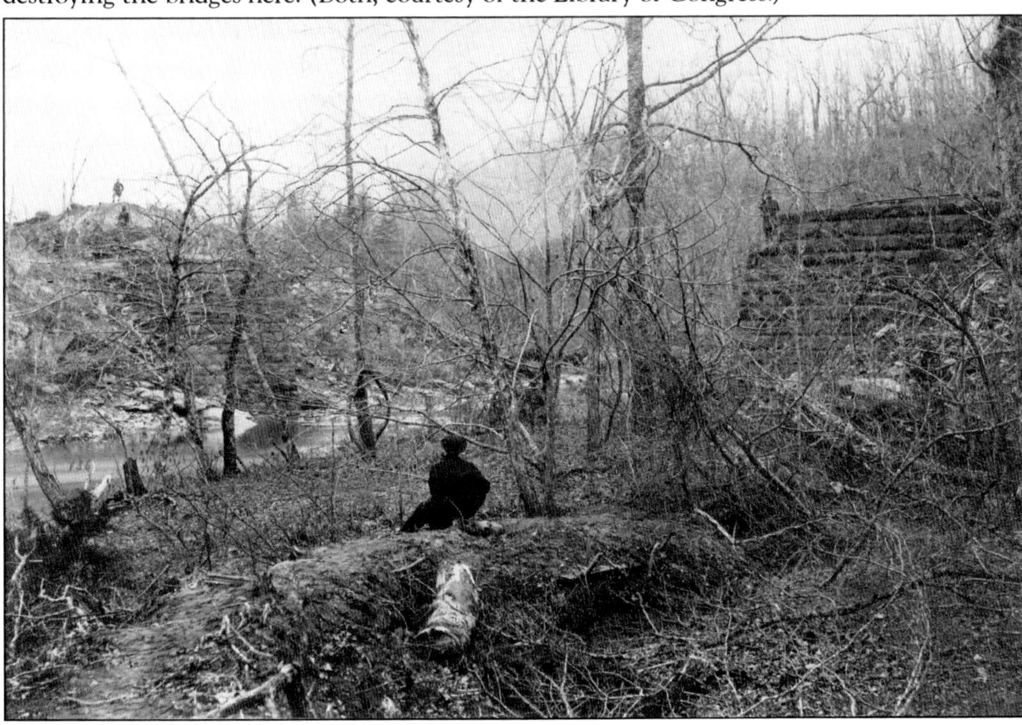

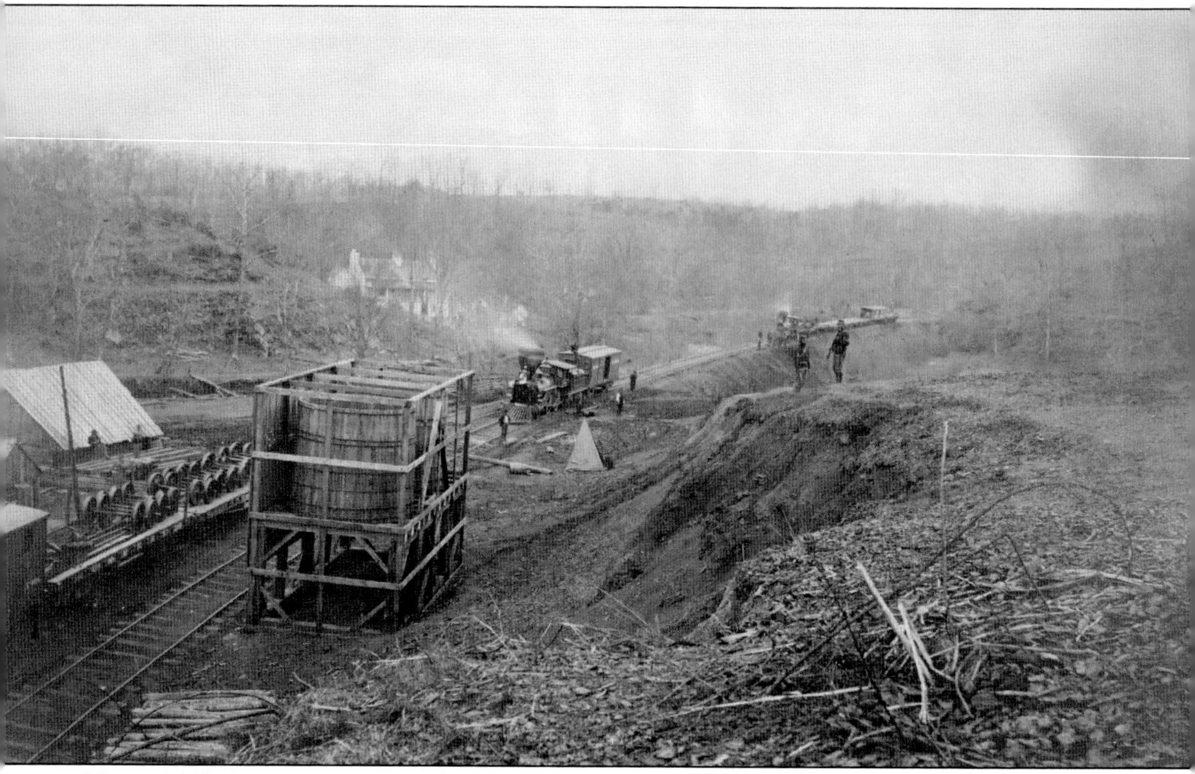

Union Mills Station was situated a few miles outside of Centreville. During the Civil War, it transformed from a quiet rural area into a bustling center of military activity. "During the first year of the war, the Confederates made the Union Mills area part of the defense line that ran from Centreville to Manassas Junction. After the Confederates departed in early 1862, Federal troops were stationed at Union Mills to protect the Bull Run railroad bridge (destroyed and rebuilt seven times during the war) and they expanded the fortifications and constructed a number of new ones," wrote Karl Reiner in *Remembering Fairfax County, Virginia.* (Courtesy Library of Congress.)

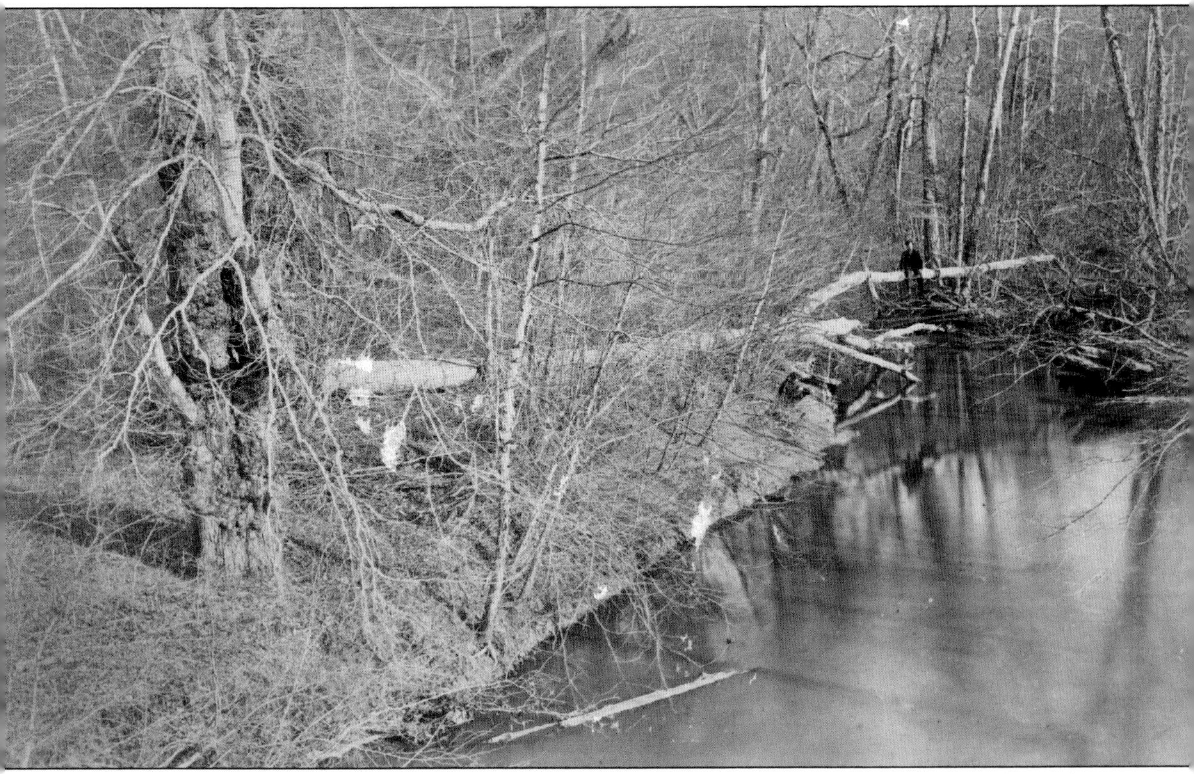

This photograph shows two men sitting on and near a fallen tree over Pope's Head Creek in nearby Clifton, Virginia. The tree was located close to a destroyed railroad bridge on the Orange & Alexandria Railroad. (Courtesy of the Library of Congress.)

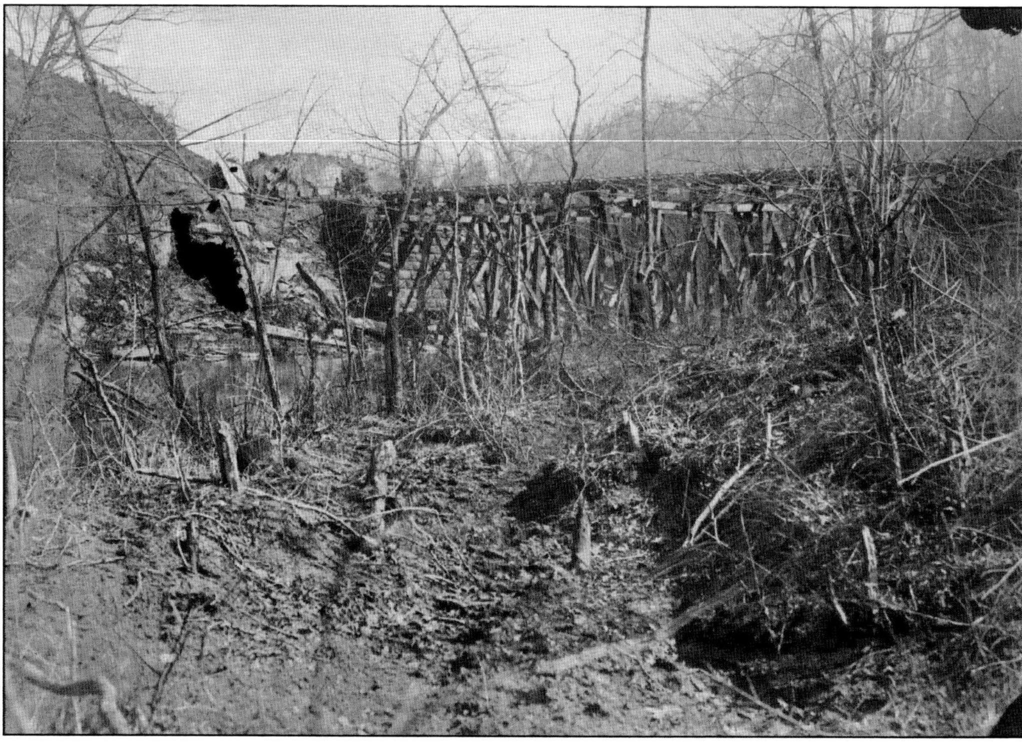

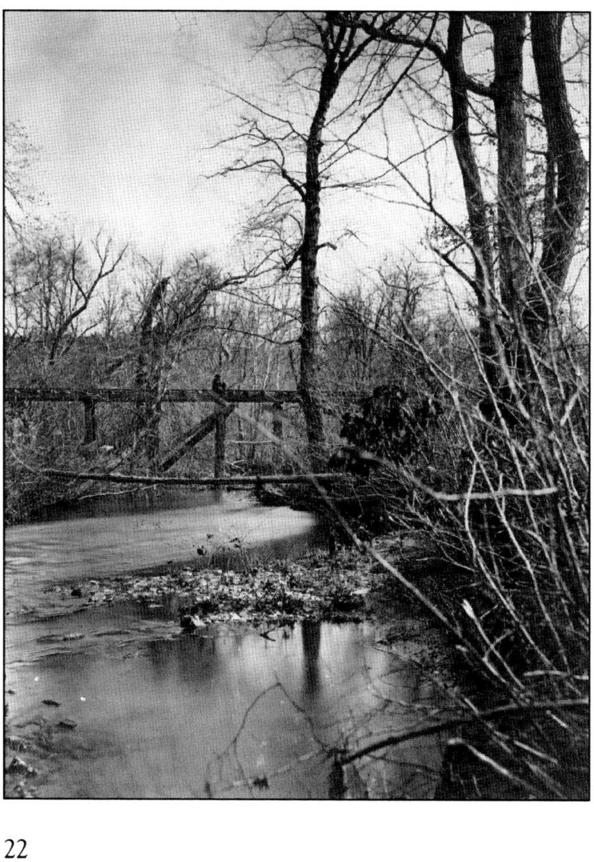

These are photographs of the Orange & Alexandria Railroad's trestle bridge across Bull Run as it appeared before the freshet of April 1863 (above), and near a burned bridge over Pope's Head, near Devereaux Station, Clifton (left). (Both, courtesy of the Library of Congress.)

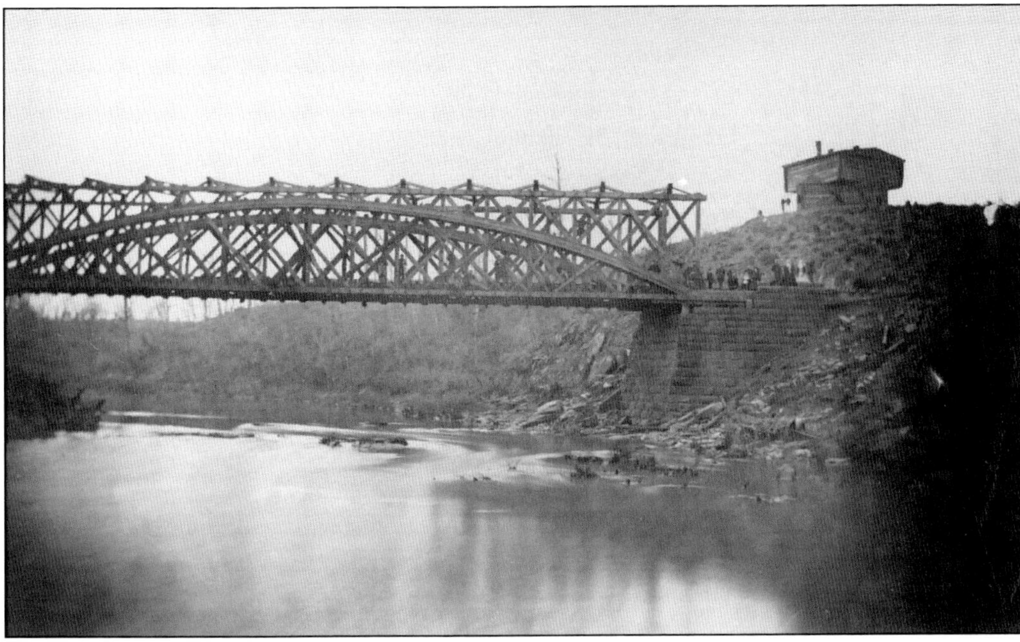

The Orange & Alexandria Railroad, pictured in both images, crossed Bull Run. The railroad line was part of what made Centreville and the surrounding area such a desirable place for both sides to try to capture during the Civil War. (Both, courtesy of the Library of Congress.)

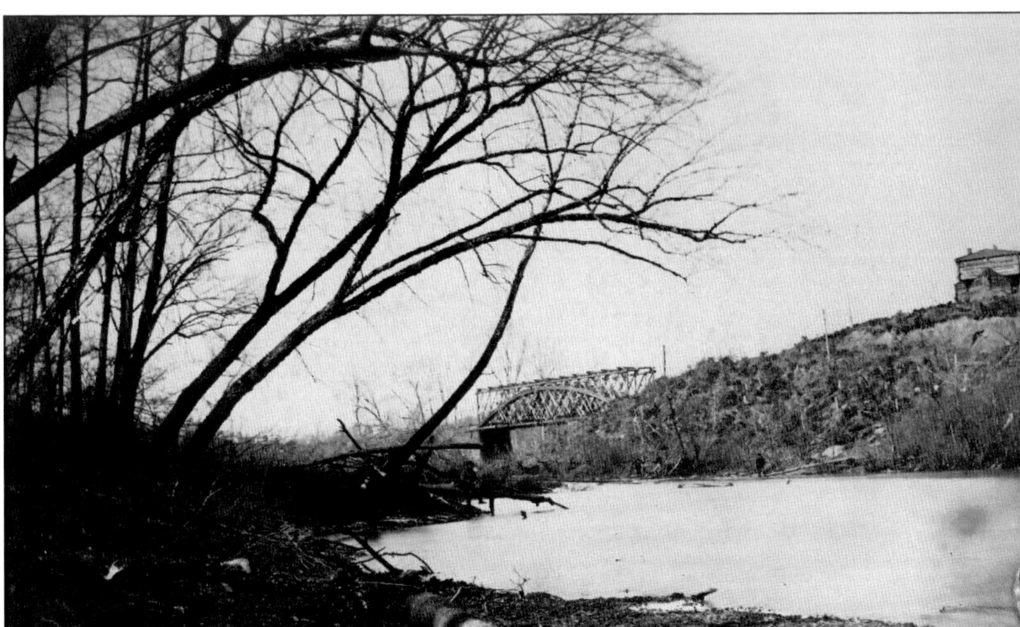

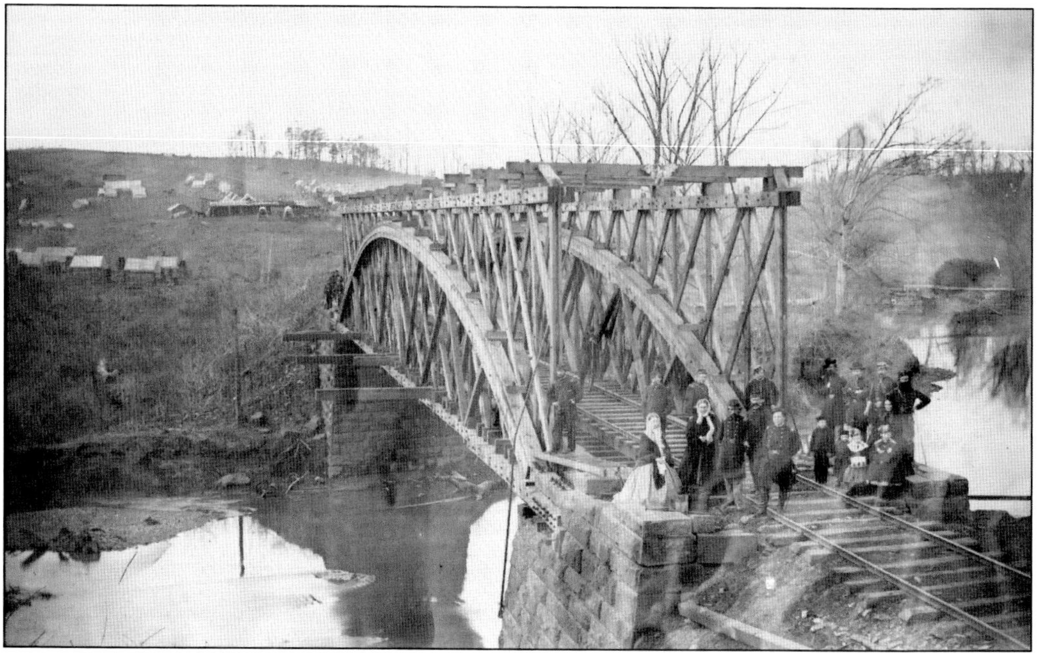

The Orange & Alexandria Railroad over Bull Run is pictured above, and the ruins of the same bridge at Union Mills are seen below. The railroad crossed the Bull Run near Union Mills, which consisted mostly of a few houses and set of mills near the river. (Both, courtesy of the Library of Congress.)

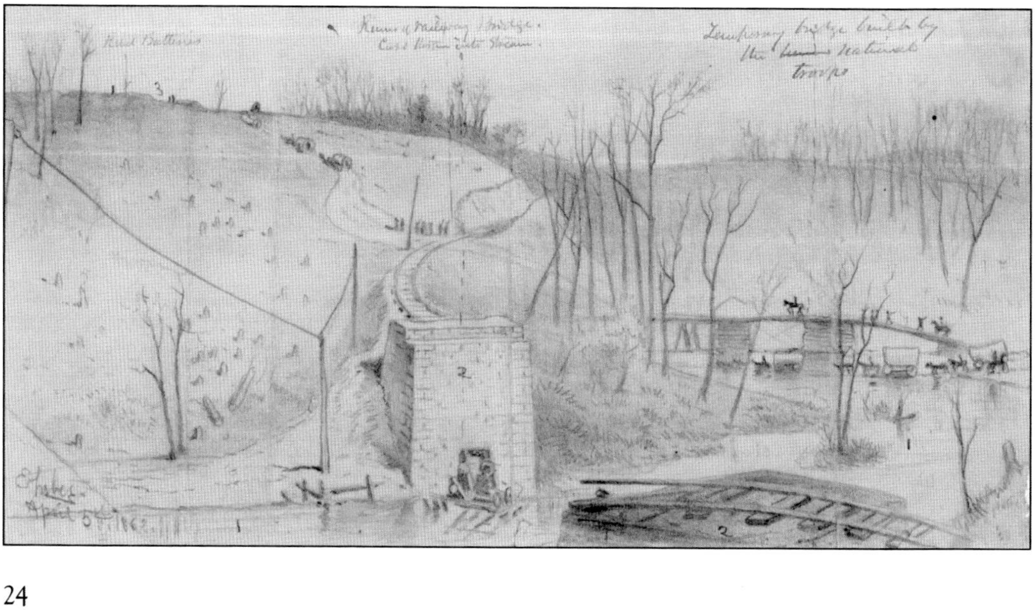

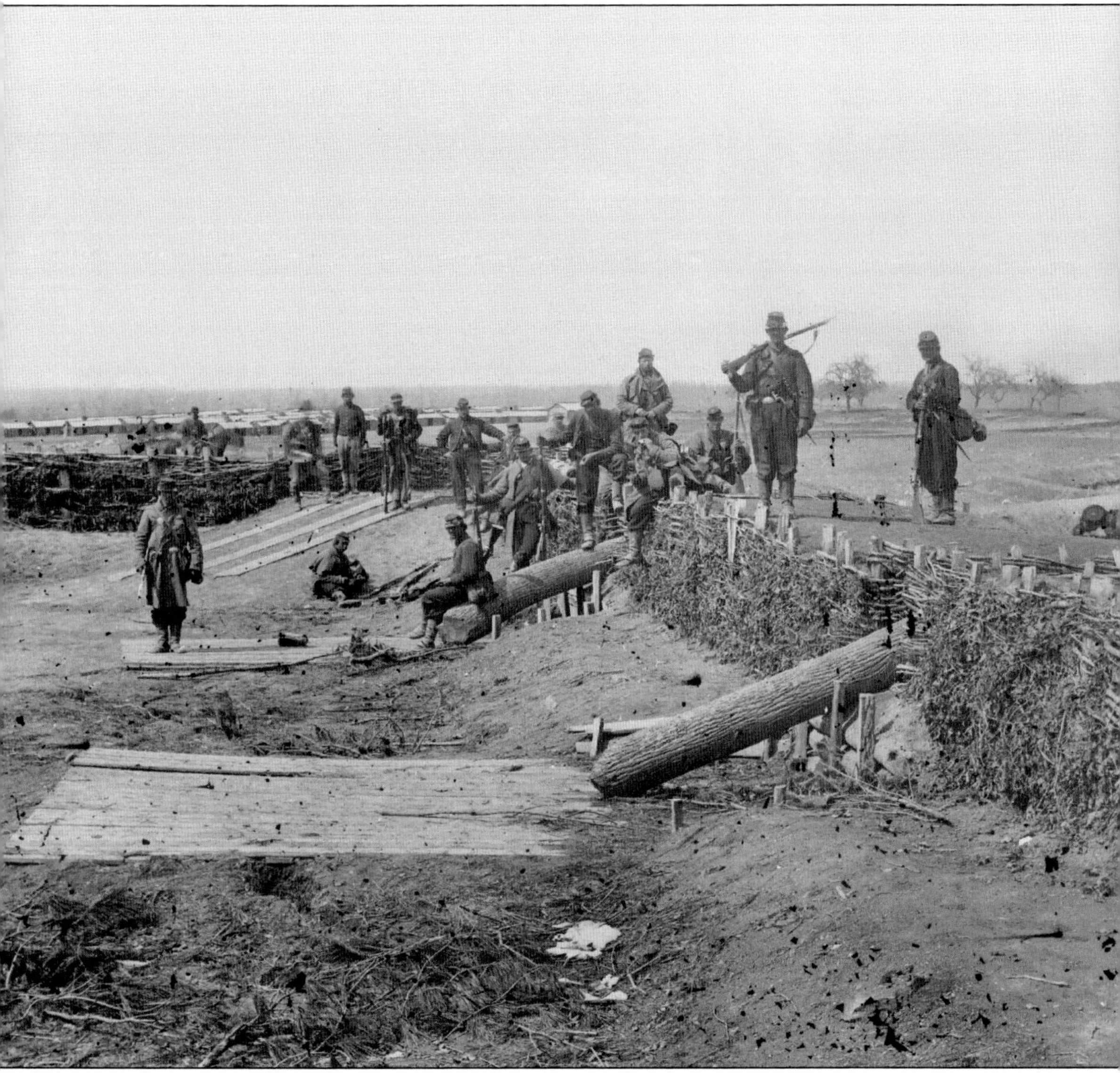

A group of Federal soldiers stands in a Confederate fort on the heights of Centreville with "Quaker guns"—logs designed to look like cannons. George N. Barnard or James Gibson took the photograph in March 1862. (Courtesy of the Library of Congress.)

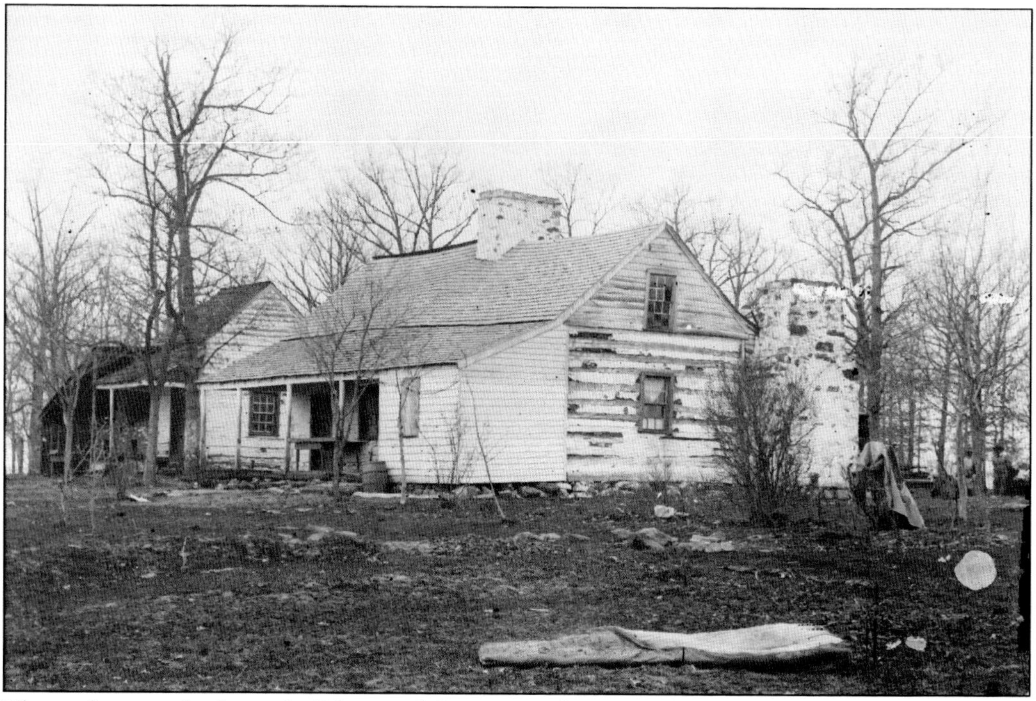

These photographs from the Library of Congress refer to a Mrs. Spinner's house, but the home pictured is very likely that of a Mrs. Spindle, who lived on the western edge of Centreville. Mrs. Spindle's home was turned into an impromptu hospital during the fighting at Bull Run. (Both, courtesy of the Library of Congress.)

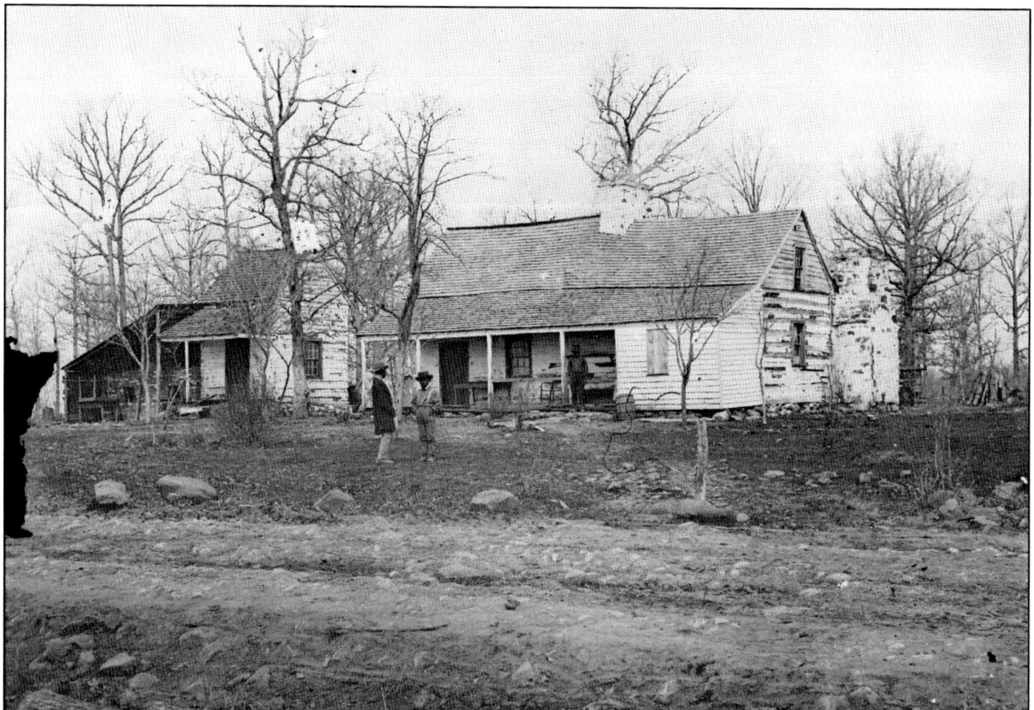

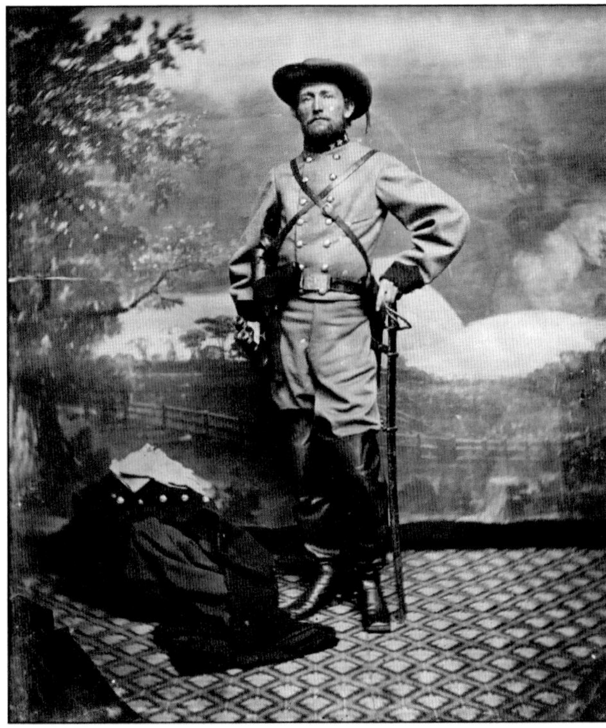

Col. John Singleton Mosby, the "Gray Ghost," is best known for his guerilla warfare–style raids and attacks. While Mosby was out scouting near Centreville in September 1864, five Union cavalrymen pursued him and two rangers. One of the men managed to shoot off the handle of Mosby's weapons and the bullet struck his groin. The bullet was near an artery and was never removed. (Courtesy of the Library of Congress.)

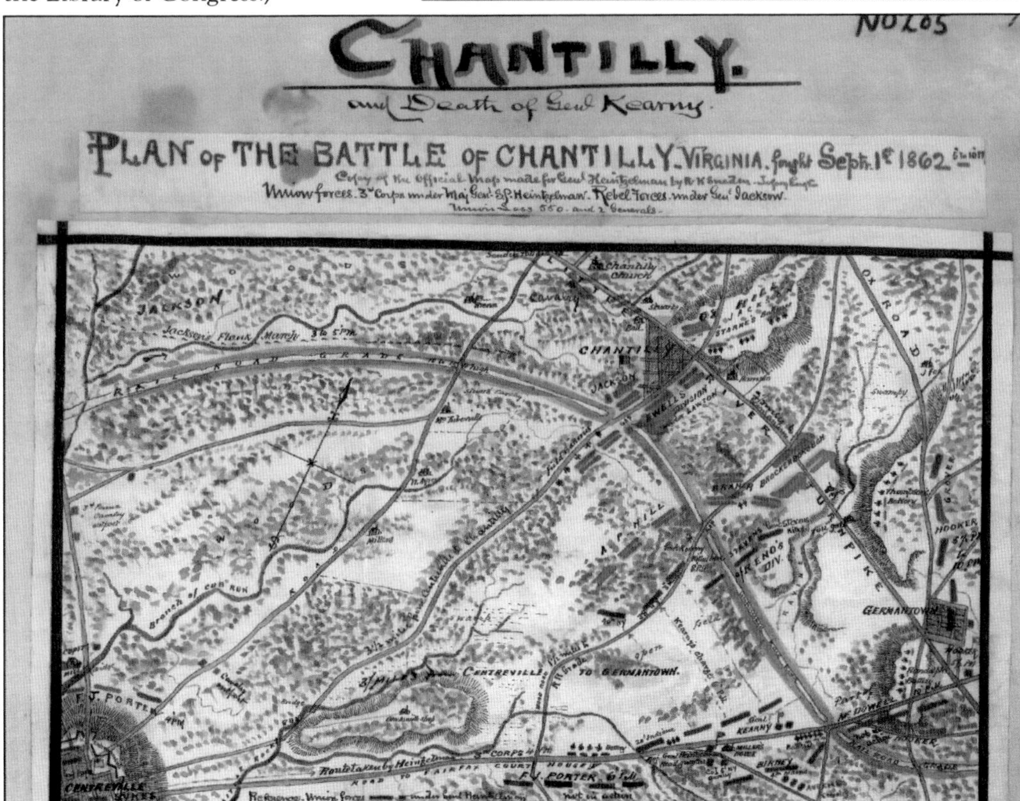

Robert Knox Sneden created this plan of the Battle of Chantilly, or Ox Hill, as it took place on September 1, 1862, during the tail end of Second Manassas. Note the fortifications at Centreville and the home of the Turbervilles, a prominent Chantilly family. (Courtesy of the Library of Congress.)

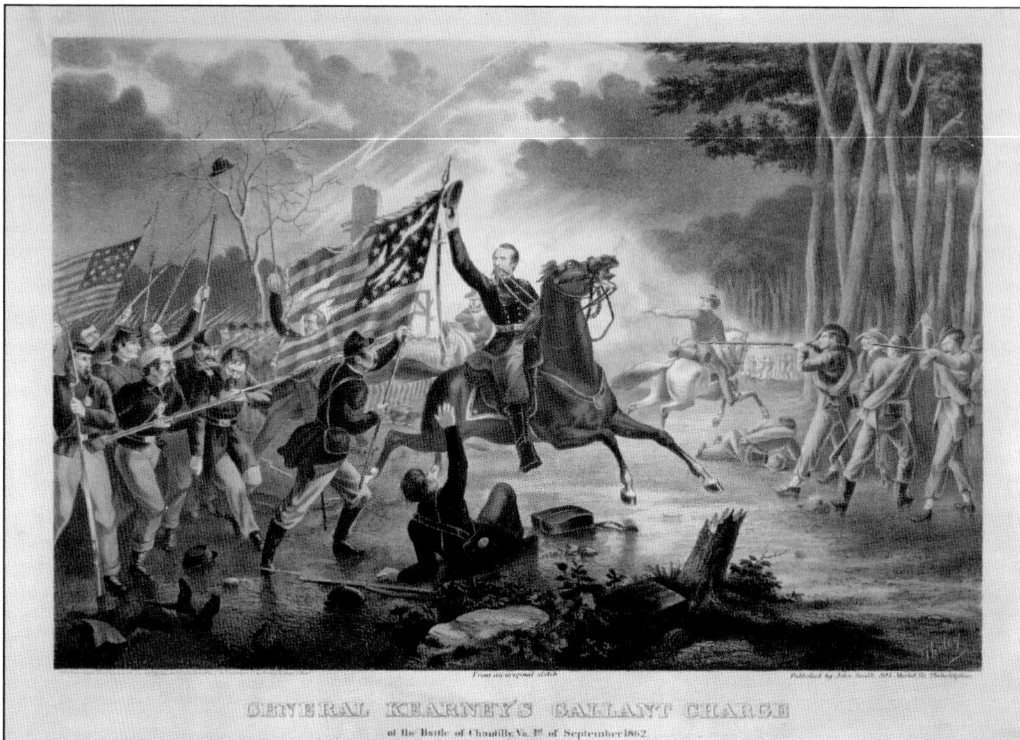

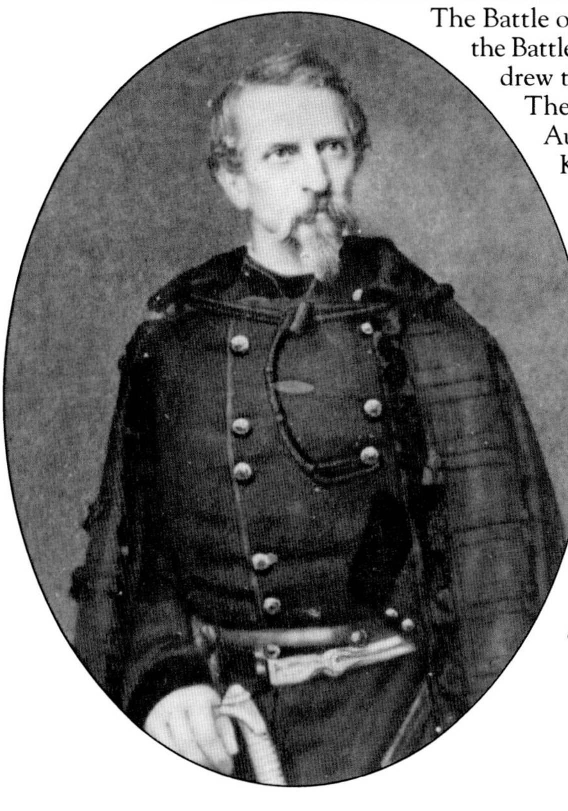

The Battle of Ox Hill, as the Confederates called it, or the Battle of Chantilly, as it was known in the Union, drew the Second Manassas campaign to an end. The c. 1867 painting above, created by artist Augustus Tholey, depicts Union general Philip Kearny. Kearny, who had been promoted to major general just months before, arrived at Ox Hill after Gen. Isaac Stevens requested his assistance. After hours of fighting in a heavy storm, Kearny rode off to investigate a report of a gap in the Federal army's defenses. He found troops from the 21st Massachusetts and ordered them into a cornfield. Under protest, the soldiers advanced but halted after capturing two Confederate soldiers. Frustrated by the delay and convinced that no Confederates were in the cornfield, Kearny roared, "Damn you and your prisoners!" and rode off into the field. His mistake was fatal. (Both, courtesy of the Library of Congress.)

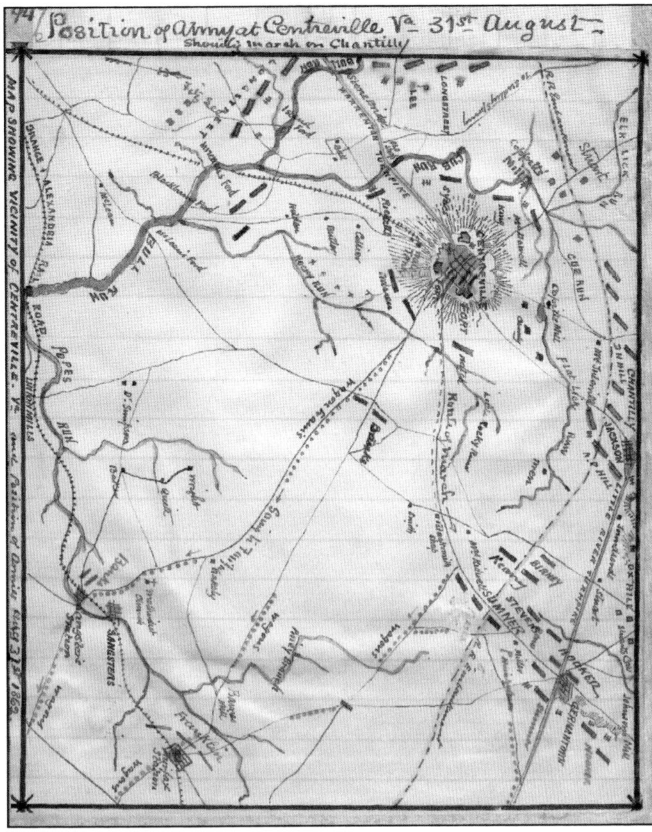

This map by Robert Knox Sneden shows movements of General Pope's Army of Virginia on August 31, 1862, just before the Battle of Chantilly (Ox Hill). The large number of troops is apparent. (Courtesy of the Library of Congress.)

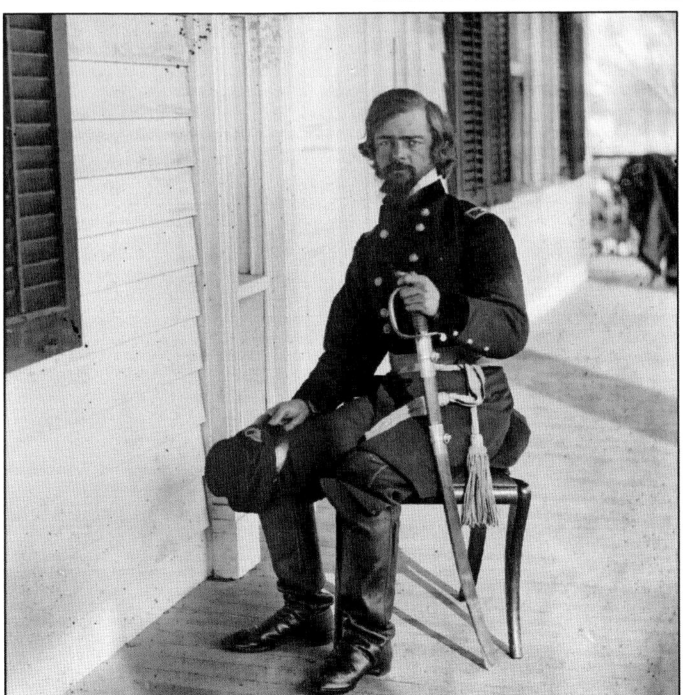

Gen. Isaac Stevens died at the Battle of Chantilly. In the midst of a losing battle, Stevens charged forward with the flag of the 79th New York Highlanders, his old regiment, crying out, "Highlanders! My Highlanders! Follow your general!" Despite this last effort, Stevens was shot in the head by opposing troops, reportedly with the flag falling over his body. (Courtesy of the Library of Congress.)

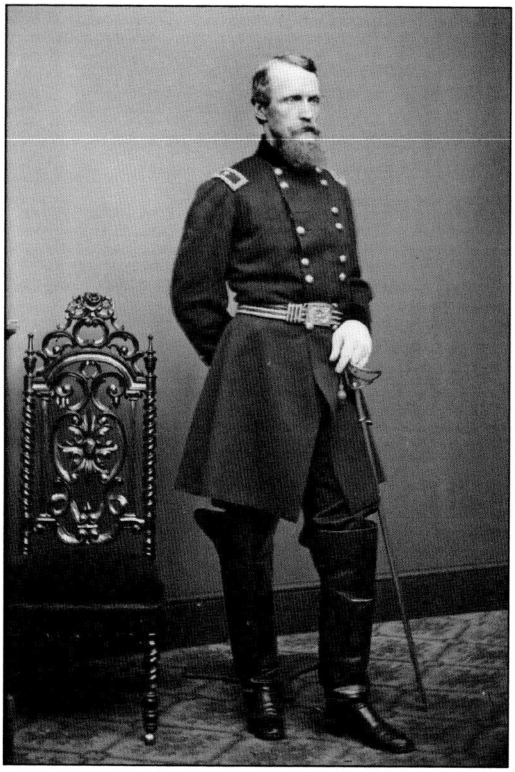

Union general David B. Birney's (left) troops fought in a fierce thunderstorm and wet cornfields at the Battle of Ox Hill against Gen. Lawrence O'Bryan Branch's (below) soldiers. The troops eventually wound up fighting with bayonets and clubbed muskets after the ammunition became too wet to fire. After Birney told Gen. Philip Kearny that there was a gap in his right flank, Kearny rode off to investigate. (Both, courtesy of the Library of Congress.)

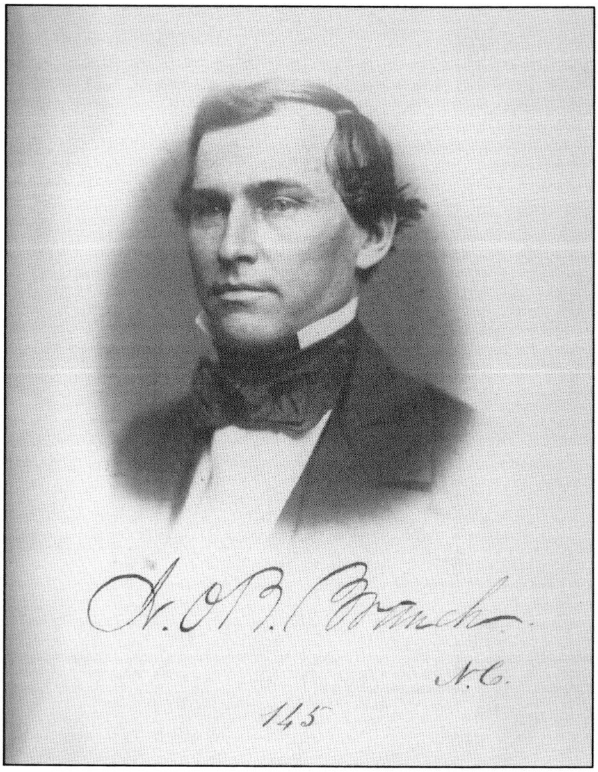

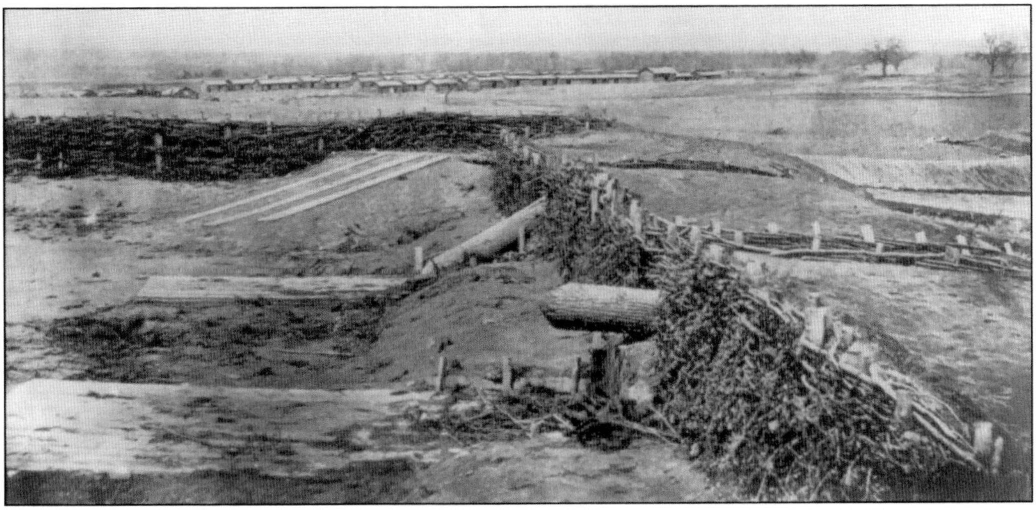

A *New York Times* correspondent commented the following in an April 3, 1862, article about the Quaker guns at Centreville: "This device of Quaker guns is one constantly and successfully used by commanders who intend to retreat from forts or entrenchments. Next to his men, an officer's first care is his artillery. But to remove his guns in sight of the enemy would be to notify him in the quickest and most unmistakable manner of the intended evacuation." (Courtesy of the Library of Congress.)

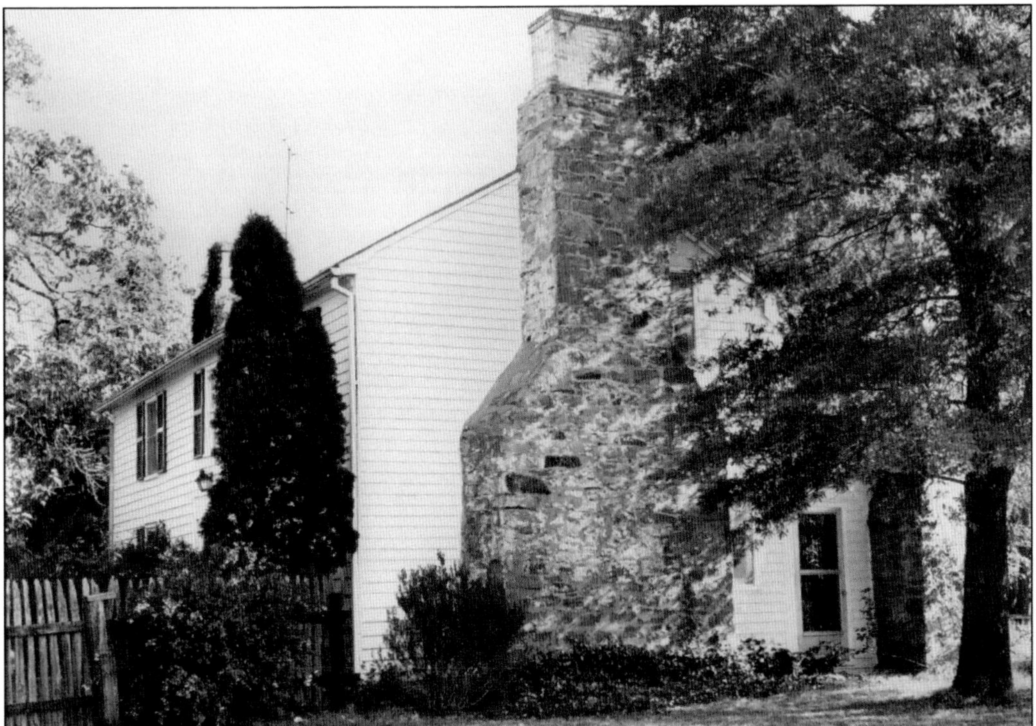

Level Green is a historic home, now situated in the middle of town houses, in the Centreville area. It was built in the early 18th century, and officers under the leadership of Confederate general P.G.T. Beauregard reportedly used it as an administrative headquarters for a short time. (Courtesy of Lee Hubbard.)

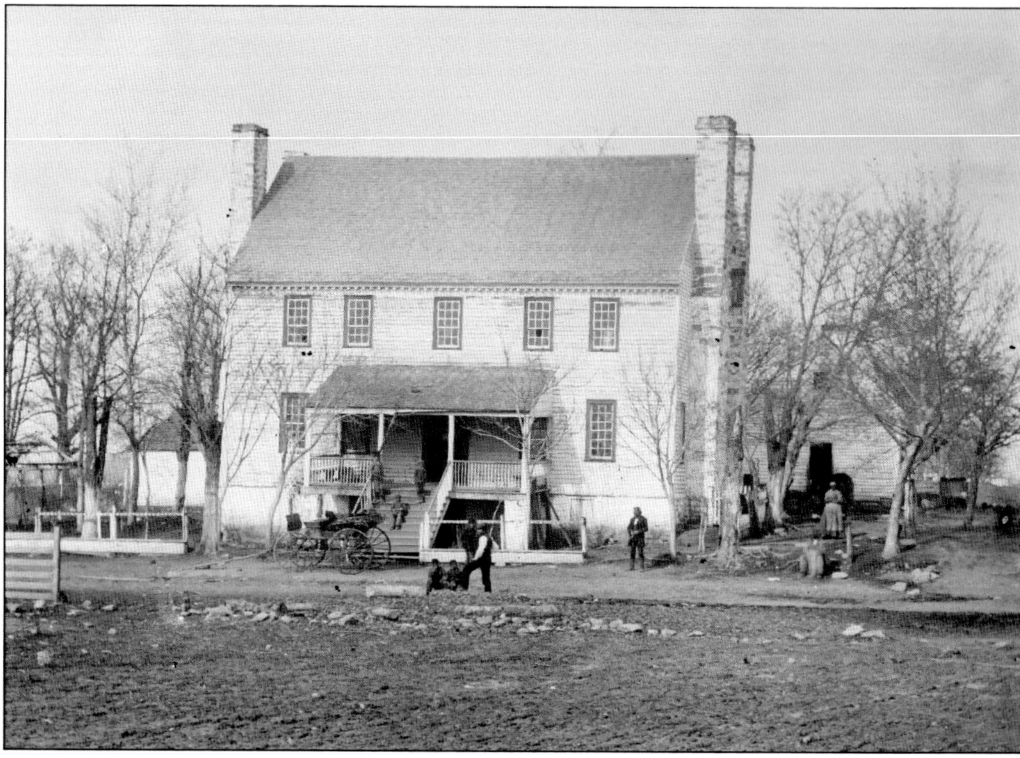

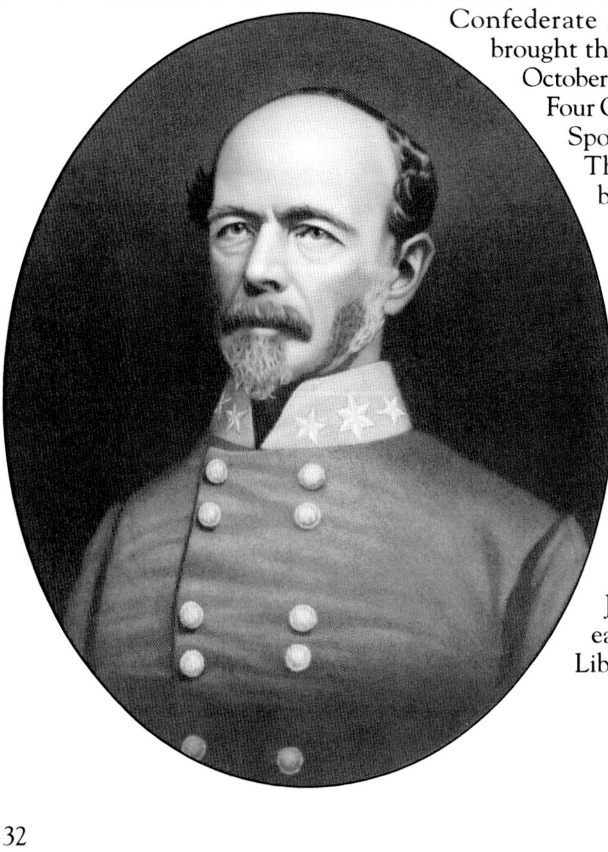

Confederate general Joseph Eggleston Johnston brought thousands of his troops to Centreville in October 1861. He set up his army's headquarters at Four Chimney House, the home of Alexander Spotswood Grigsby, a local businessman. The two-story house was built sometime between 1769 and 1787 and, true to its name, featured four large chimneys. For his personal headquarters, Johnston stayed in Mount Gilead, one of the oldest homes in Fairfax County, which is still standing today. After a meeting with Confederate president Jefferson Davis and his cabinet in mid-February 1862, Johnston made the decision to withdraw from Centreville. The withdrawal required weeks of preparation due to the large amount of food, clothing, and other supplies in and near the village. Johnston withdrew from Centreville in early March 1862. (Both, courtesy of the Library of Congress.)

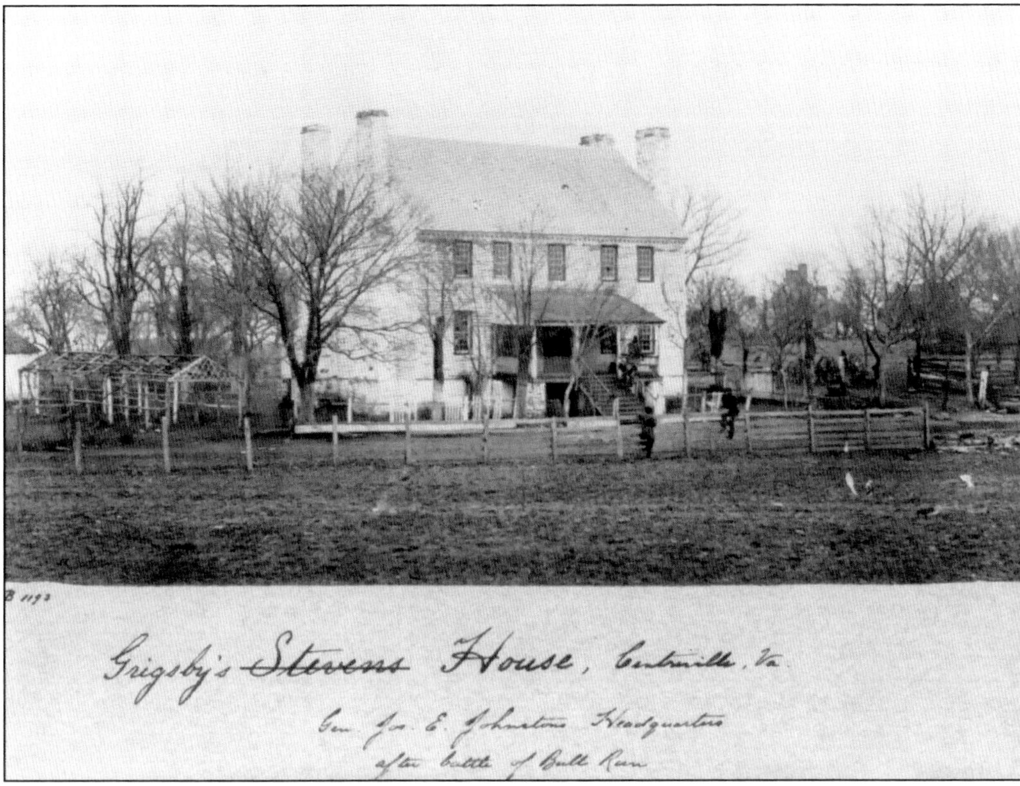

Gen. Joseph E. Johnston set up his army headquarters in the Four Chimney House, not far from where he stayed at Mount Gilead. Johnston departed Centreville in March 1862. Four Chimney fell into ruins in the ensuing years. Once an impressive two-story dwelling with the namesake stone chimneys, the home was abandoned by the early 20th century and, save some rubble, was completely demolished by the 1950s. (Both, courtesy of the Library of Congress.)

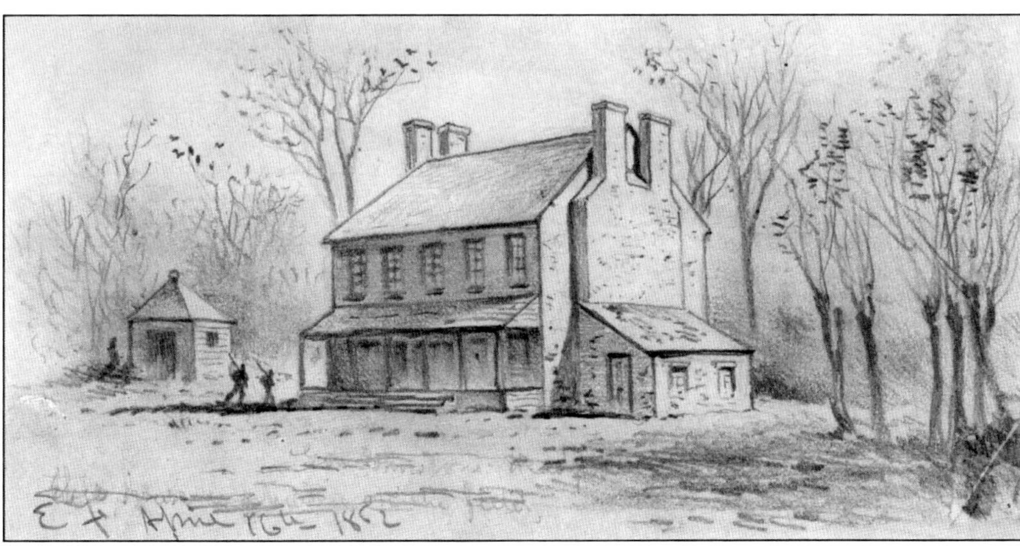

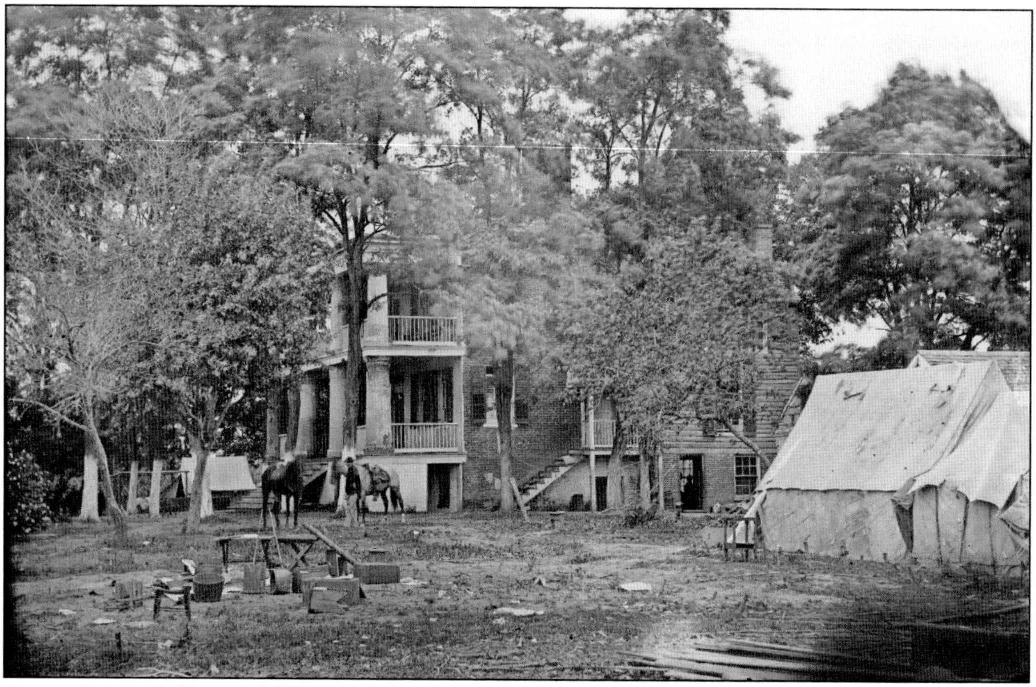

Generals McClellan and Beauregard used the Fairfax Courthouse, located a few miles away in downtown Fairfax City, as a headquarters. Fairfax became a haven for Union sympathizers, like James Barlow, who lived at Sully Plantation until the Confederates reached his very doorstep. (Courtesy of the Library of Congress.)

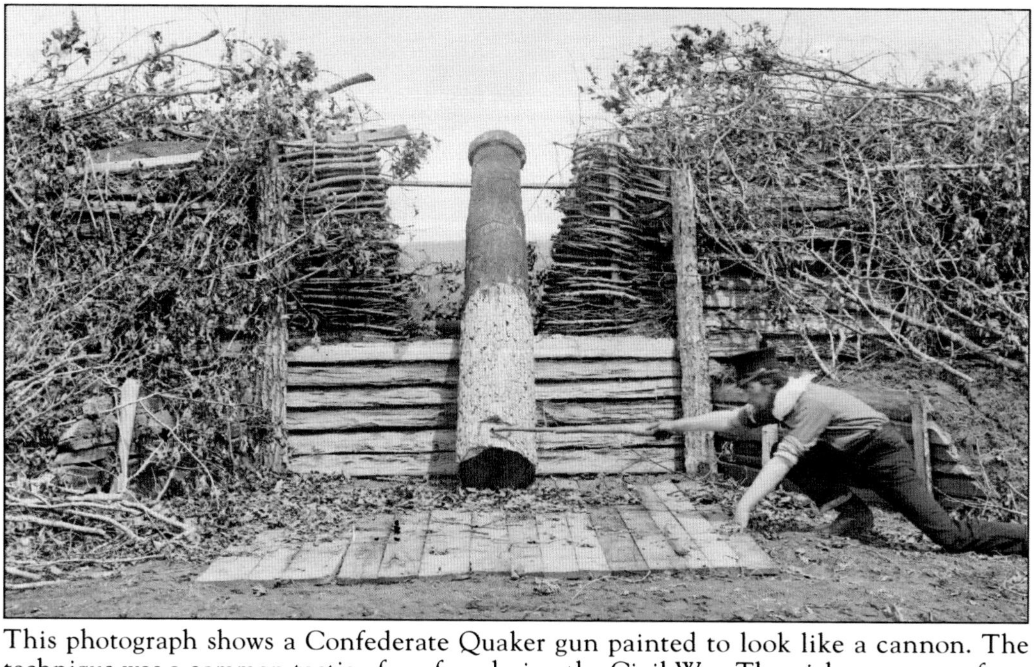

This photograph shows a Confederate Quaker gun painted to look like a cannon. The technique was a common tactic of warfare during the Civil War. The nickname came from the antiwar Quakers, because the guns obviously would not be able to kill anyone. (Courtesy of the Library of Congress.)

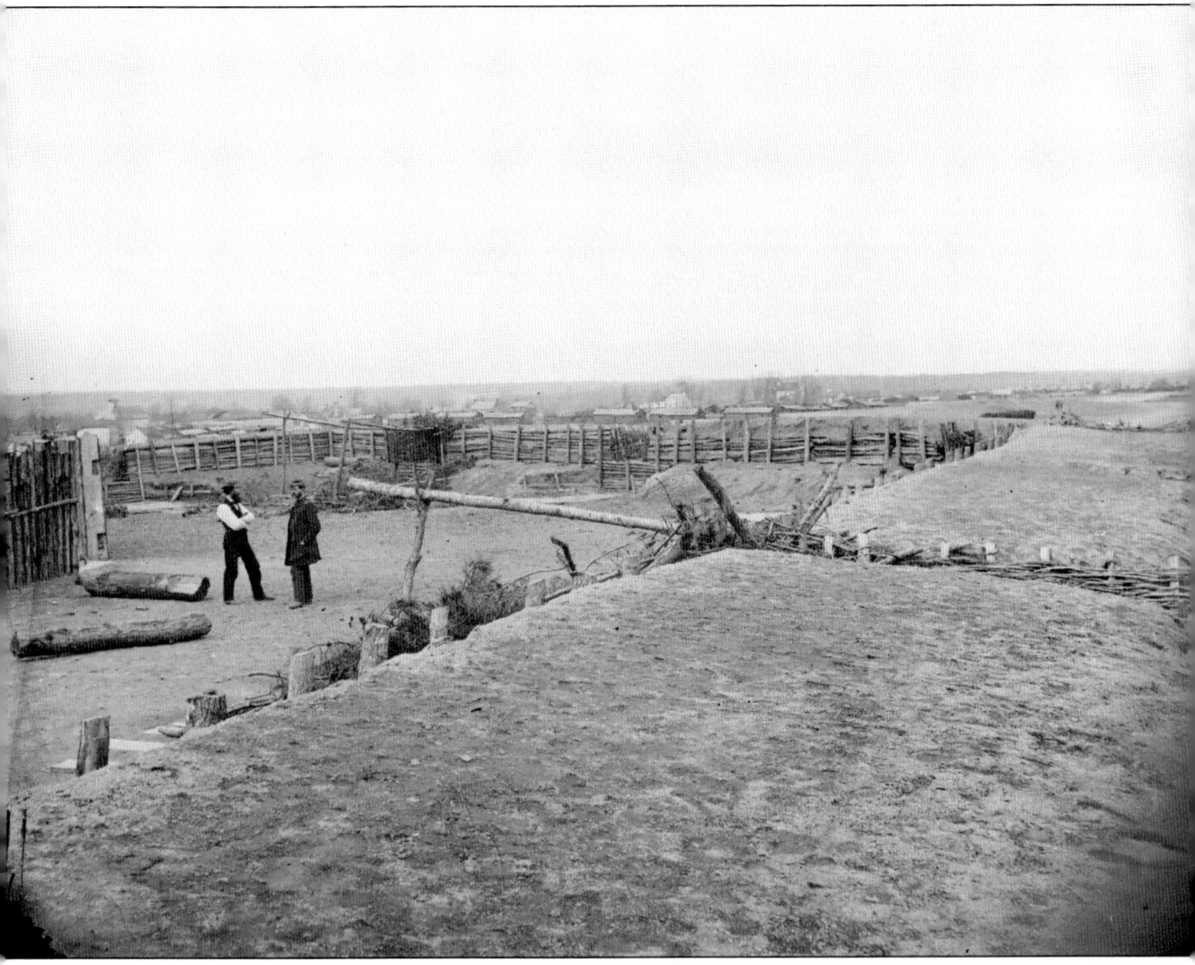

Pictured are the Confederate winter quarters and fortifications at Centreville, during the winter of 1861–1862. (Courtesy of the Library of Congress.)

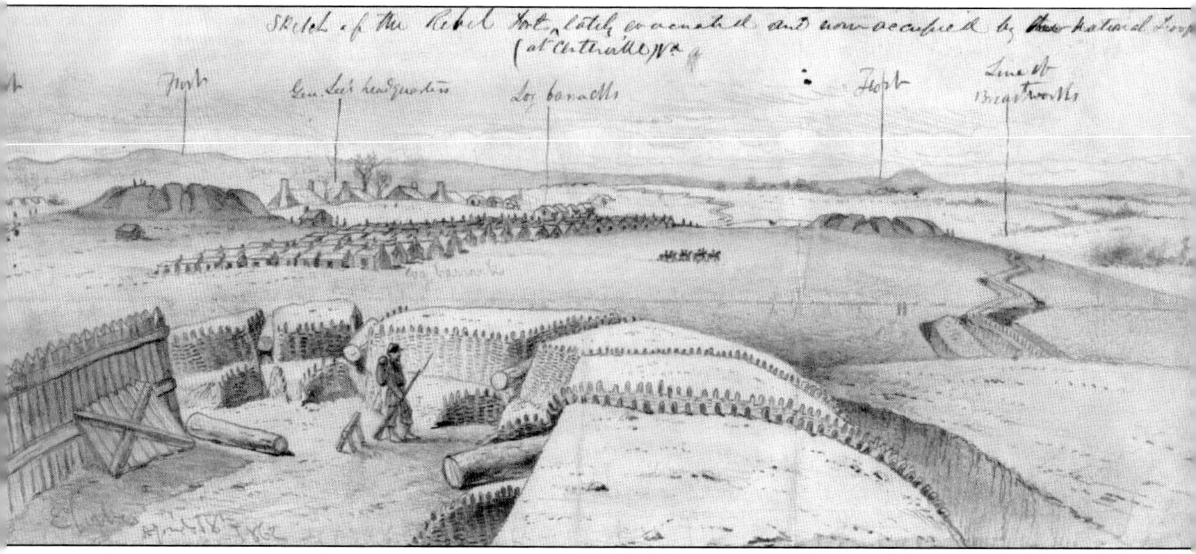

This sketch by artist Edwin Forbes depicts the rebel defenses at Centreville. It notes that the log barracks were "lately evacuated and now occupied by national troops." A fort, General Lee's headquarters, log barracks, and a line of breastworks are identified in the sketch. The handwriting was probably added years after the drawing was made and likely confuses Lee with Johnston. (Courtesy of the Library of Congress.)

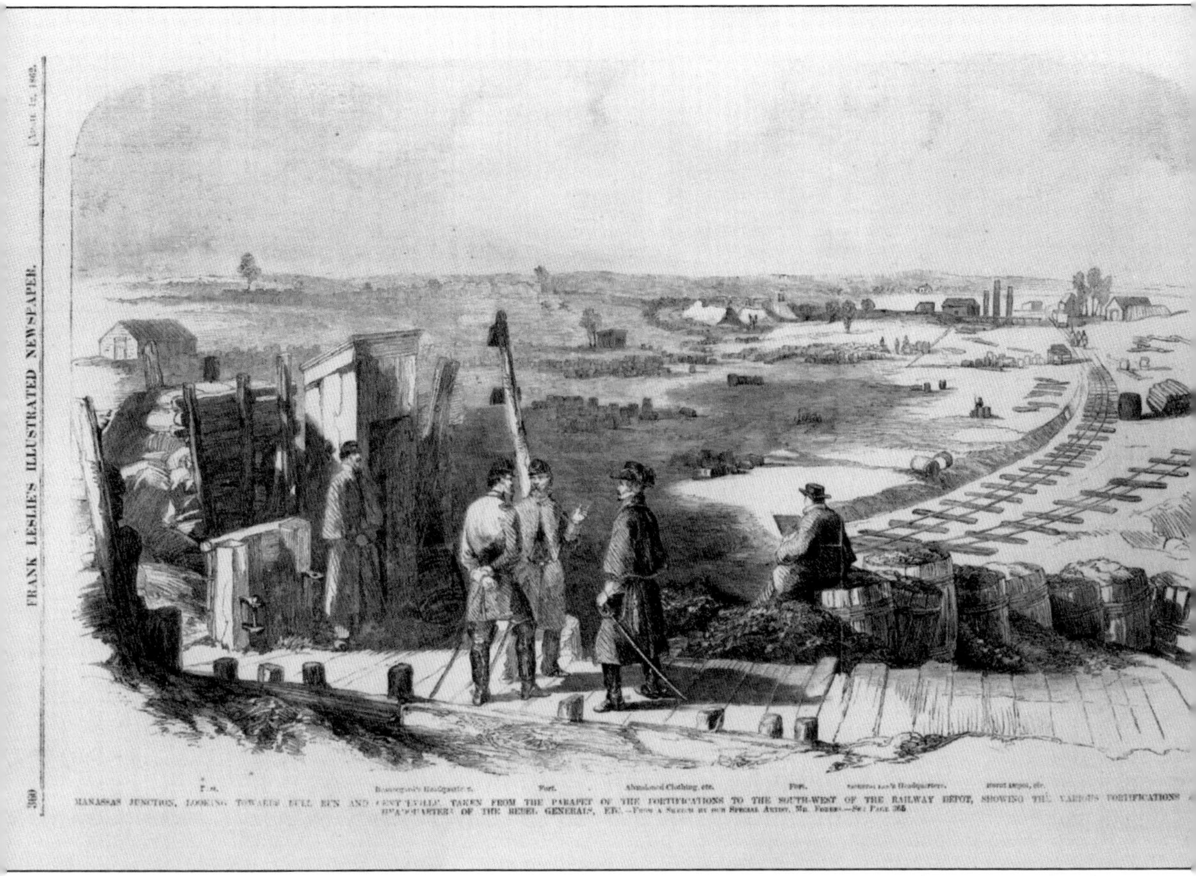

Thousands of soldiers converged in nearby Manassas Junction, a major switching point for the Orange & Alexandria and Manassas Gap Railroads. (Courtesy of the Library of Congress.)

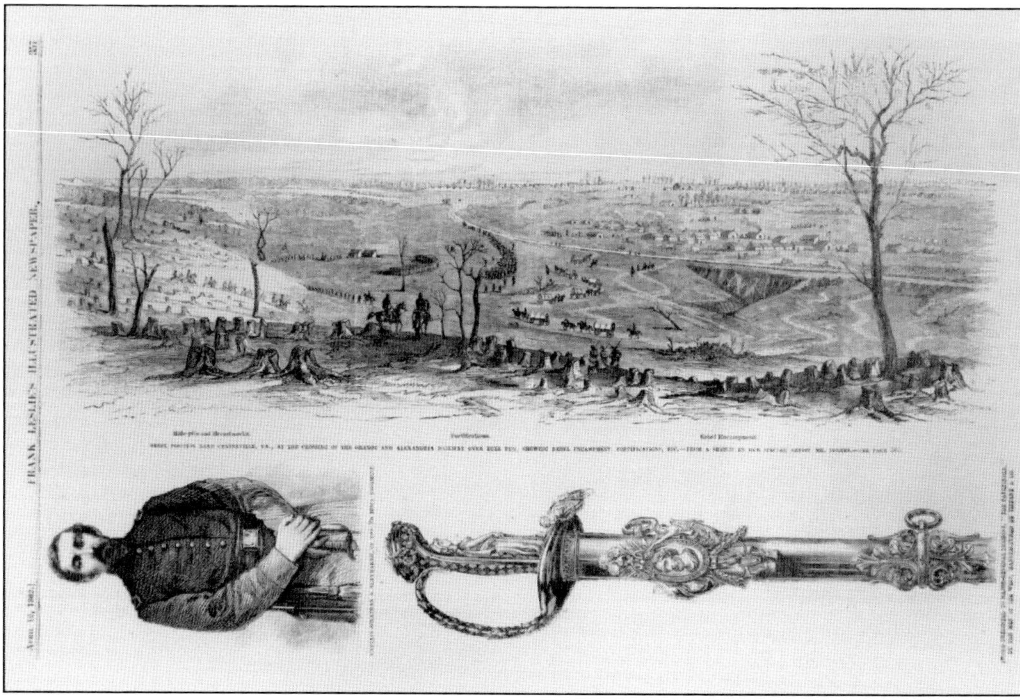

The war continued to affect Centreville, with troop movements nearby, as seen in this sketch of the Confederate position at the crossing of the Orange & Alexandria Railway over Bull Run. Created by artist Edwin Forbes, this sketch was published in *Frank Leslie's Illustrated Newspaper* on April 12, 1862. (Courtesy of the Library of Congress.)

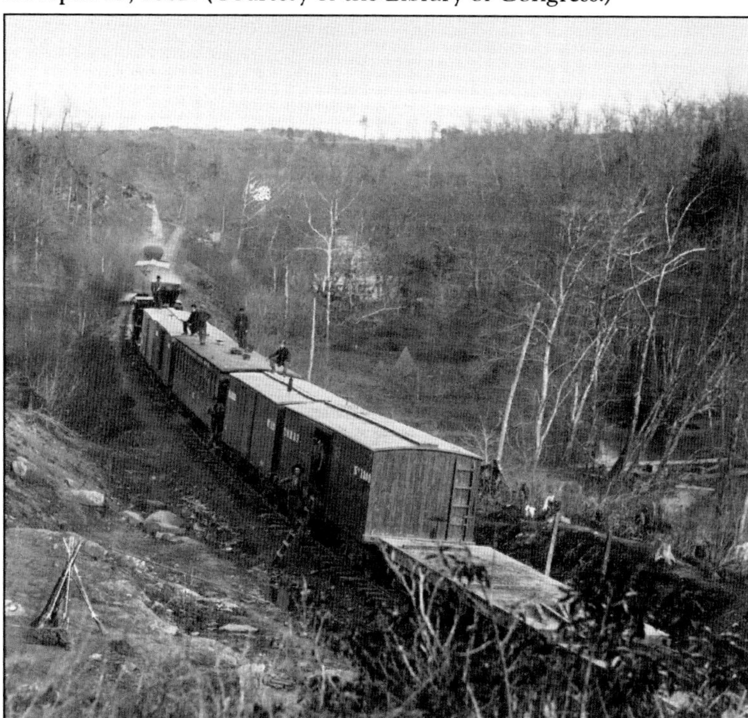

Union Mills Station, a formerly insignificant country railroad station, just a few miles out of Centreville—off Union Mill Road near Clifton—became an important logistical consideration for Civil War commanders due to its location on the Orange & Alexandria Railroad tracks. Both armies were situated near Union Mills over the course of the war. (Courtesy of the Library of Congress.)

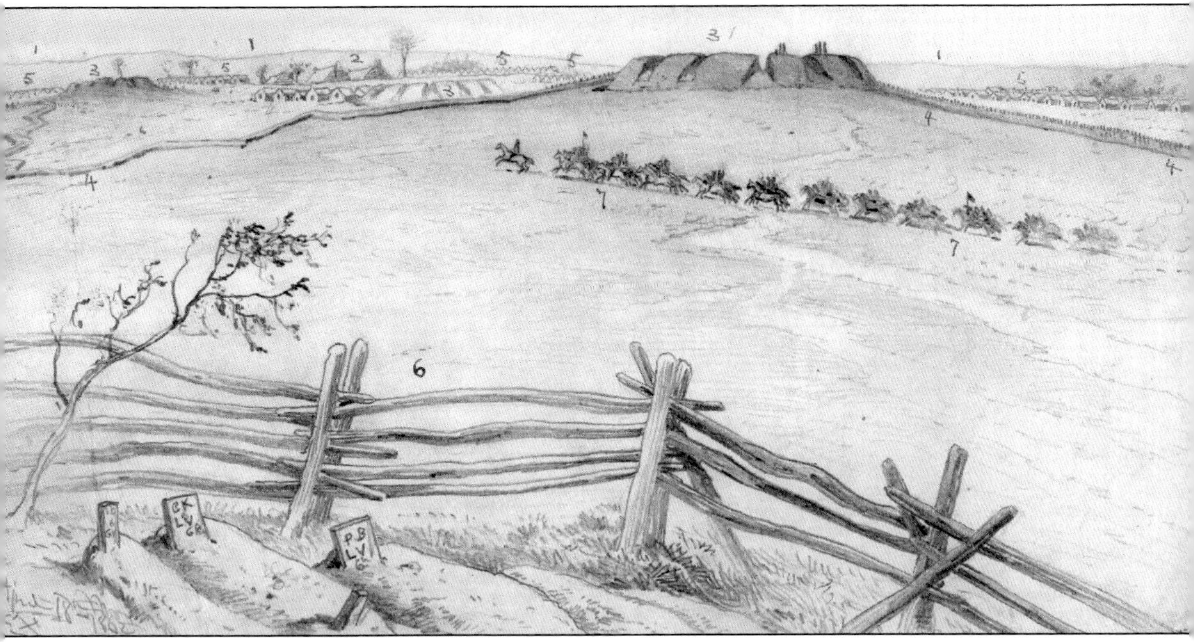

From a point south of the Warrenton Turnpike, artist Edwin Forbes sketched the defenses of Centreville, forts, breastworks, and more. (Courtesy of the Library of Congress.)

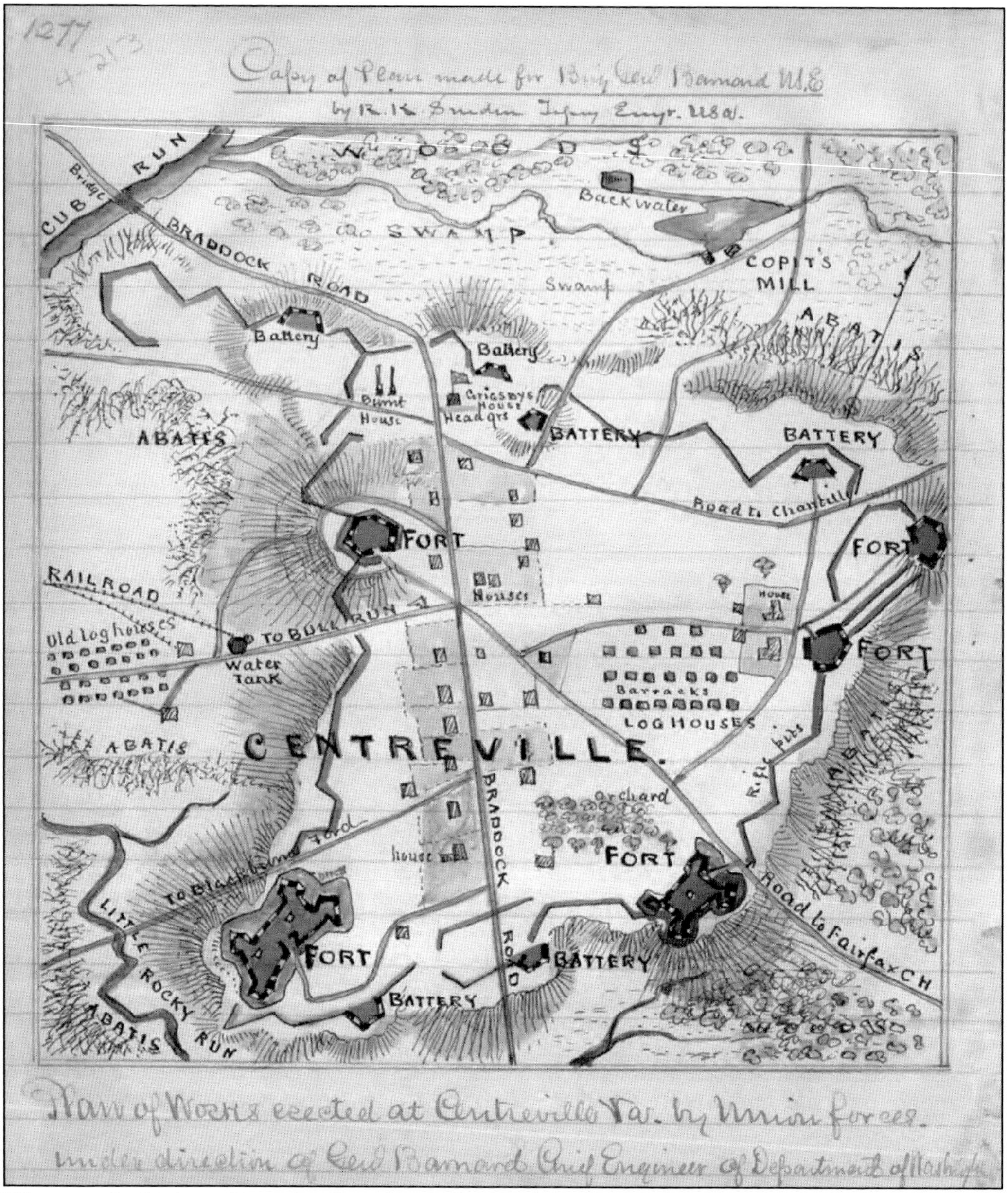

This map by Robert Knox Sneden shows the earthworks that Union forces created under the direction of General Barnard. Grigsby House (Four Chimney House) is show at the top center. (Courtesy of the Library of Congress.)

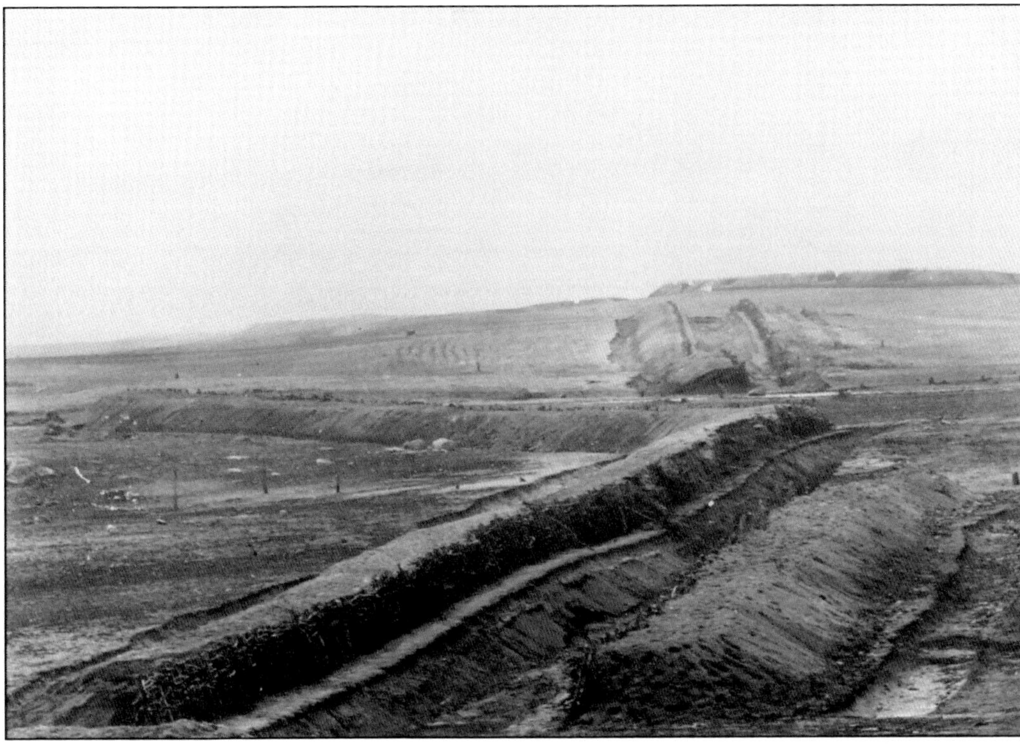

The Confederate fortifications at Centreville are shown here. Gen. Joseph E. Johnston's army left Centreville by March 1862. His army's winter barracks are visible in the distance. (Courtesy of the Library of Congress.)

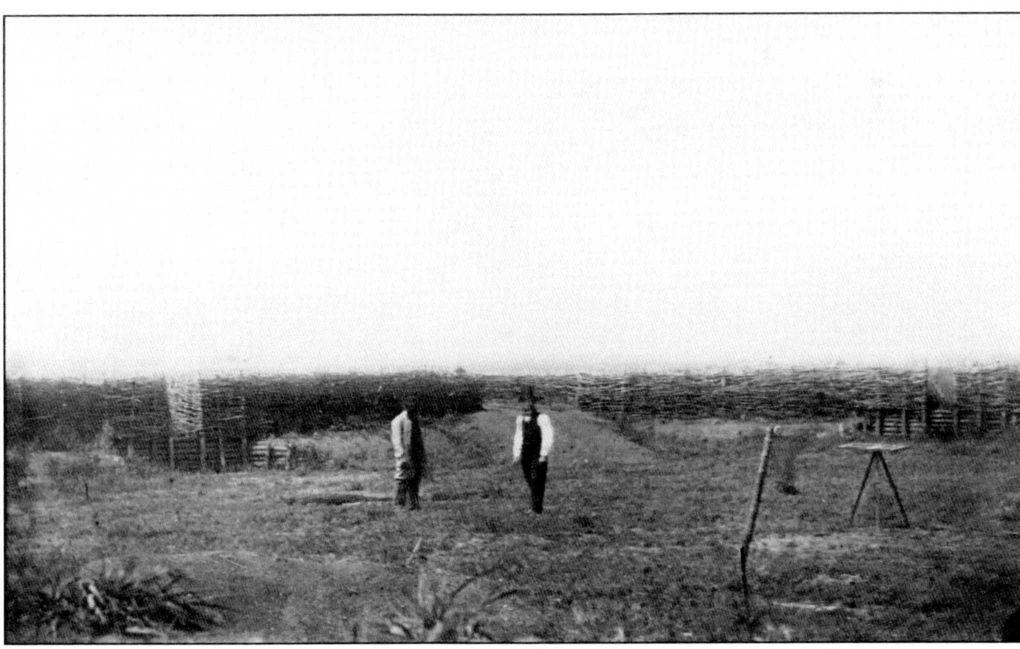

Two men are shown in this photograph at a Confederate fort at Centreville in August 1862. (Courtesy of the Library of Congress.)

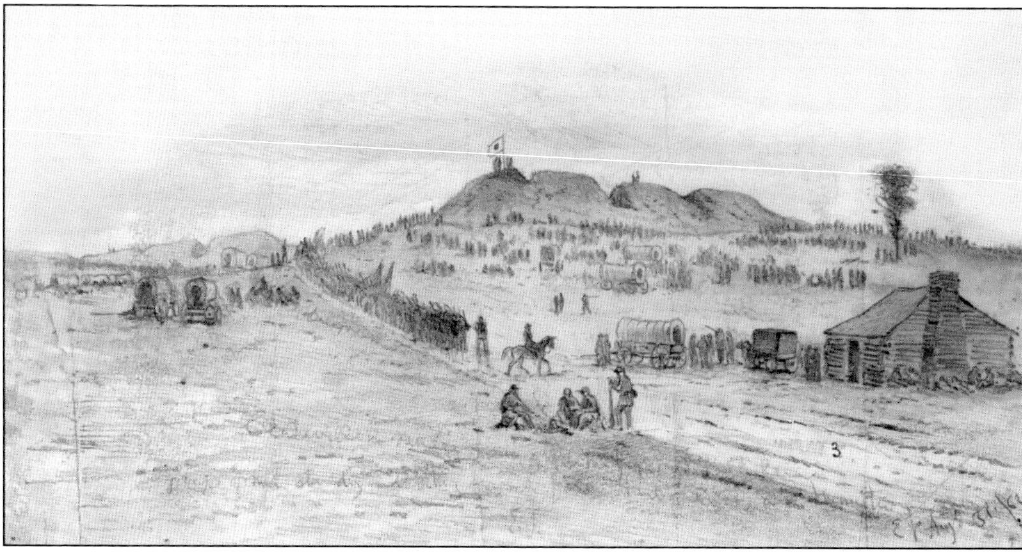

Gen. Louis Blenker's brigade covers the retreat near Centreville in 1862. Artist Edwin Forbes depicted the Union's retreat through Centreville after its defeat at the Second Battle of Manassas in the sketch below from August 1862. The 1862 retreat from Second Manassas is shown in the Forbes drawing above; the below drawing is Blenker's brigade covering the retreat during First Manassas in 1861. (Both, courtesy of the Library of Congress.)

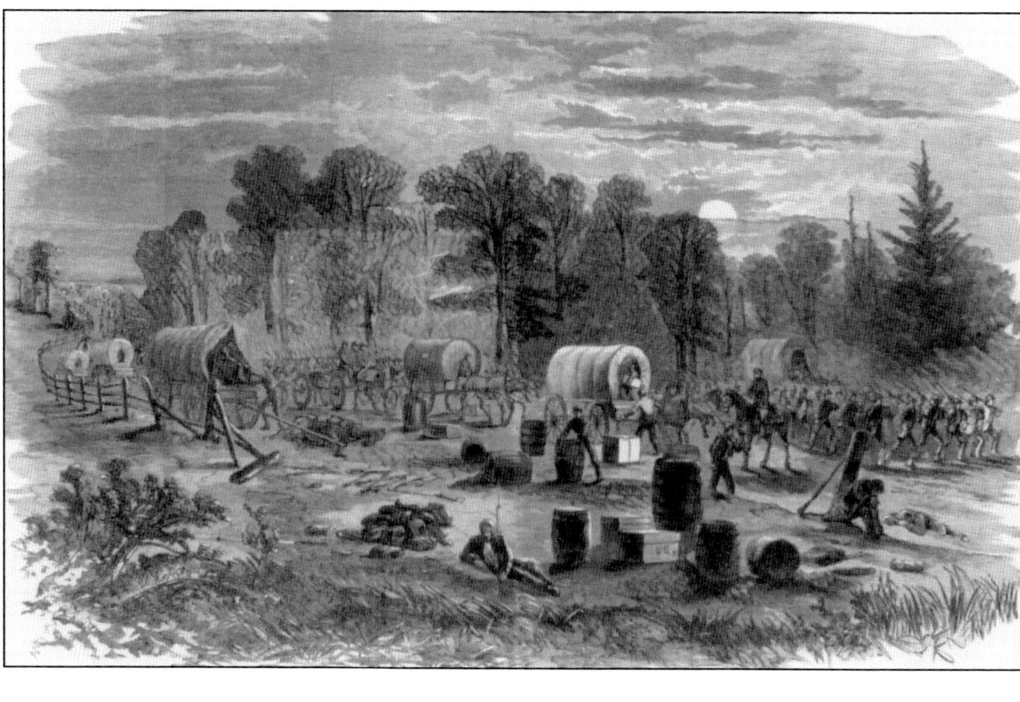

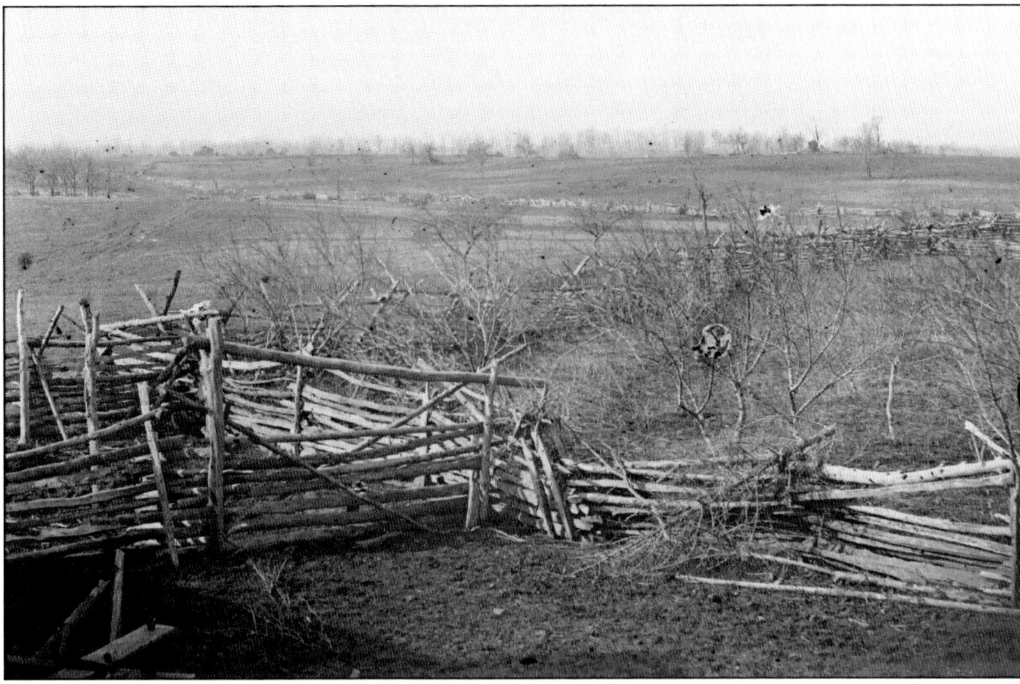

This view is of the Manassas Battlefield in 1861. The destruction is plain to see for miles around. (Courtesy of the Library of Congress.)

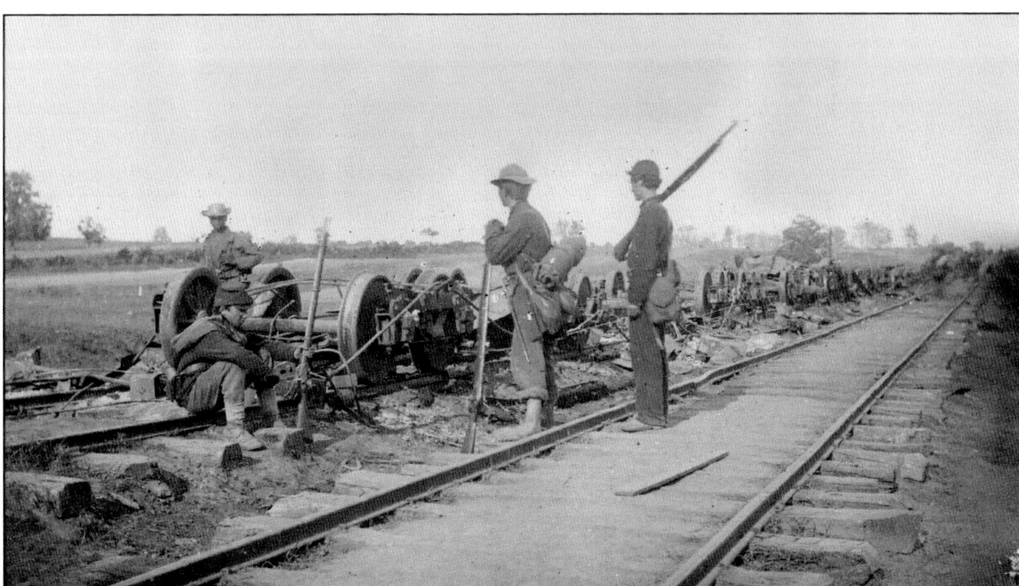

Soldiers are seen beside damaged rolling stock of the Orange & Alexandria Railroad at Manassas Junction in August 1862. (Courtesy of the Library of Congress.)

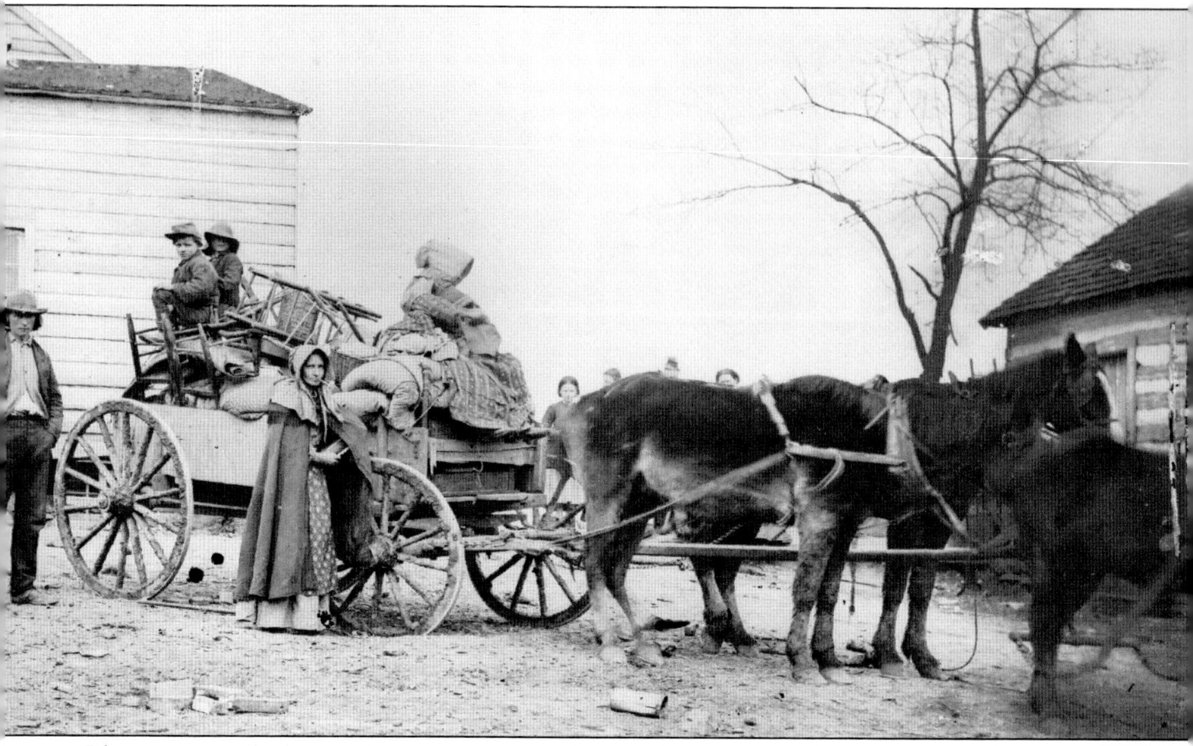

The woman in the bonnet is smoking a pipe as her family prepares to depart from their homestead, likely in Centreville. Many local families were displaced by the war. (Courtesy of the Library of Congress.)

Two

Around Historic Centreville and Chantilly

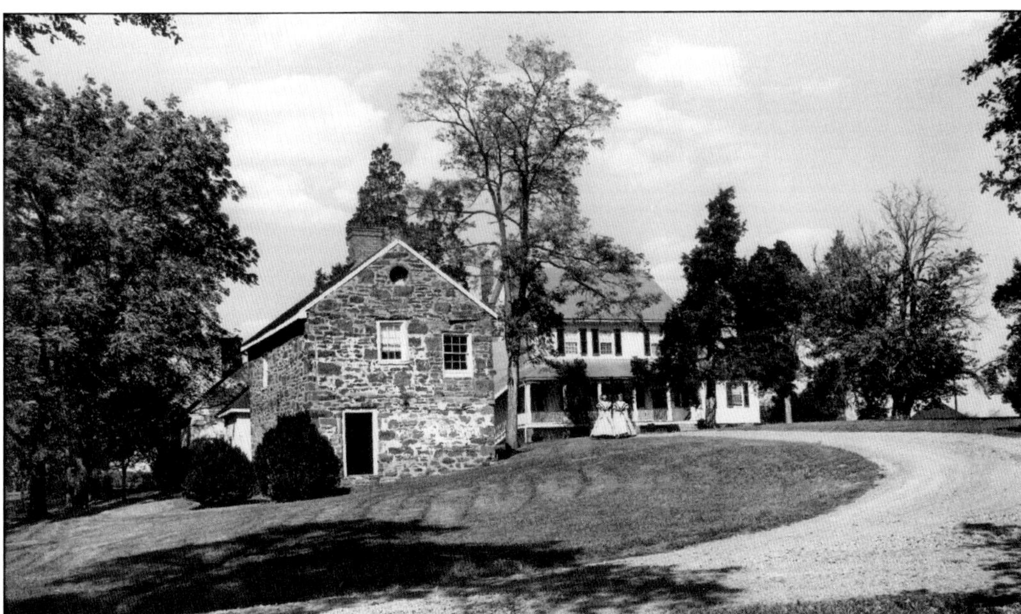

There are many hidden gems in Centreville and Chantilly—historic homes that managed to survive the ravages of the Civil War and the neglect of the ensuing years. Some, however, fell into disrepair and were torn down. Not all of the community's important homes are in this chapter; yet images of places like the Sully Plantation, pictured here with reenactors in front of the porch in 1965, paint a picture of what life was like centuries ago. (Courtesy of the Fairfax County Public Library Photographic Archive.)

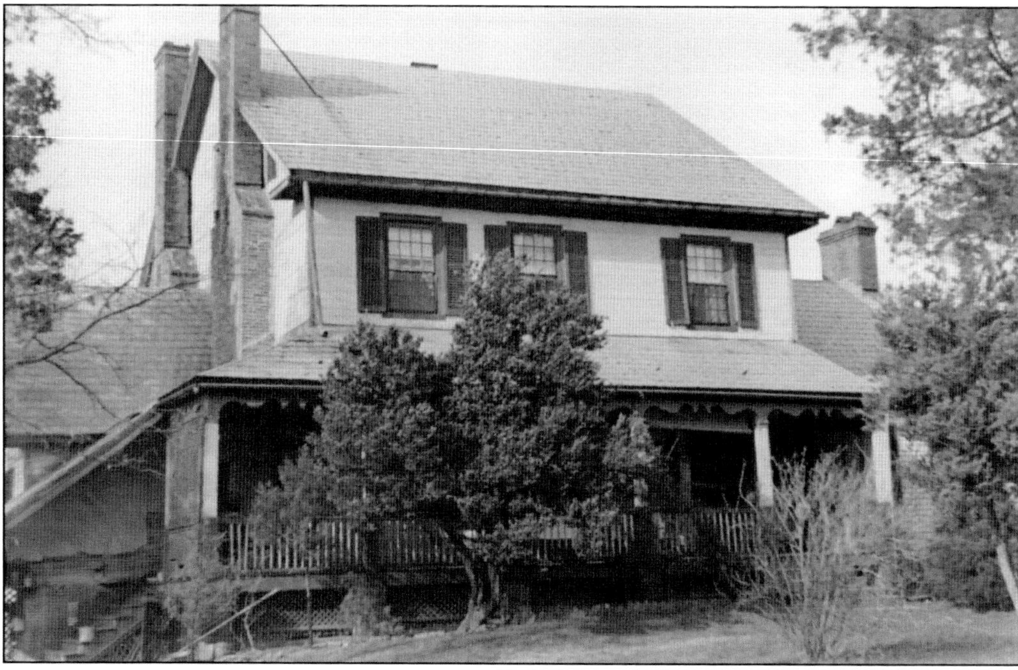

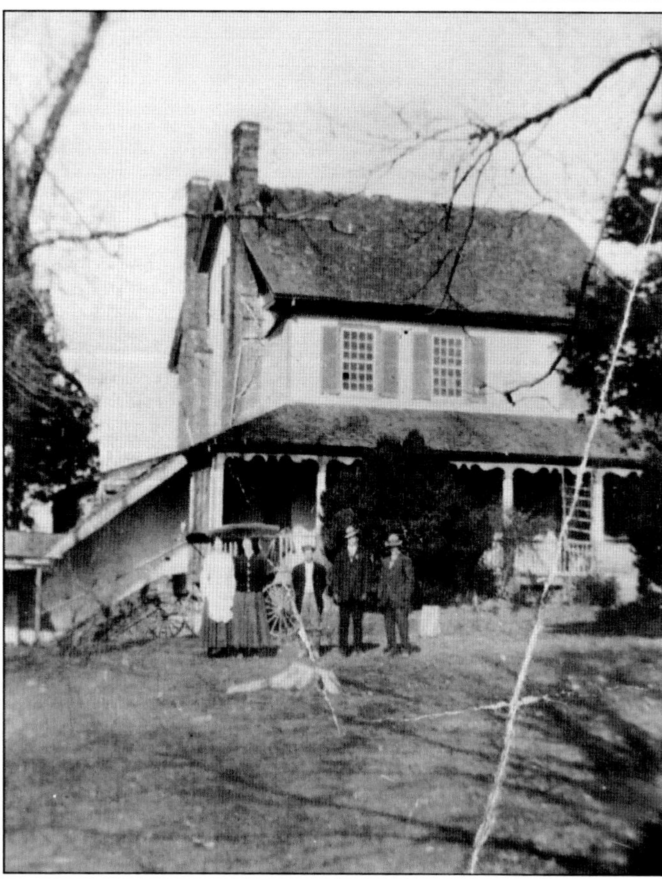

Sully Plantation was the home of Elizabeth and Richard Bland Lee, Northern Virginia's first congressman and the uncle of Gen. Robert E. Lee. It was built in 1794, and Lee added a small east wing in 1799. The Fairfax County Park Authority now owns the property, which is called Sully Historic Site. Robert Bray took this photograph in 1939. (Courtesy of the Fairfax County Public Library Photographic Archive.)

Gilbert McLearen (middle) and his wife (far left), along with visiting relatives Mrs. J.A. Seaton (second from left), William Smith, and Ralph Rose (far right), pose for a photograph at Sully in 1912. McLearen was the manager of Sully when William Eads Miller owned the property. (Courtesy of the Library of Congress.)

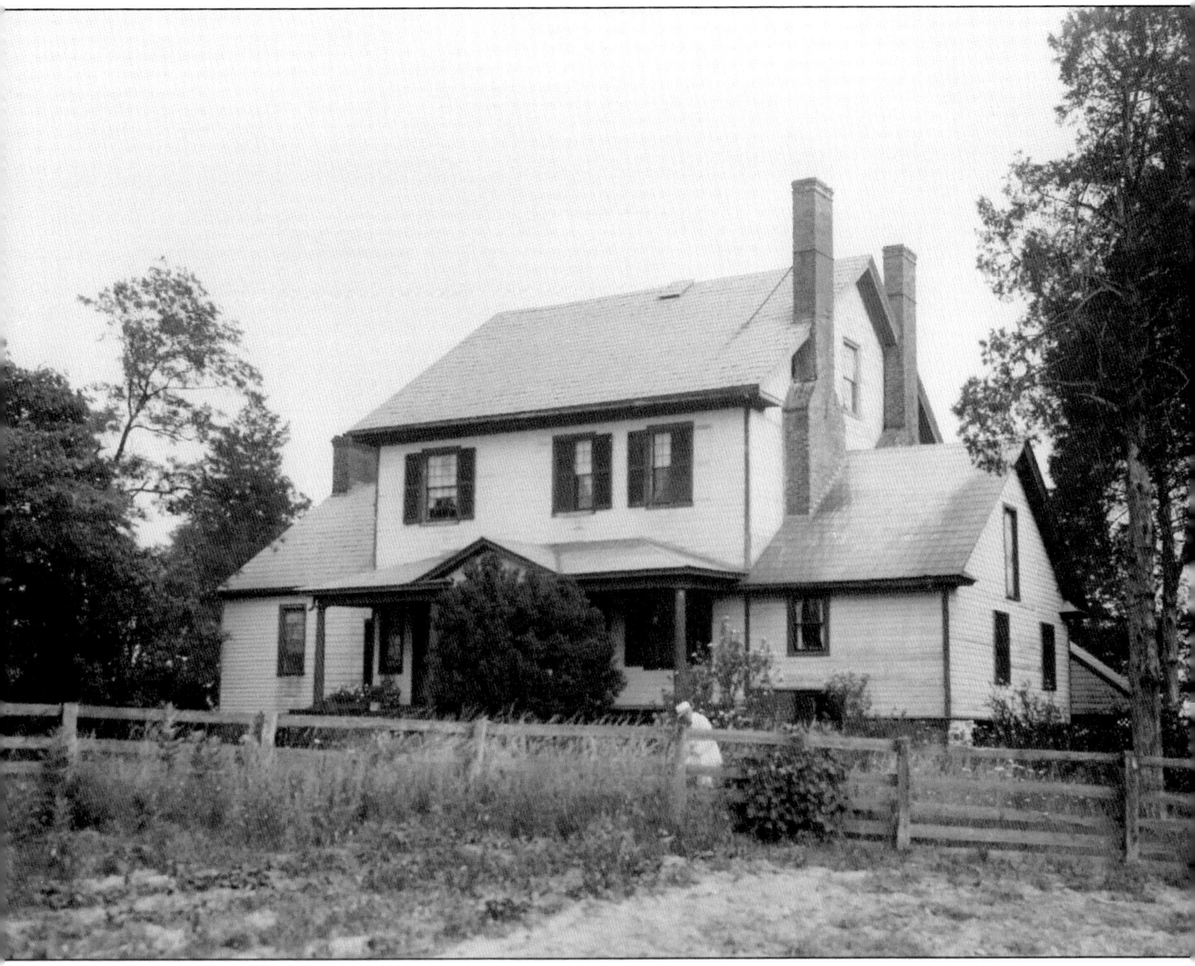

Richard Bland Lee sold Sully to his cousin Francis Lightfoot Lee in 1811. Over the next century and a half, the land passed through the hands of many families, including dairy farmers King and Rebecca Poston from 1919 to 1939 and diplomats Walter Thurston and Frederick E. Nolting Jr. (Courtesy of the Library of Congress.)

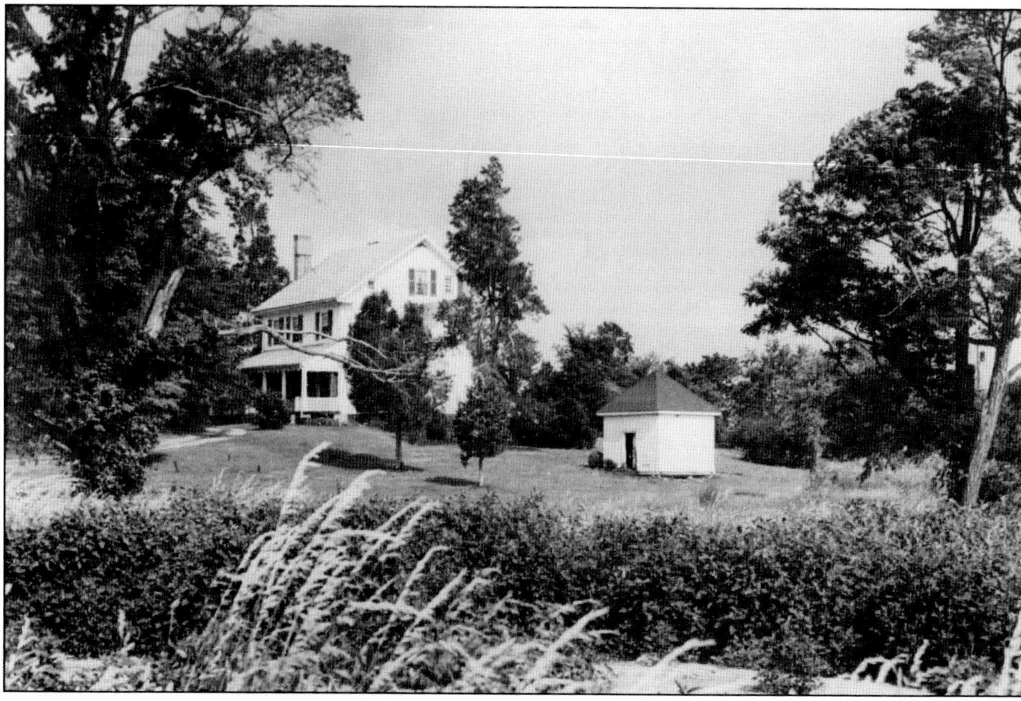

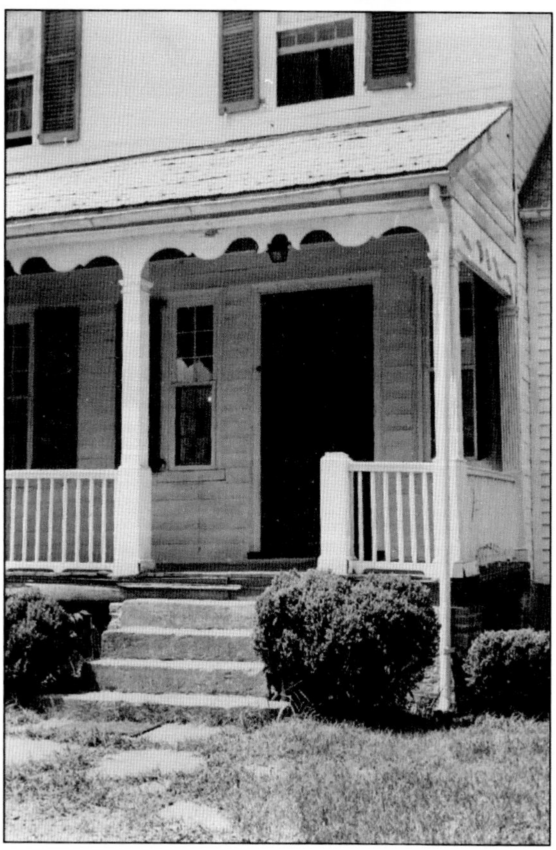

"Two-and-a-half stories high and three bays wide, Sully bears a resemblance to the town houses of Philadelphia, the city where Lee met and married Elizabeth Collins, the daughter of a Quaker merchant," the Fairfax County Park Authority notes on its website. Lee built Sully during the Federal Period. He ordered two marble hearths, plaster of Paris, window weights, and other items and had them shipped by wagon from the port at Alexandria to Sully. (Both, courtesy of the Library of Congress.)

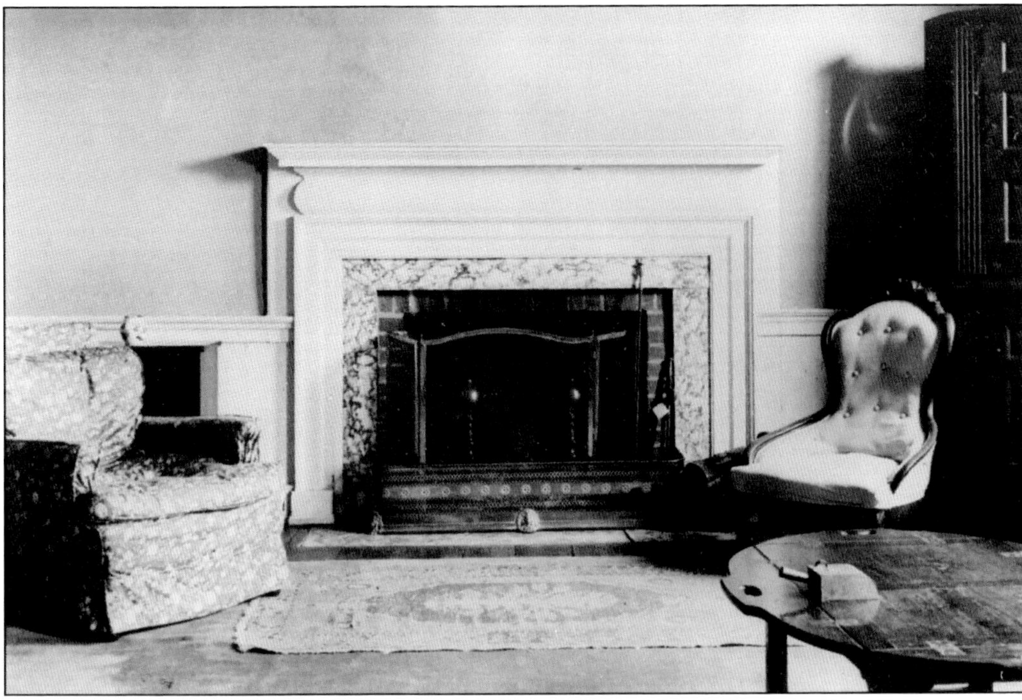

The Sully home had living space and sitting rooms on the first floor. The home was luxuriously furnished with items including mahogany chairs, exported porcelain, a desk, silver, and flatware with green Ivory handles. Outside, Lee had a dairy (pictured below), a kitchen, smokehouse, and another small building constructed. (Courtesy of the Library of Congress.)

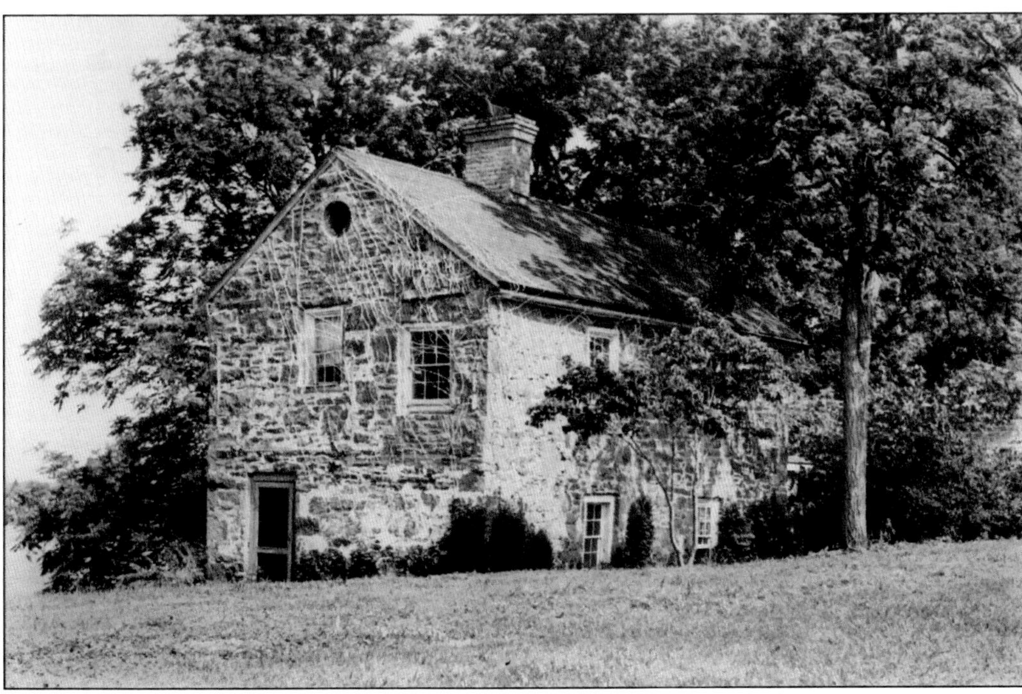

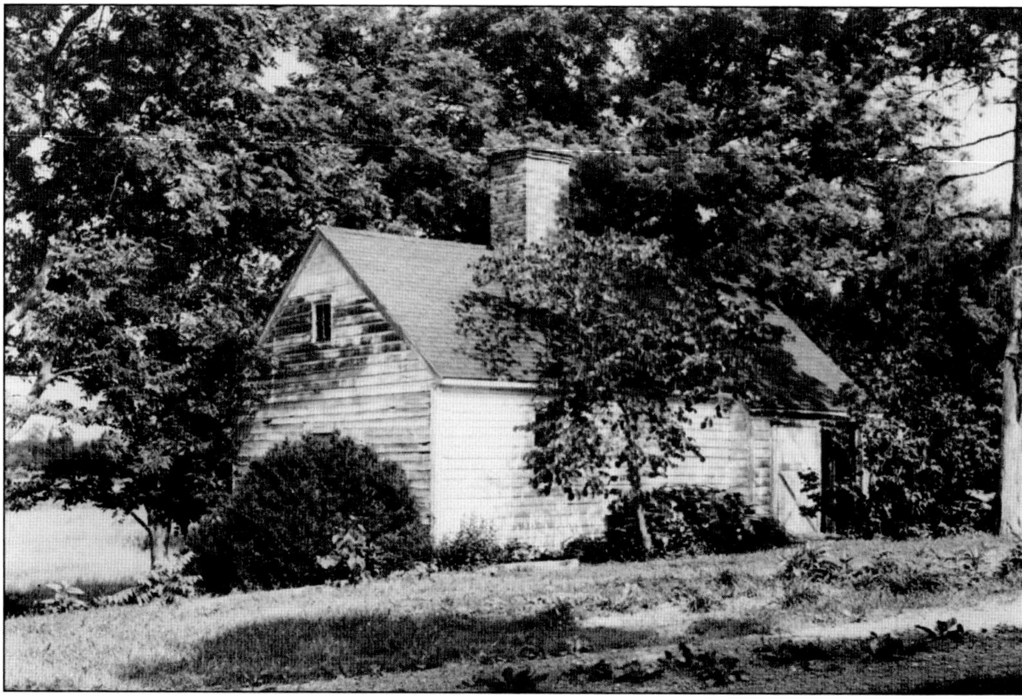

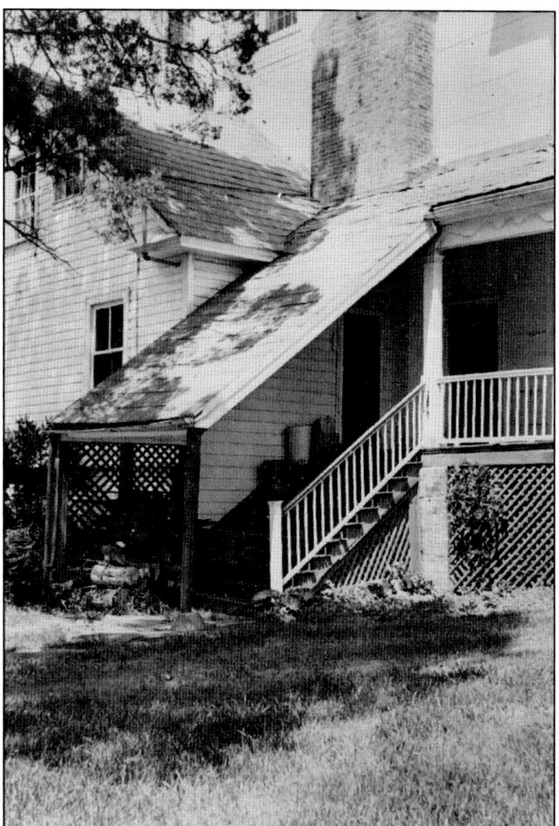

Slaves worked both inside and outside the home at Sully, keeping the farm running. They included John, a manservant; Sam, a blacksmith; Caine and Eave; Prue, a mother; and Thornton, the cook, according to the Fairfax County Park Authority. Lee inherited 29 slaves from his father in 1787. There were also four tenant farmers at Sully. (Courtesy of the Library of Congress.)

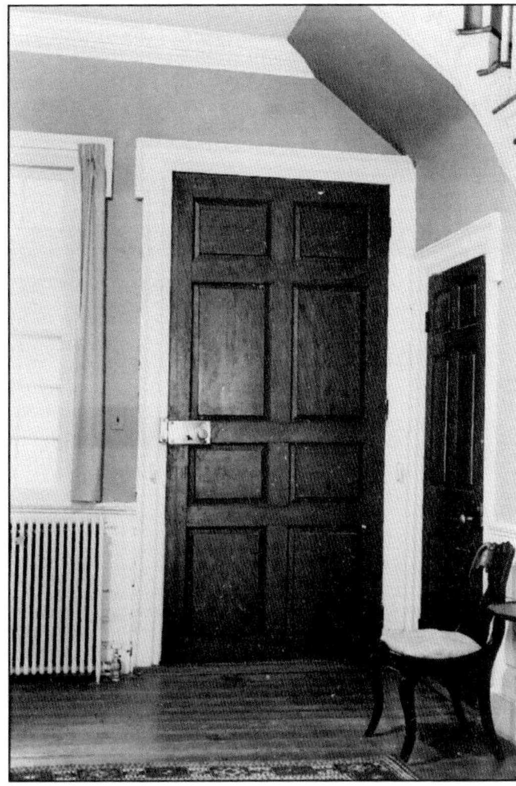

This is a view inside the Sully Plantation. Richard Bland Lee probably sold the house because of changes in his financial situation and possibly because of the demands on his schedule due to his being in public office. (Courtesy of the Library of Congress.)

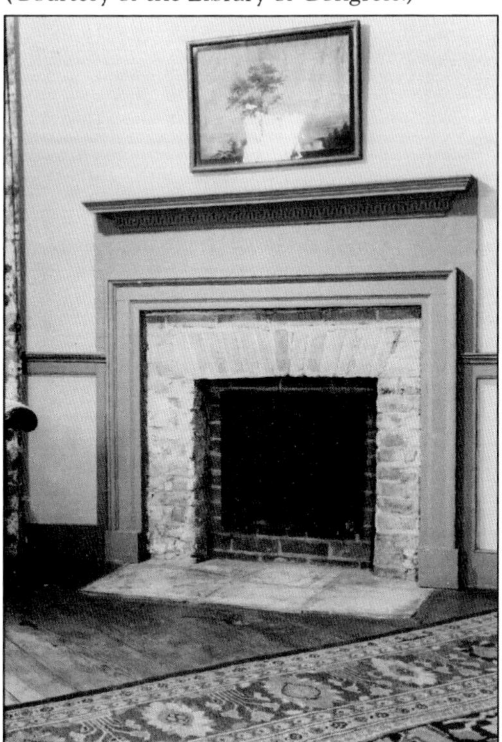

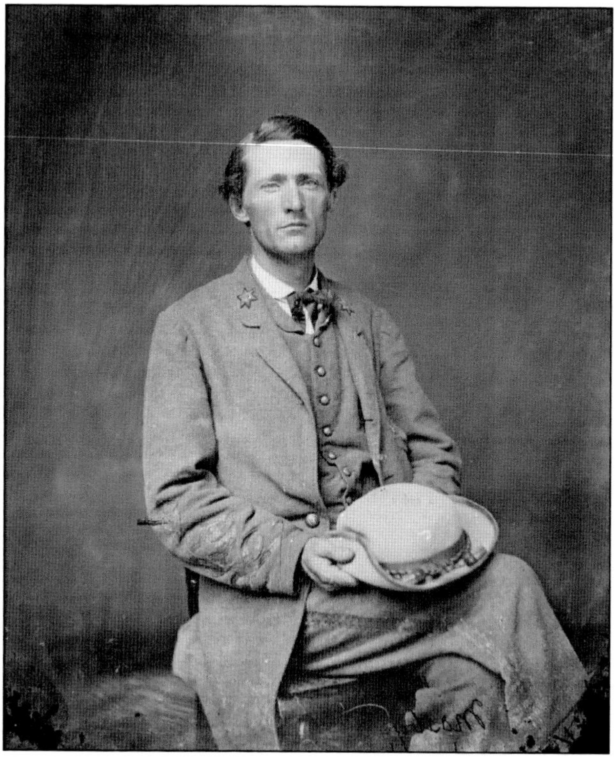

John Mosby, the Confederacy's Gray Ghost, became well-known to the Union-sympathizing Haight and Barlow families who lived at Sully during the Civil War. In fact, after the war, Mosby once told a newspaper that he had asked Maria Barlow on her way to Washington to cut off a piece of his hair and deliver it to President Lincoln. Maria felt that Mosby had embellished the story a bit, but said it was true that he had presented the lock to her—which she never took to the White House. (Courtesy of the Library of Congress.)

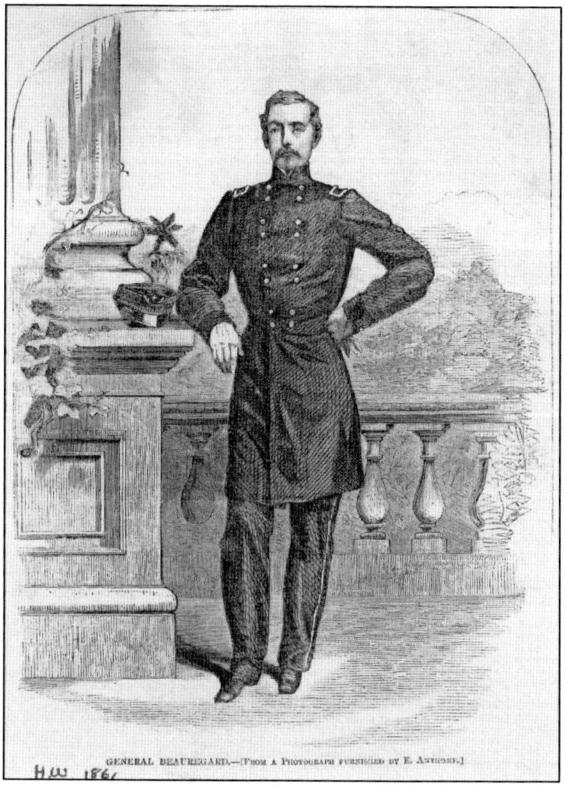

Gen. Pierre Gustave Toutant-Beauregard was a guest at Little Sully. Beauregard reportedly presented Phebe Haight with a spur out of gratitude for the dinner. The spur remained in the family for nearly 60 years. (Courtesy of the Library of Congress.)

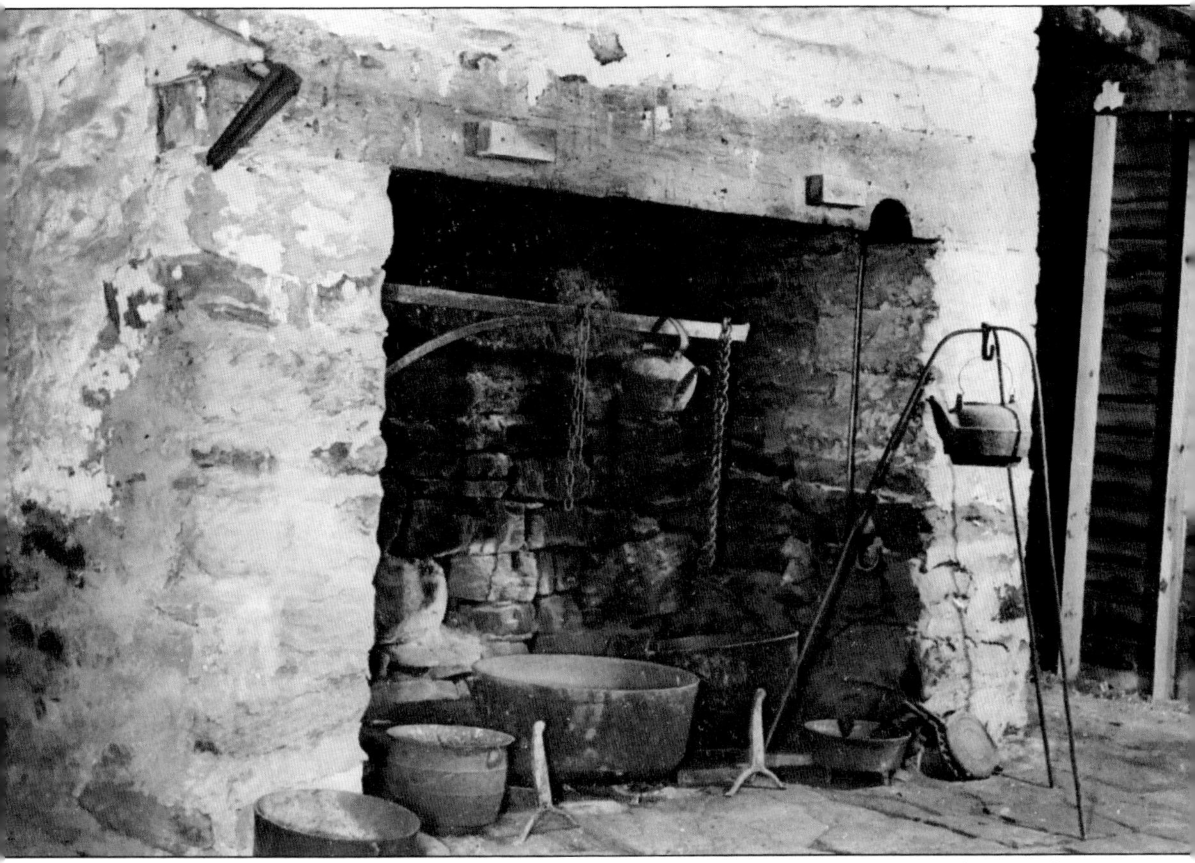

A slave cook ran this kitchen at Sully Plantation. This building was separate from the main house and had a laundry room with a huge wash pot. (Courtesy of the Library of Congress.)

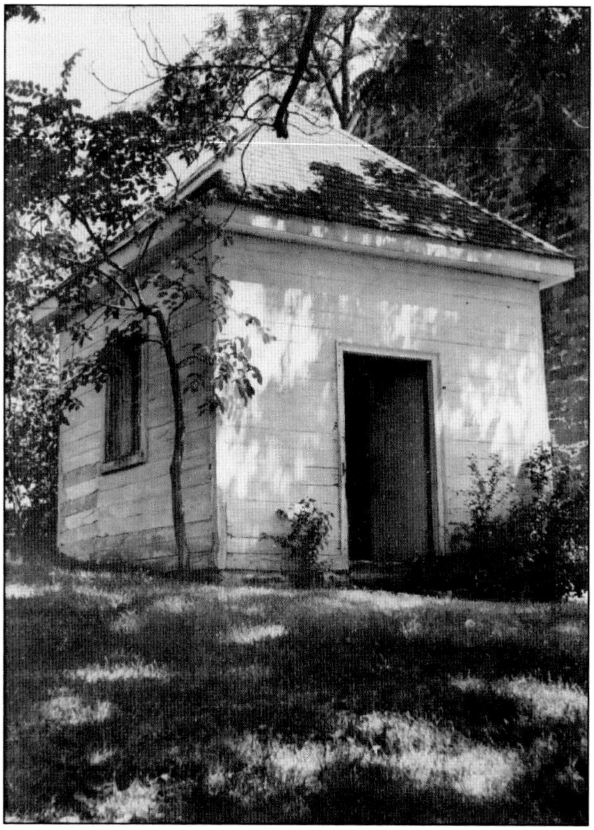

This small building on Sully was an office where the family kept records and did business. As noted in *Sully: Biography of a House*, this was a common feature on most large estates in Virginia. (Courtesy of the Library of Congress.)

Leeton was originally on land that was part of the historic Sully Plantation. Despite some appeals from local residents, the home was demolished in 1960 to make way for Dulles International Airport. The home at Sully was preserved because it was in better condition, after protests from a group of concerned citizens. (Courtesy of the Library of Congress.)

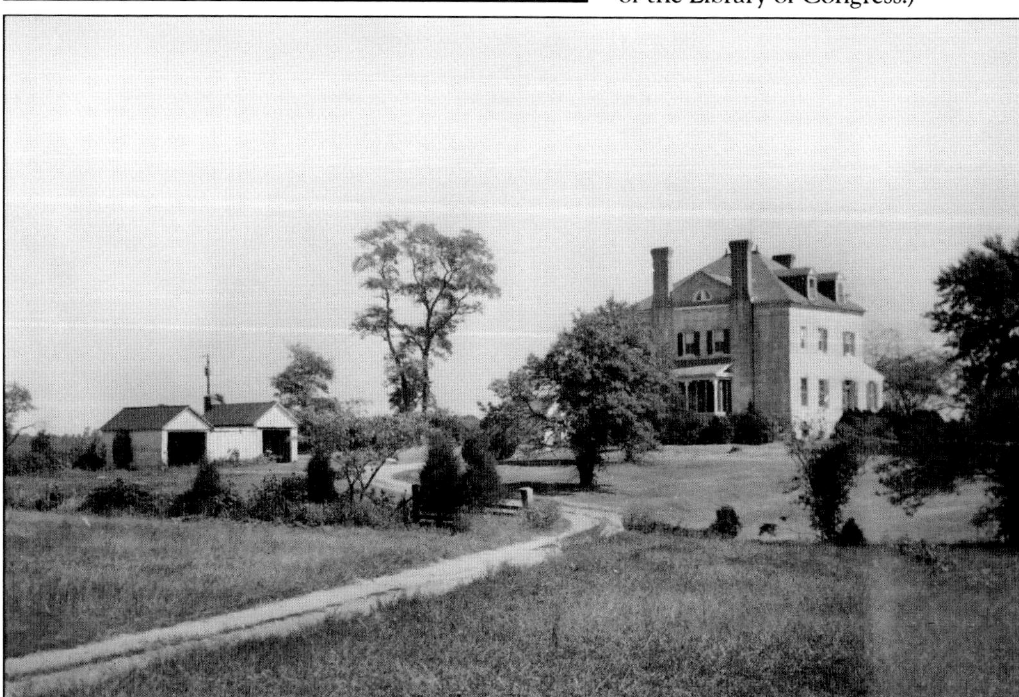

Gov. Mills E. Godwin Jr., the 62nd governor of Virginia, signs the guest book in this undated photograph at the Sully Historic Site. (Courtesy of the Fairfax County Public Library Photographic Archive.)

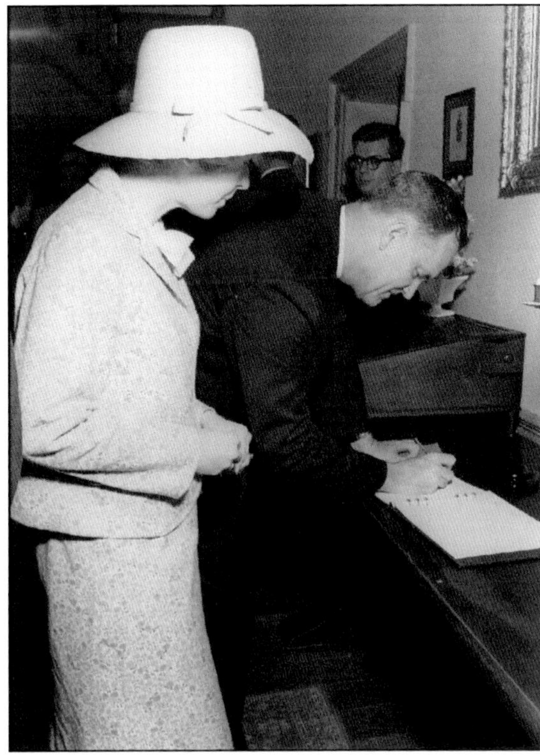

Mount Gilead was built in the mid- to late 1700s. The owner, Joel Beach, operated it as an inn, the House at the Sign of the Black Horse. Malcolm Jamesson, a tanner, bought it in 1837. (Courtesy of the Library of Congress.)

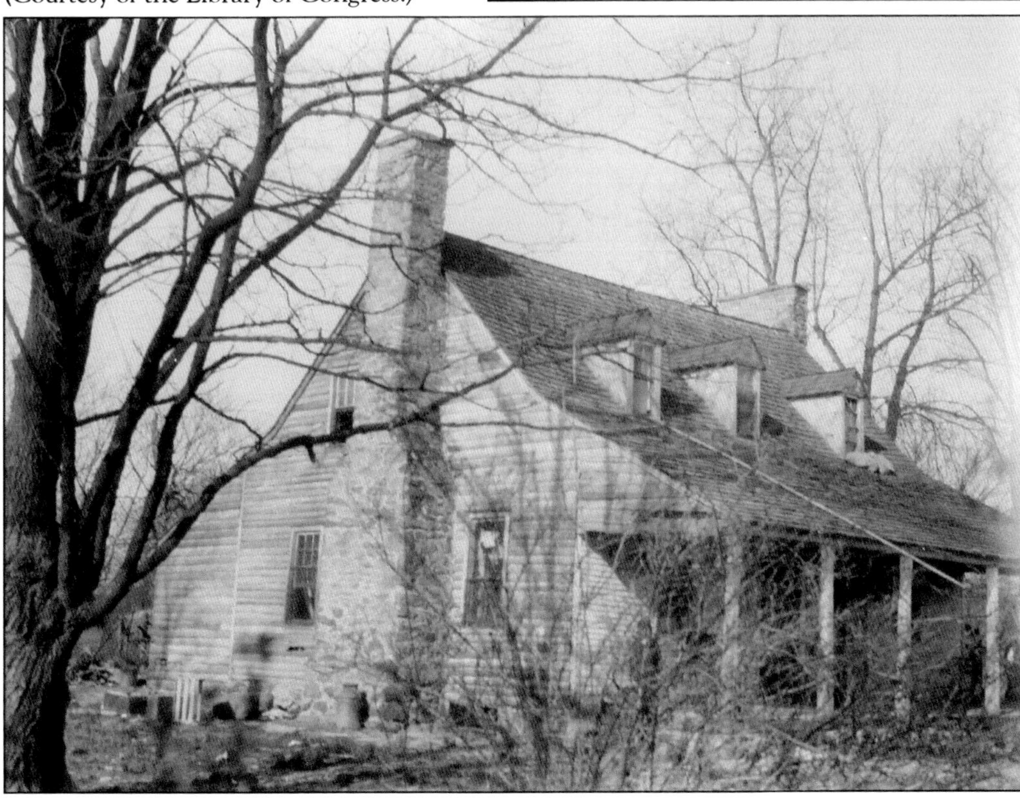

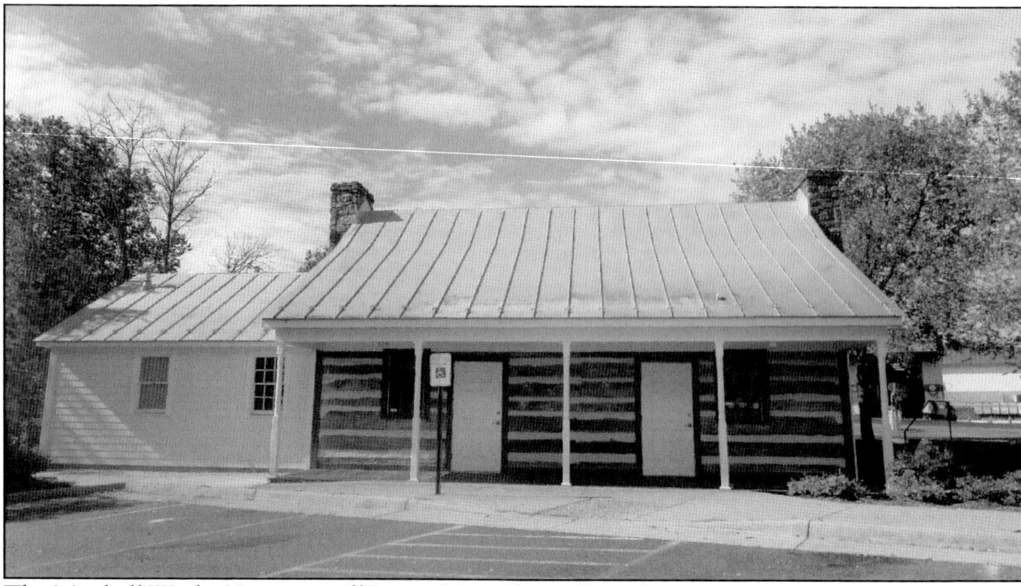

The Mitchell-Weeks House sits off Route 50 in Chantilly and may have been built as early as 1789. Benjamin Mitchell was granted the land in 1797. It remained in the family until 1887. During the Battle of Chantilly, the house was used as a hospital. In 1952, Charles and Edith Weeks bought the house and did considerable work on it. (Author's collection.)

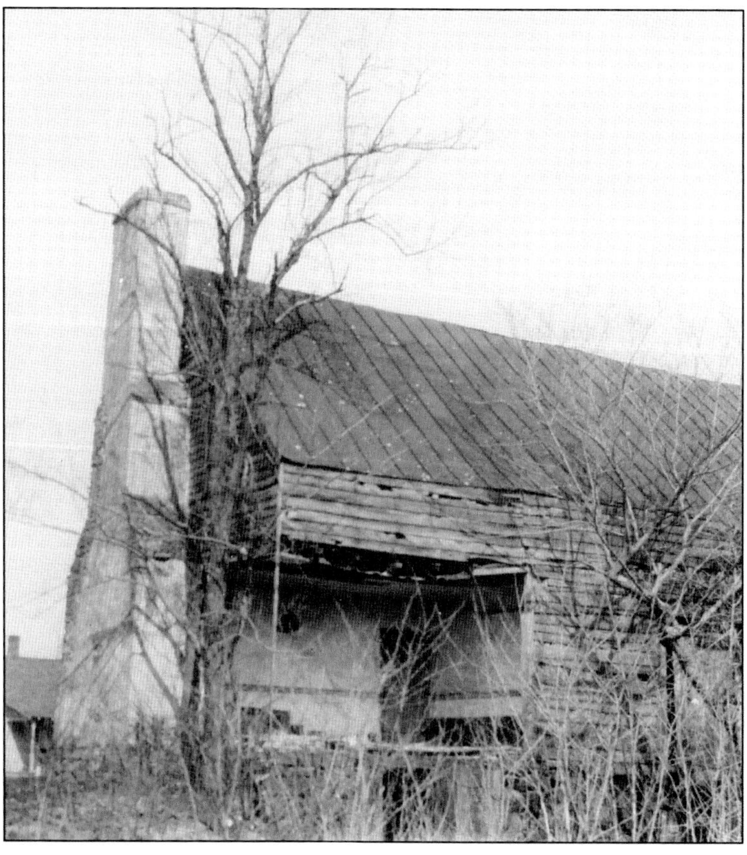

William Carr Lane opened Newgate Tavern in Centreville in the 1760s. The tavern was successful and attracted visitors like George Washington, who stopped by multiple times during his trips, and Thomas Jefferson. By the early 1900s, the tavern was in ruins. (Courtesy of the Fairfax County Public Library Photographic Archive.)

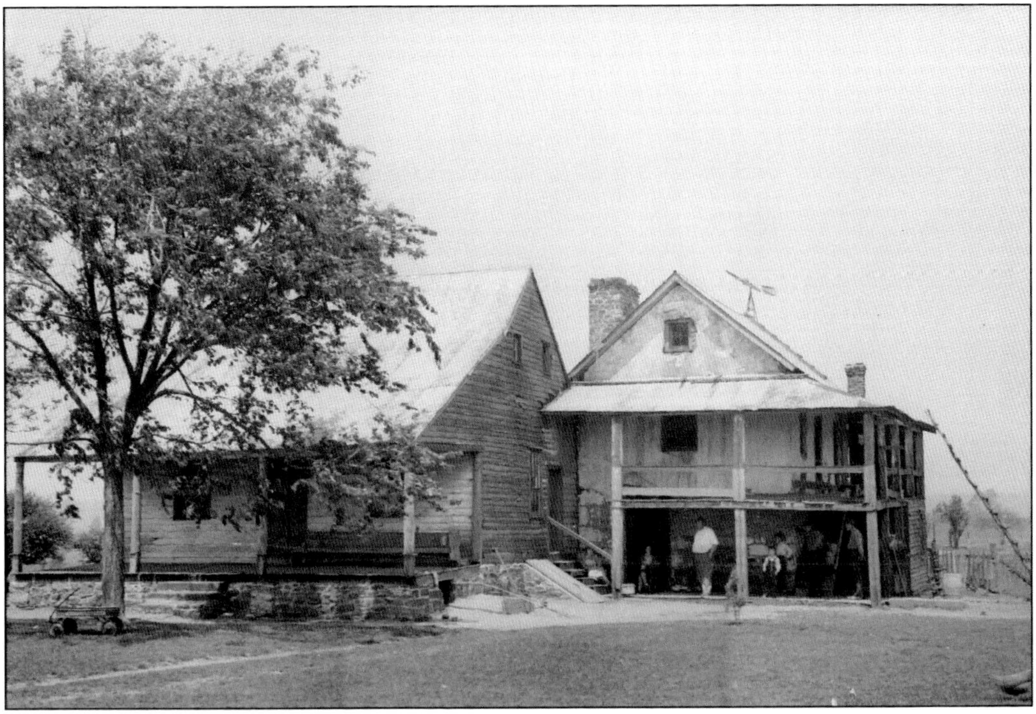

This photograph, likely taken around 1936, is of the Mountain View home at 6421 Bull Run Post Office Road. The home is no longer in existence. The area near Bull Run Post Office Road is one of the few places left in Centreville that has retained much of its rural character in the present day, with horse farms, a small Fairfax County Park, and the Southwestern Youth Association sports park, surrounded by woods. (Both, courtesy of the Library of Congress.)

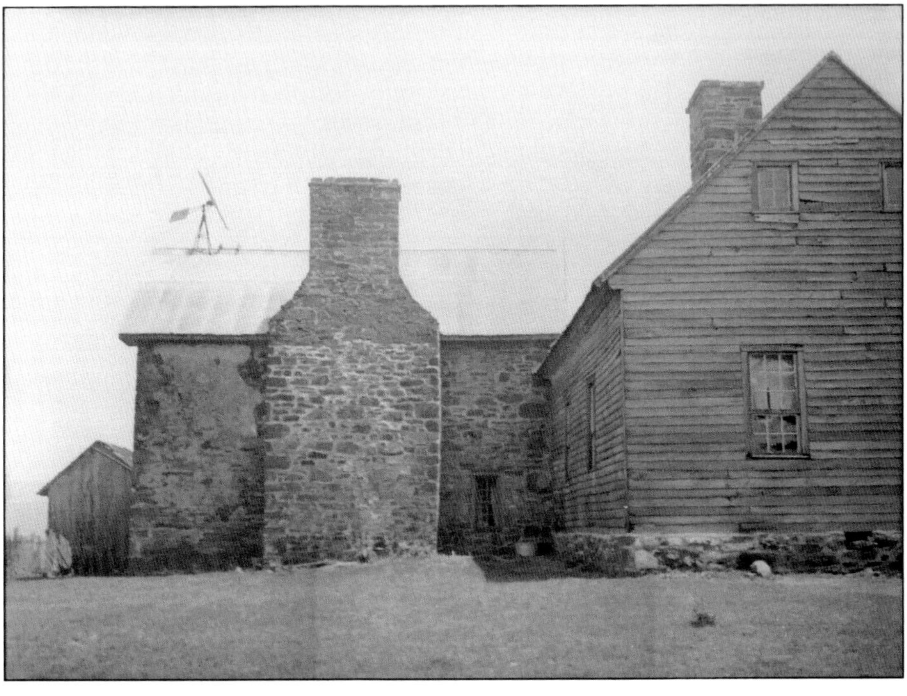

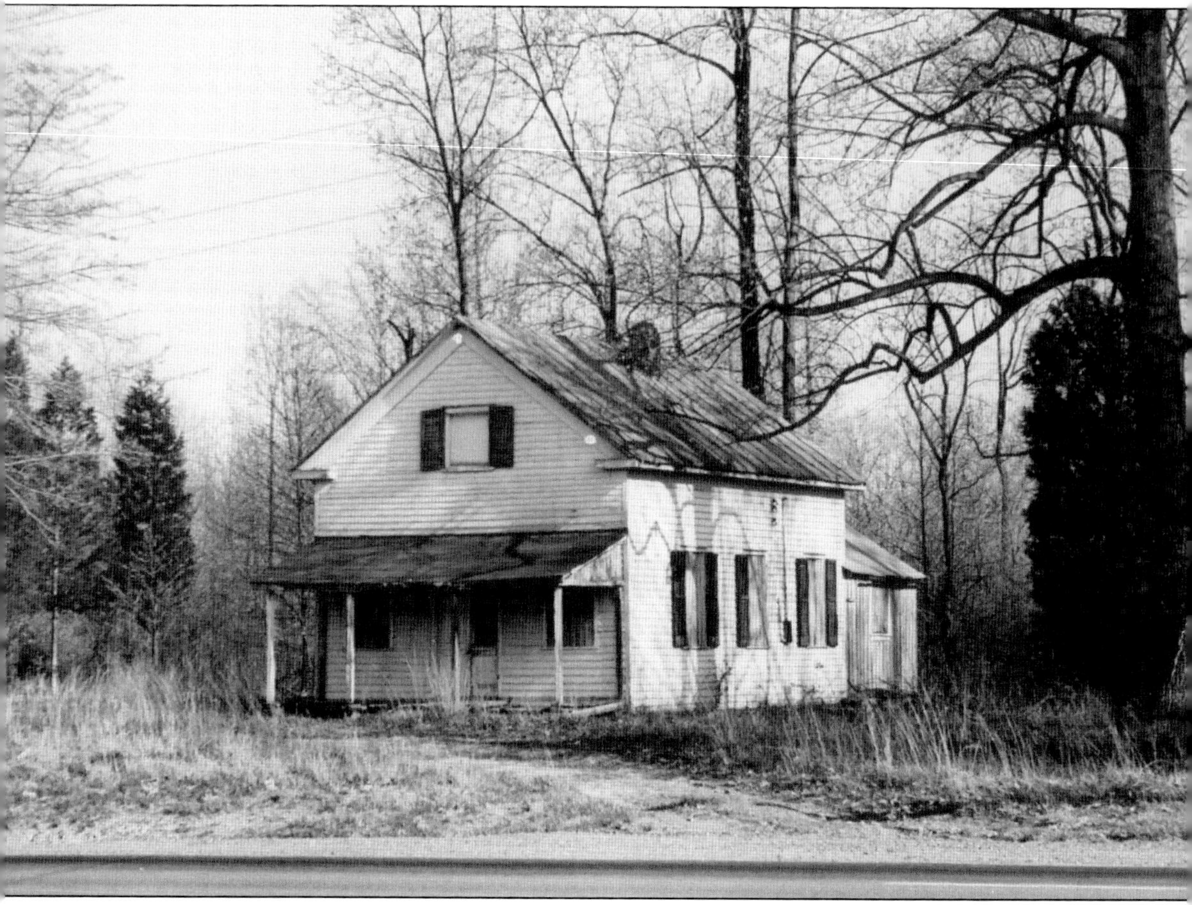

Legato School stood on the south side of Lee Highway where the present Pheasant Ridge Road intersects the service road east of Fairfax County Parkway. This picture, taken by Lee Hubbard in 1968 shows the school, which was typical of Fairfax County's one-room schoolhouses. Rock Hill schoolhouse in Centreville, just a few miles away, would have been a very similar style. The Legato School still stands but was moved to the Fairfax County Government Center complex. (Courtesy of Lee Hubbard.)

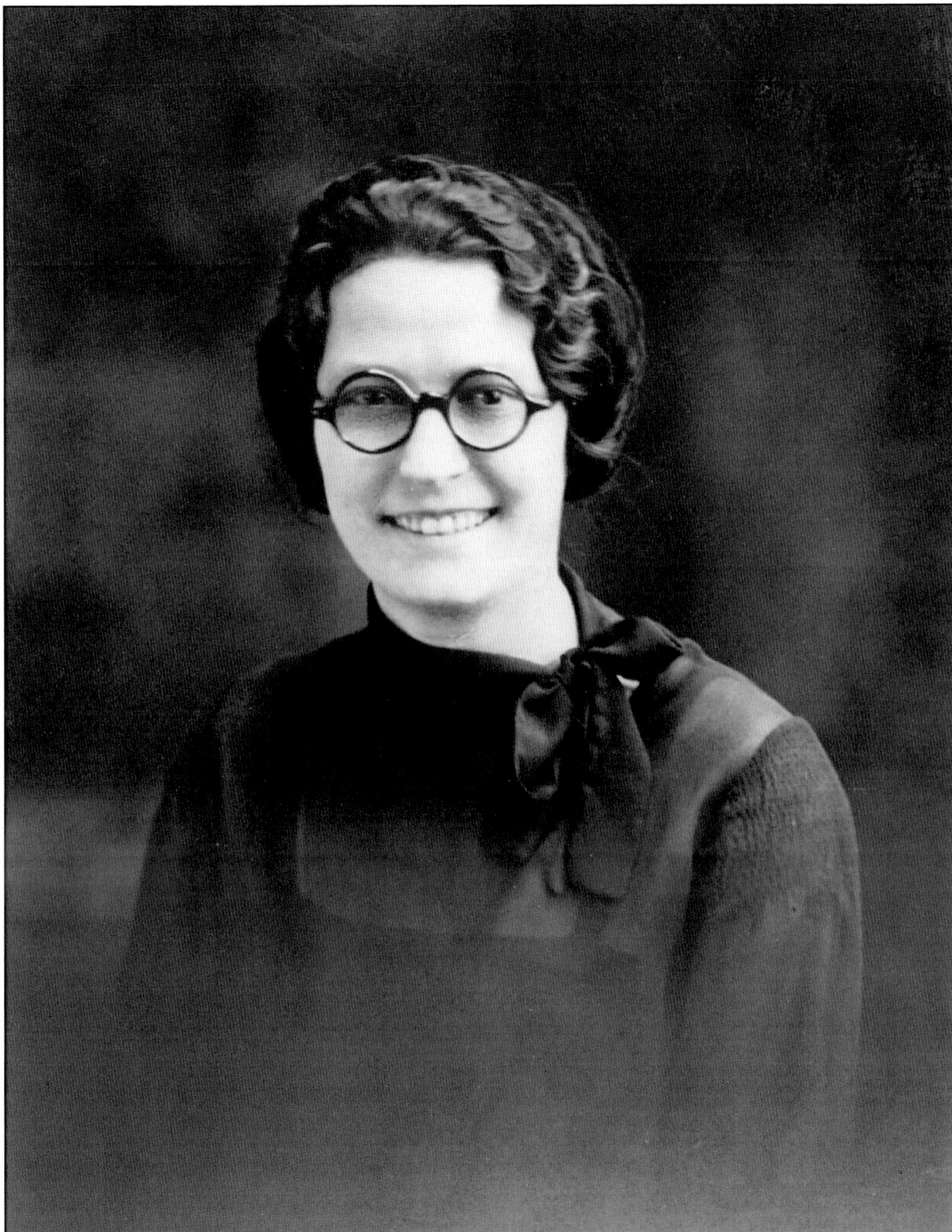

Sue (Rigg) Murph was a teacher at the Rock Hill schoolhouse around 1920. She drove to the school every day in a horse and buggy (Courtesy of Lee Hubbard.)

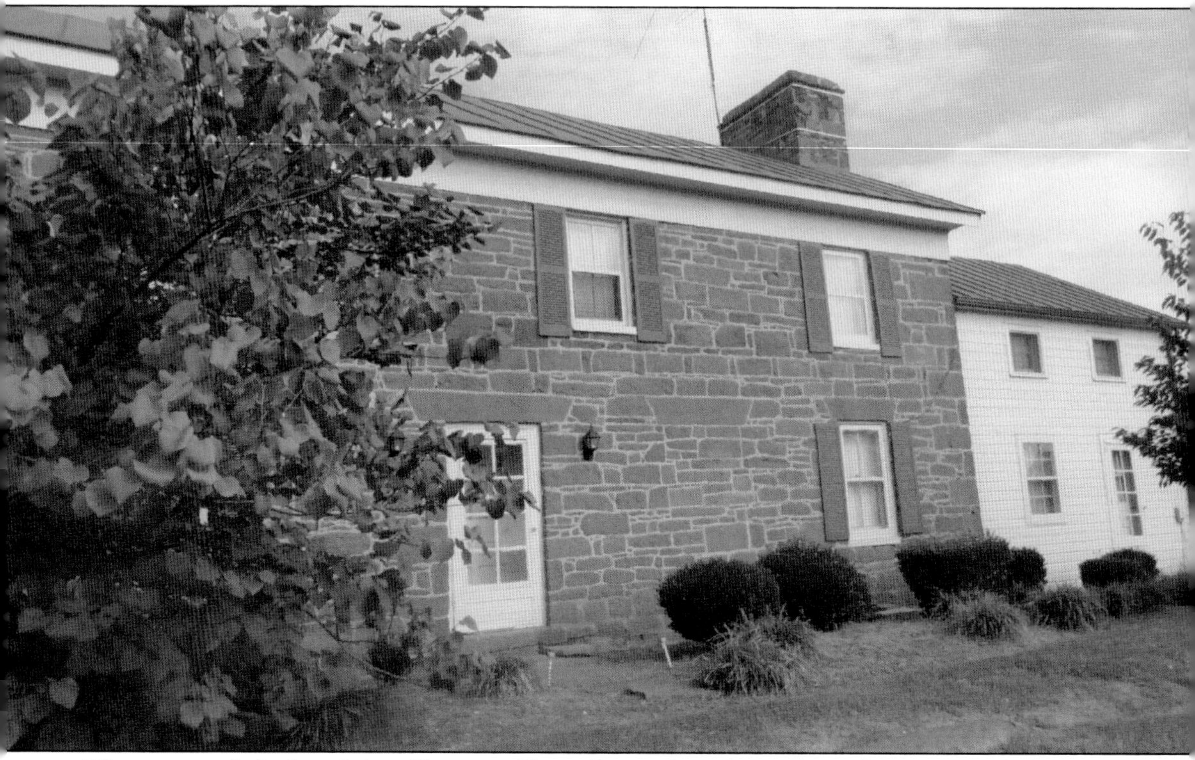

The stone-and-clapboard Ayre House in Chantilly may have been where the overseer of Chantilly farm lived. It was built sometime between 1771 and 1820. The International Country Club now owns the house and surrounding property, though a historical marker testifies to the significance of the house. (Author's collection.)

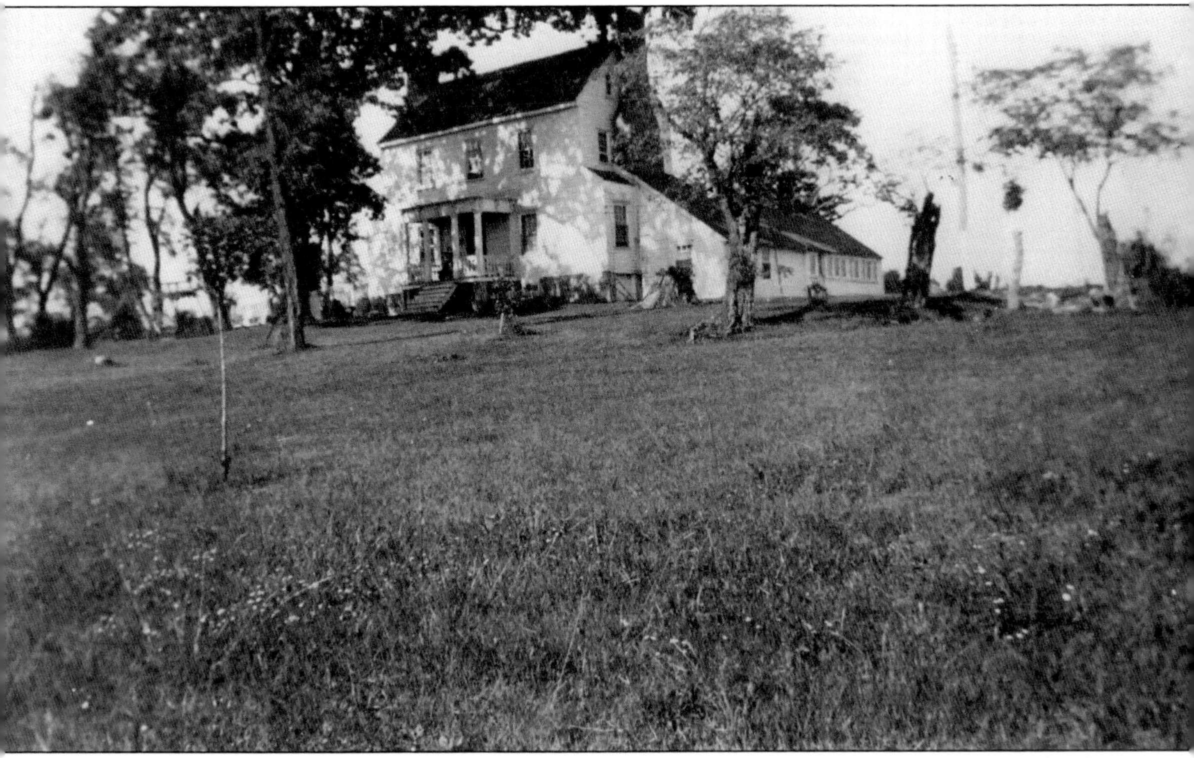

The Royal Oaks House was situated in the heart of historic Centreville—with 10 rooms. Col. John Singleton Mosby may have hid in Royal Oaks during one of his raids, and Generals McDowell and Pope may have also used the house as a headquarters. (Courtesy of the Fairfax County Public Library Photographic Archive.)

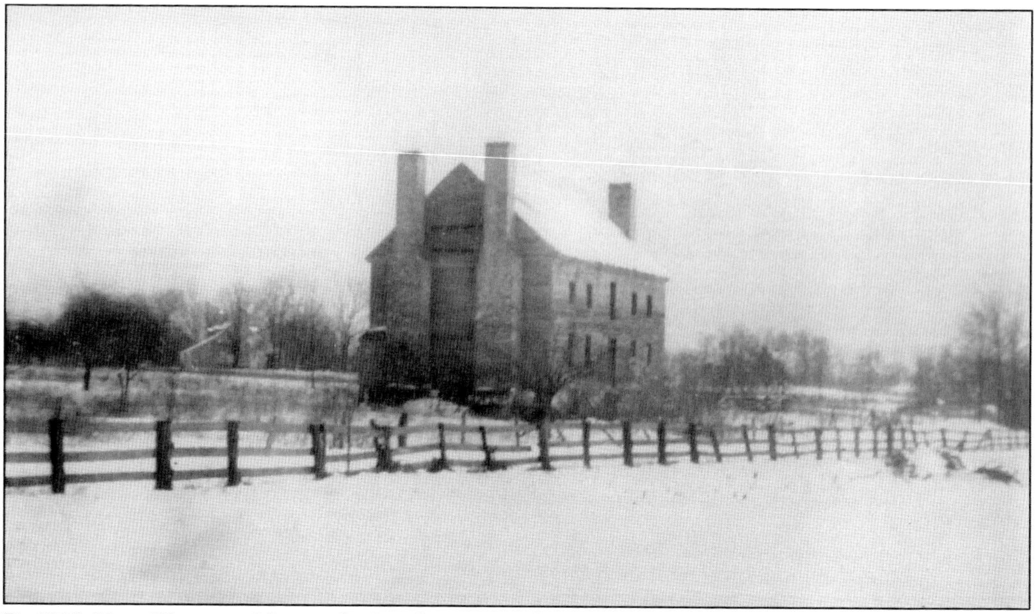

By 1918, Four Chimney House, the headquarters of General Johnston in the Civil War, had fallen into disrepair. The once carefully whitewashed home with dark window framing and enormous front porch was now a ruin. By the 1940s, only the cellar remained. Eventually, someone removed the stones from the foundation to build a gas station near Lee Highway. (Courtesy of the Library of Congress.)

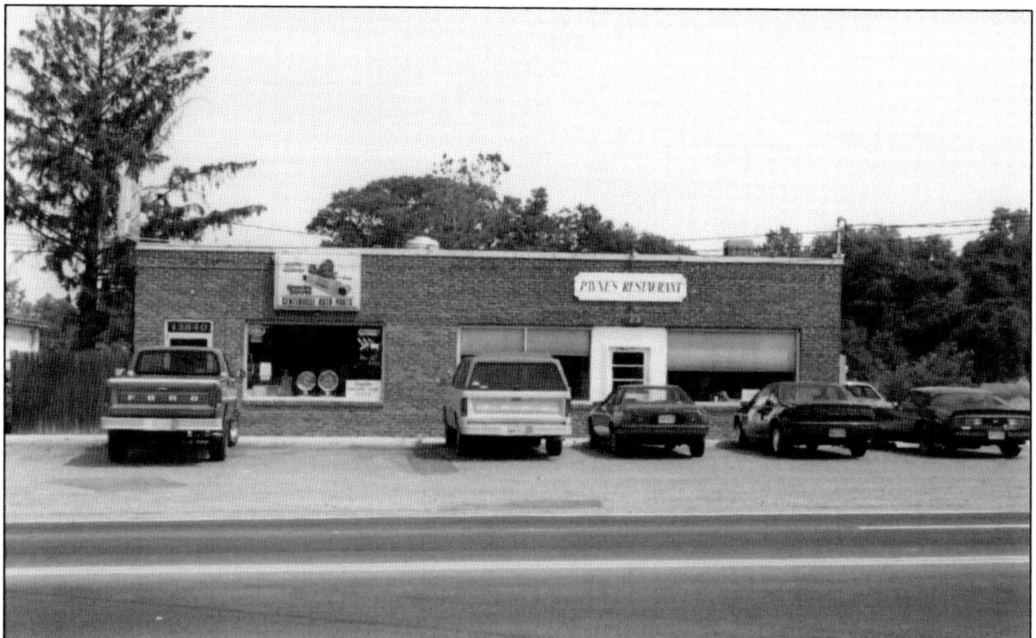

Payne's Restaurant was a popular hangout that closed in 2009, after 50 years in business. The building was constructed in 1908. The Payne family turned it into a restaurant. Abdo and Nancy Abdo ran it for the last 31 years of its existence. It is now used as a Verizon cell phone store. (Courtesy of the Fairfax County Public Library Photographic Archive.)

Three

Down on the Farm

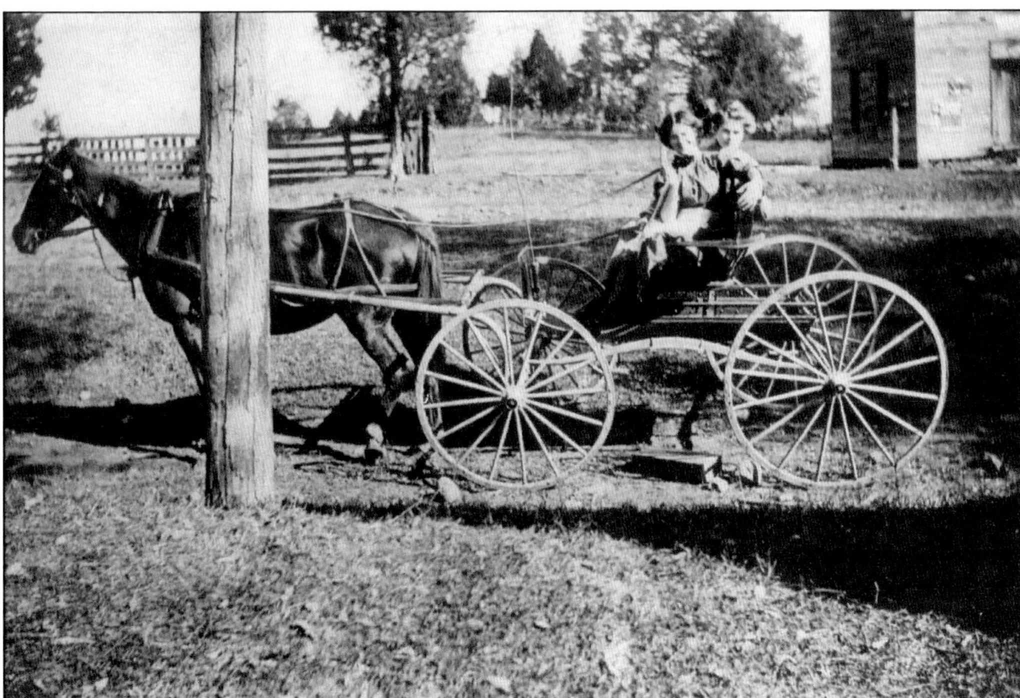

Rural life once defined Centreville and Chantilly, but now little trace remains of the area's rich agricultural heritage. Farming was once the backbone of the local economy, with Fairfax County even boasting its own brand of corn. Here, Martha Hoppe and Nellie Lee Cockerille ride in a horse-drawn buggy in Chantilly around 1900. (Courtesy of the Fairfax County Public Library Photographic Archive.)

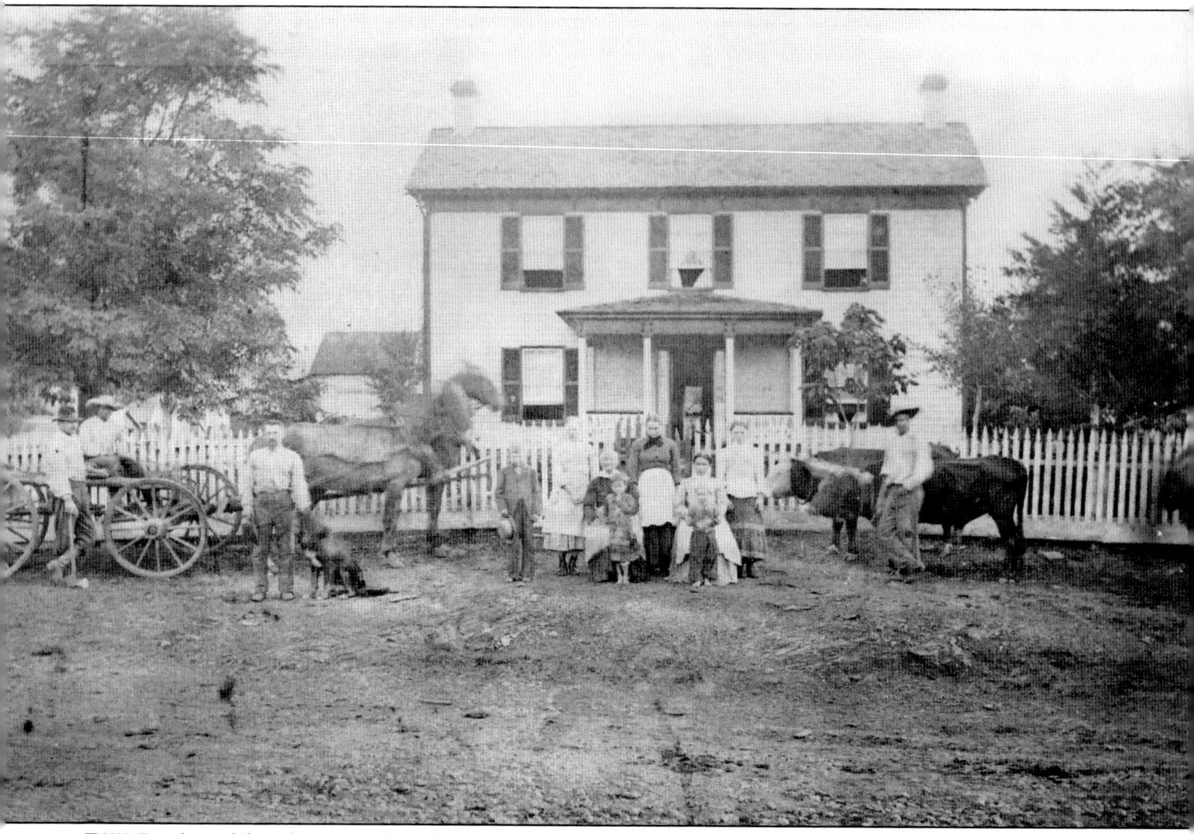

E.W. Birch and family are at their farm in Chantilly, around 1880. E.W. Birch, a farmer, wheelwright, and blacksmith, married Mary Catherine Virginia Davis in 1860. They lived in a home on her parents' farm by Route 50. After Mary died in 1864, E.W. married her younger sister, Frances Emiline America Davis. (Courtesy of the Fairfax County Public Library Photographic Archive.)

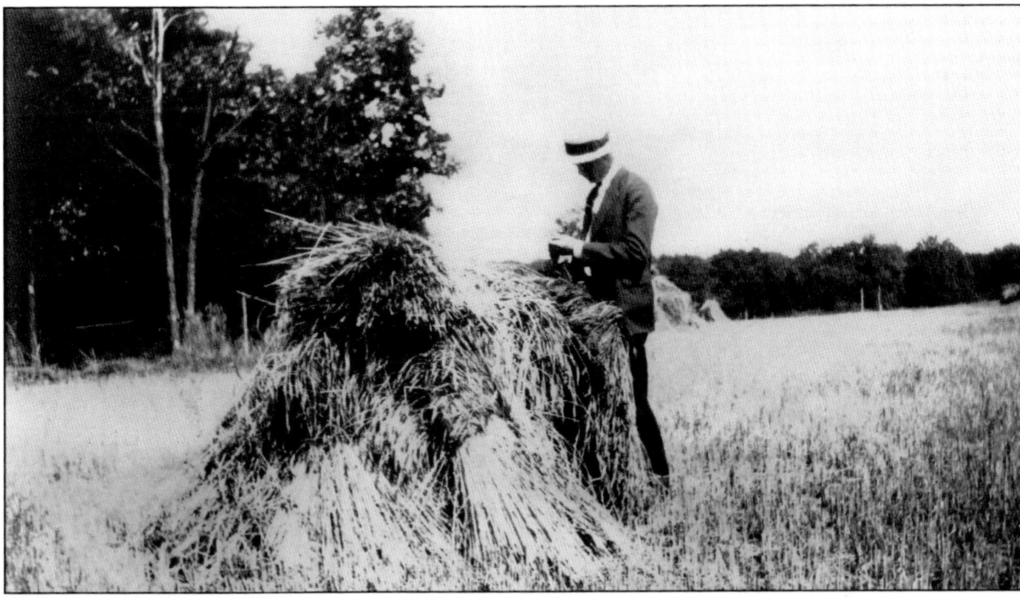

Pictured is county agent Harry B. Derr inspecting vascular puncture inoculation (VPI) wheats in Fairfax County, around 1925. "The majority of the improved fields of wheat were not inspected as the seed was all to be sold in the county where the purchaser could do his own inspecting," Derr noted. (Courtesy of the Fairfax County Public Library Photographic Archive.)

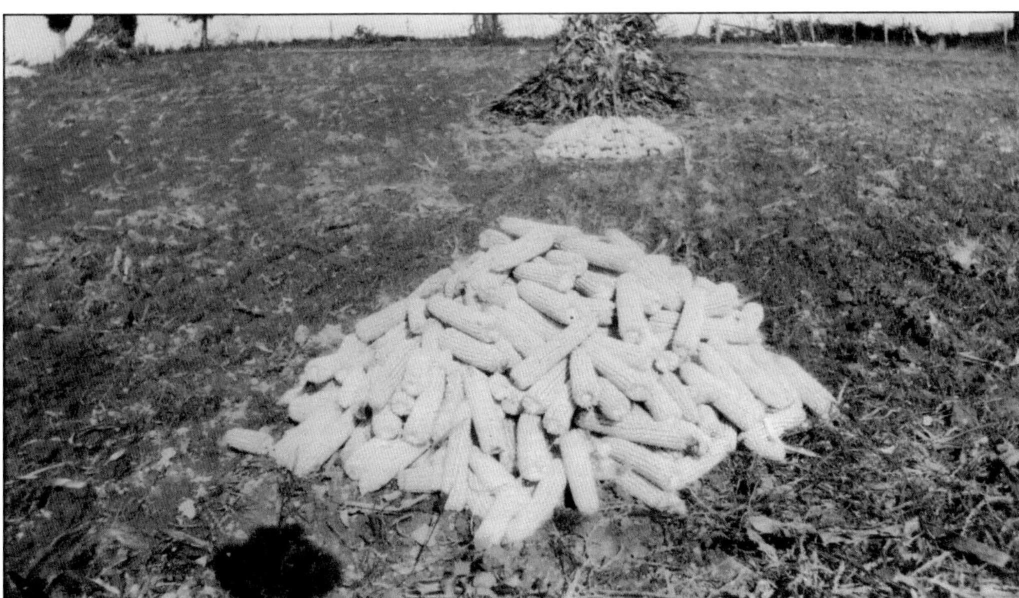

"For the past six years the writer has been working with the corn project and has made a number of selections from Boone county white corn. The Boone corn in the old farm was not adapted to a large portion of the soil. A selection was made and called Fairfax County white which has given splendid results," county extension agent Harry B. Derr wrote in his annual report. This picture is of Fairfax County white corn on the farm of Robert Wrenn, off Centreville Road. (Courtesy of the Fairfax County Public Library Photographic Archive.)

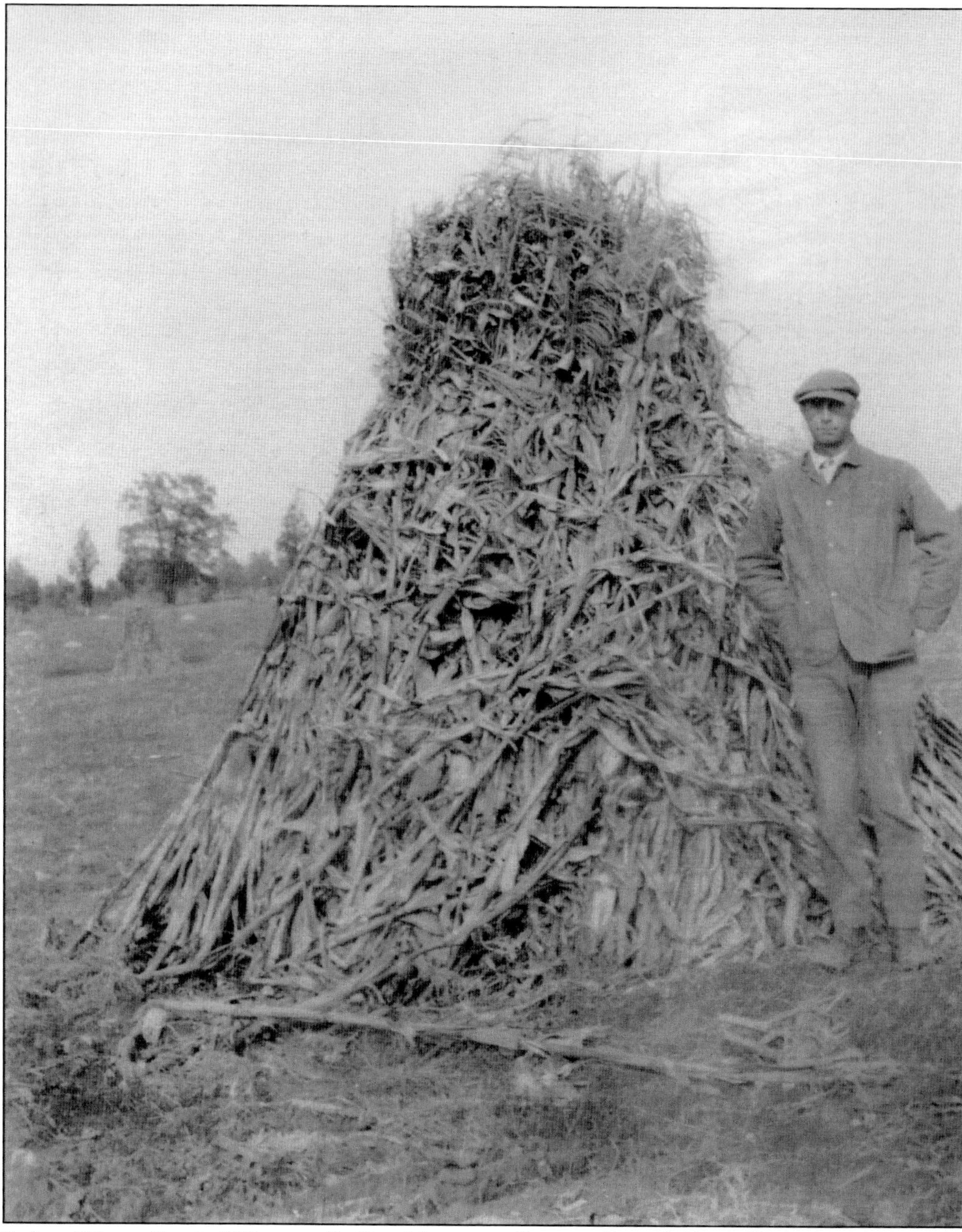

Robert Wrenn lived off Centreville Road, between Centreville and Chantilly. He grew seed corn, barley, and oats and then sold them to his neighbors. "Mr. Robt. Wrenn the demonstrator who has had splendid success with the Fairfax county white sel. His best field will yield at least 80 bushels per acre," county demonstration agent Harry B. Derr noted in his 1925 annual report. (Courtesy of the Fairfax County Photographic Archive.)

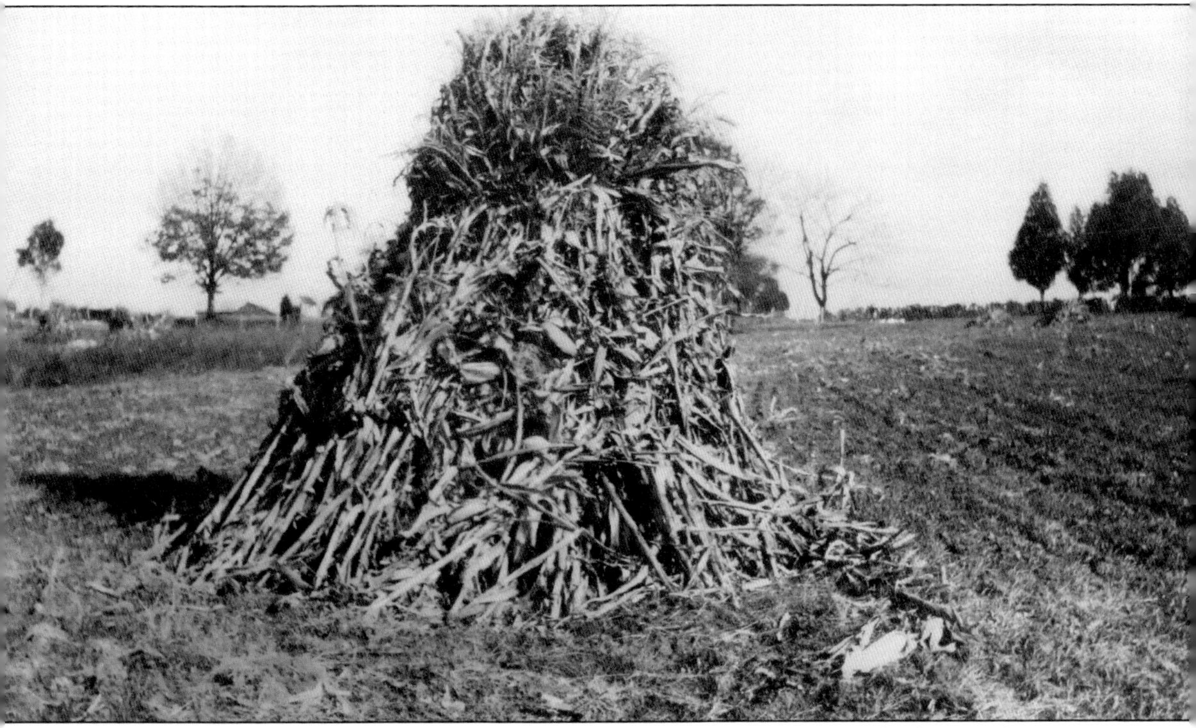

"A ten-acre field with shocks like this has some corn in sight. Is it any wonder that Fairfax county is in the corn belt of the state," county extension agent Harry B. Derr remarked in his 1925 annual report. (Courtesy of the Fairfax County Public Library Photographic Archive.)

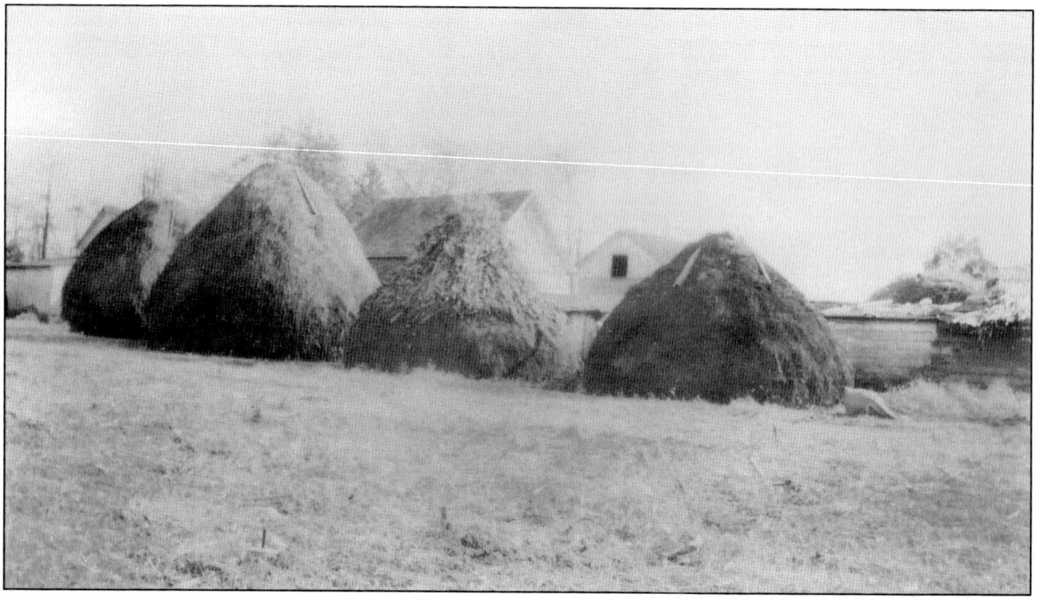

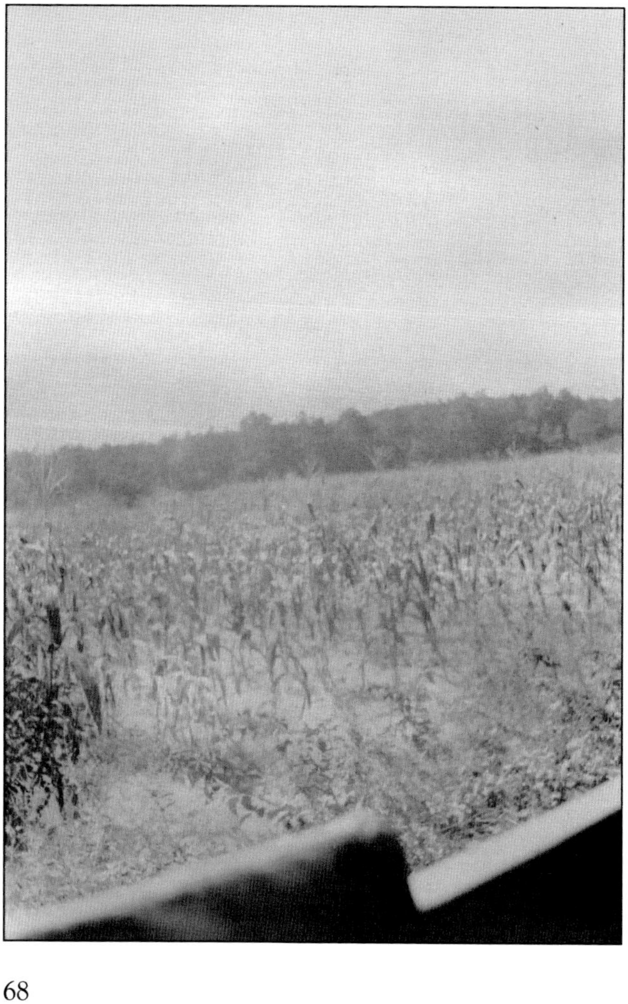

Clover and mixed hay are seen on the farm of Robert Wrenn in Chantilly. County demonstration agent Harry B. Derr notes that Wrenn had tried out some hay mixtures he recommended, especially adapted to his type of soil. The stacks in the photograph are the result. (Courtesy of the Fairfax County Public Library Photographic Archive.)

"This is a picture of a field that has been in corn continuously for many years. Little or no seed selection has been practiced. The soil a sandy loam has been depleted, nothing being added except a small amount of fertilizer each year," county demonstration agent Harry B. Derr noted in his 1925 annual report. This photograph is likely of Robert Wrenn's farm. (Courtesy of the Fairfax County Public Library Photographic Archive.)

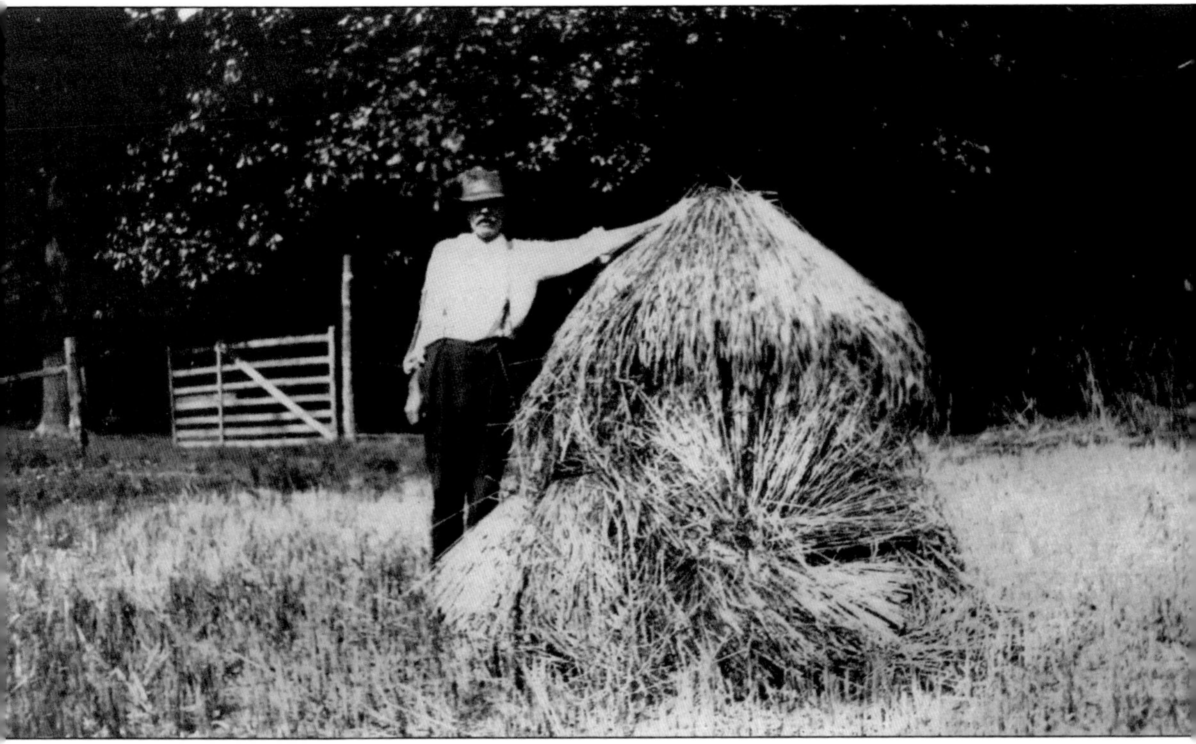

T.E. Reeves is shown with his VPI 131 wheat at a farm at the intersection of Centreville Road and Route 50 in Chantilly. The photograph is from extension agent Harry B. Derr's 1925 annual report. (Courtesy of the Fairfax County Public Library Photographic Archive.)

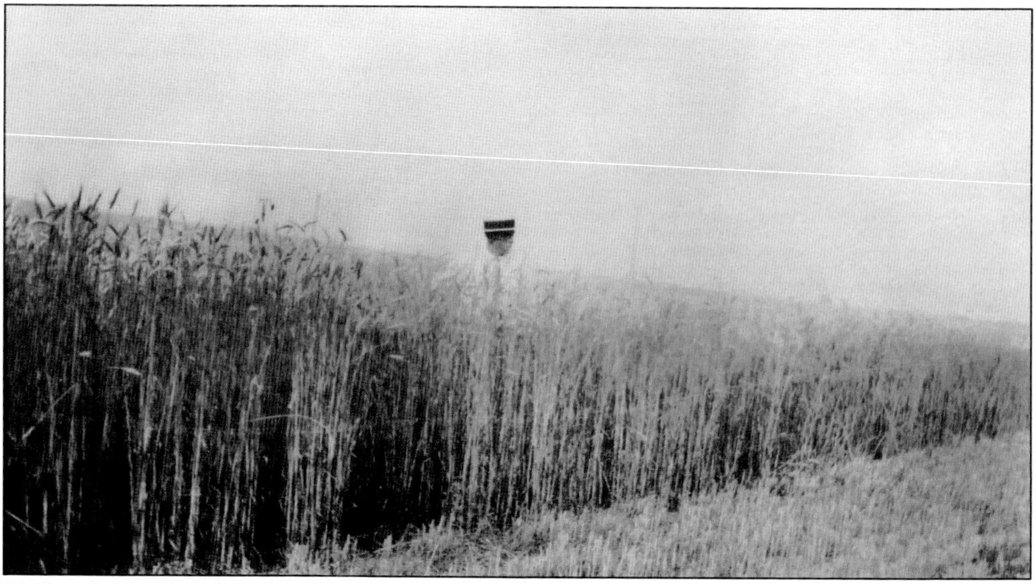

"A fine field of 131 that would pass any inspection," county agent Harry Derr wrote in his 1925 annual report. The field is from T.E. Reeves land by Centreville Road and Route 50 in Chantilly. (Courtesy of the Fairfax County Public Library Photographic Archive.)

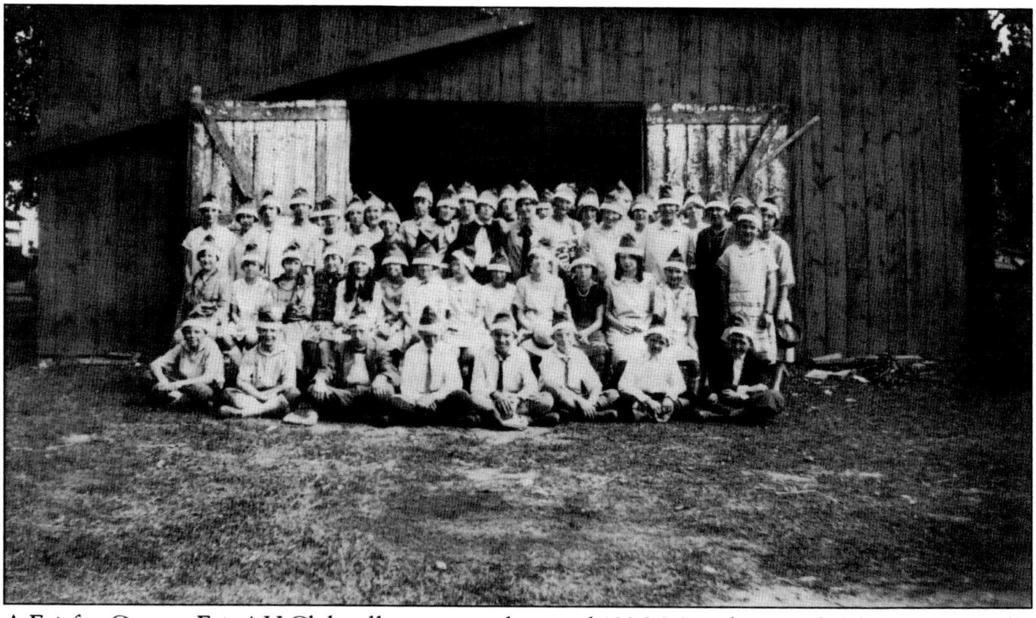

A Fairfax County Fair 4-H Club rally is pictured around 1926. Many boys and girls in Centreville and Chantilly would have been part of the 4-H Club to learn about agriculture. (Courtesy of the Fairfax County Public Library Photographic Archive.)

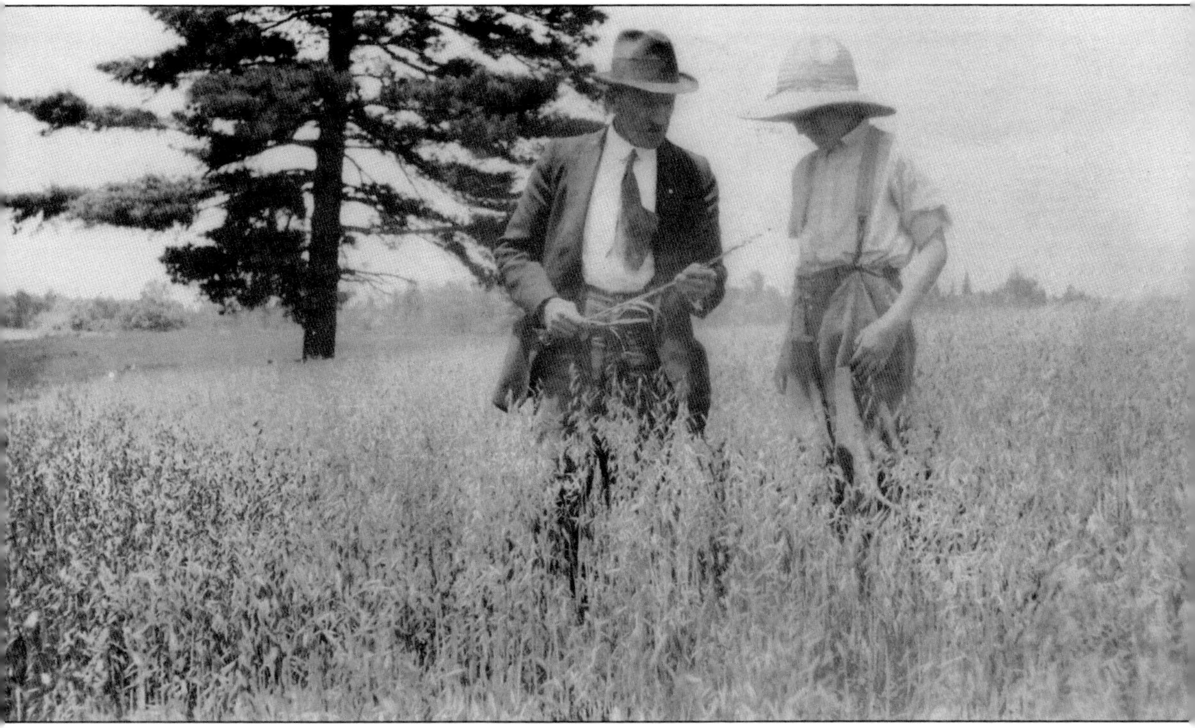

Here, county agent Harry Derr, frequent visitor to Centreville and Chantilly area farms, is showing a boy the damage done by oat smut in 1926. (Courtesy of the Fairfax County Public Library Photographic Archive.)

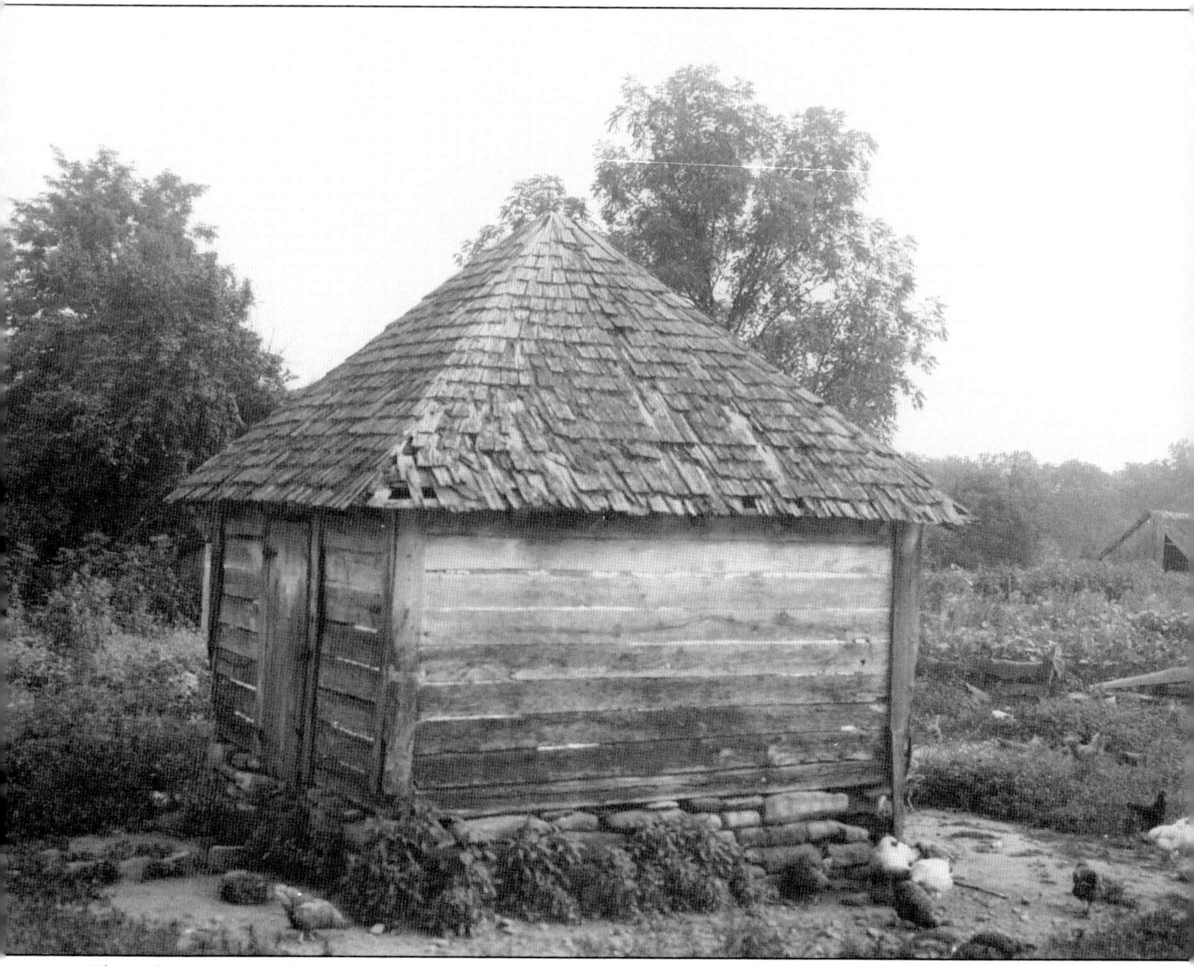

This photograph of the meat plank house at Ellanor C. Lawrence Park may have been taken in the 1930s. It was used to smoke meats. (Courtesy of the Library of Congress.)

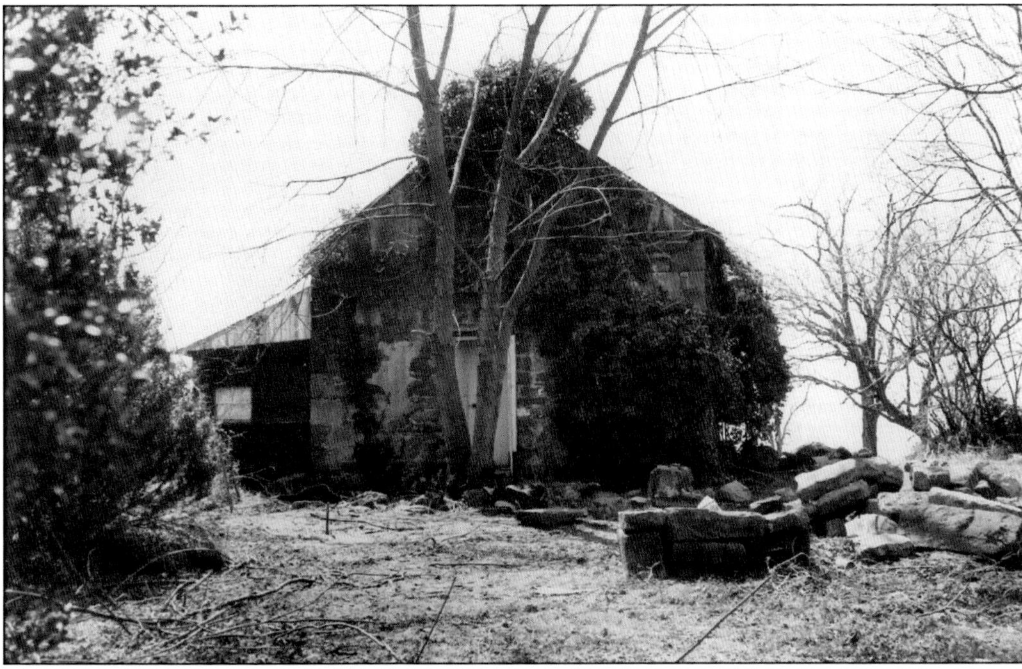

This rear view of a home is of 14015 Braddock Road in Centreville. (Courtesy of the Fairfax County Public Library Photographic Archive.)

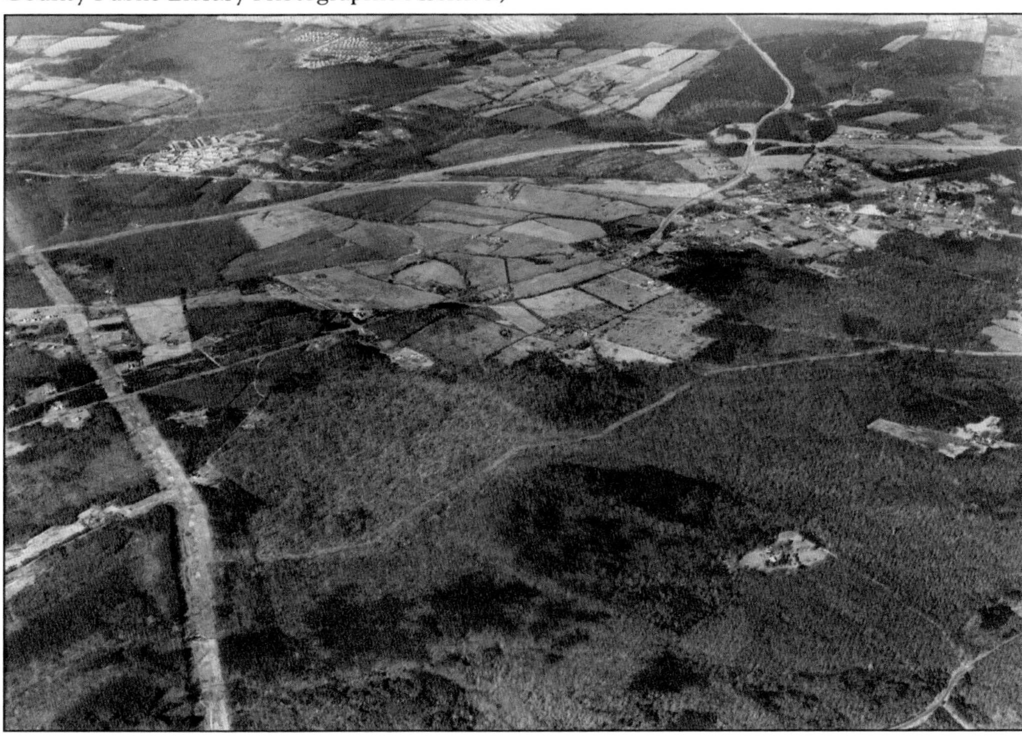

A 1950s aerial view of Centreville shows how rural the area remained, even after the community became more attractive to commuters. (Courtesy of the Fairfax County Public Library Photographic Archive.)

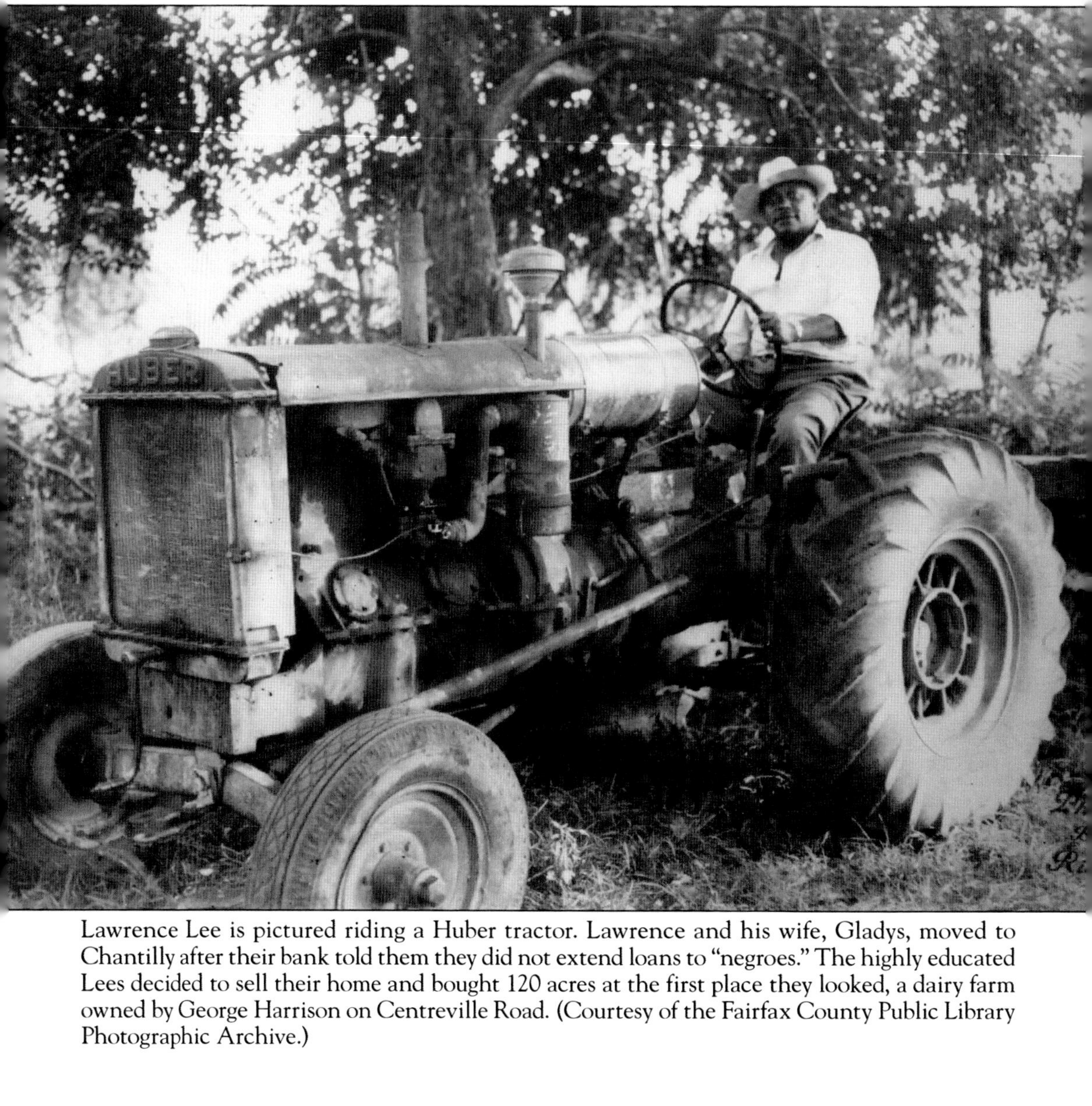

Lawrence Lee is pictured riding a Huber tractor. Lawrence and his wife, Gladys, moved to Chantilly after their bank told them they did not extend loans to "negroes." The highly educated Lees decided to sell their home and bought 120 acres at the first place they looked, a dairy farm owned by George Harrison on Centreville Road. (Courtesy of the Fairfax County Public Library Photographic Archive.)

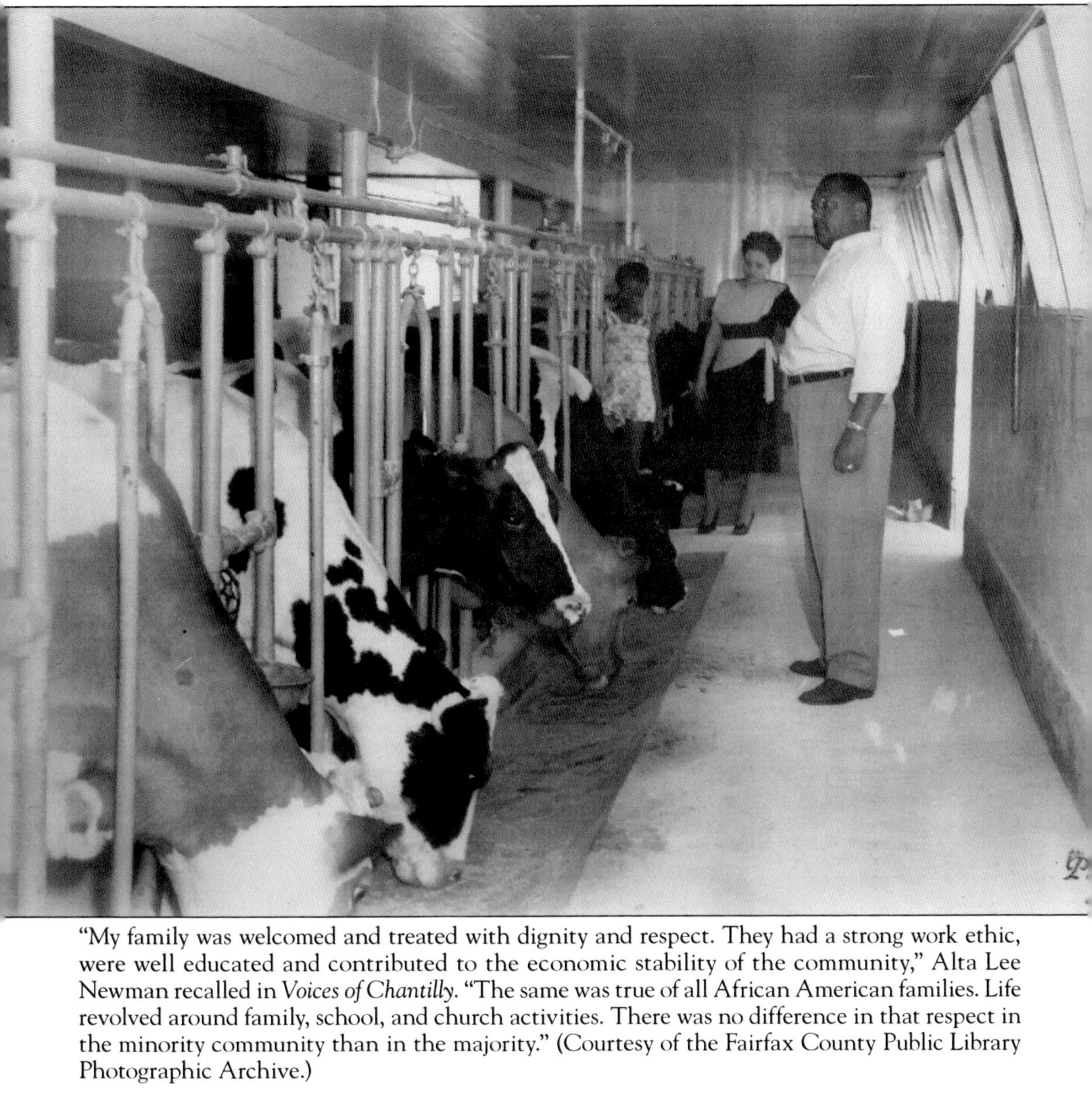

"My family was welcomed and treated with dignity and respect. They had a strong work ethic, were well educated and contributed to the economic stability of the community," Alta Lee Newman recalled in *Voices of Chantilly*. "The same was true of all African American families. Life revolved around family, school, and church activities. There was no difference in that respect in the minority community than in the majority." (Courtesy of the Fairfax County Public Library Photographic Archive.)

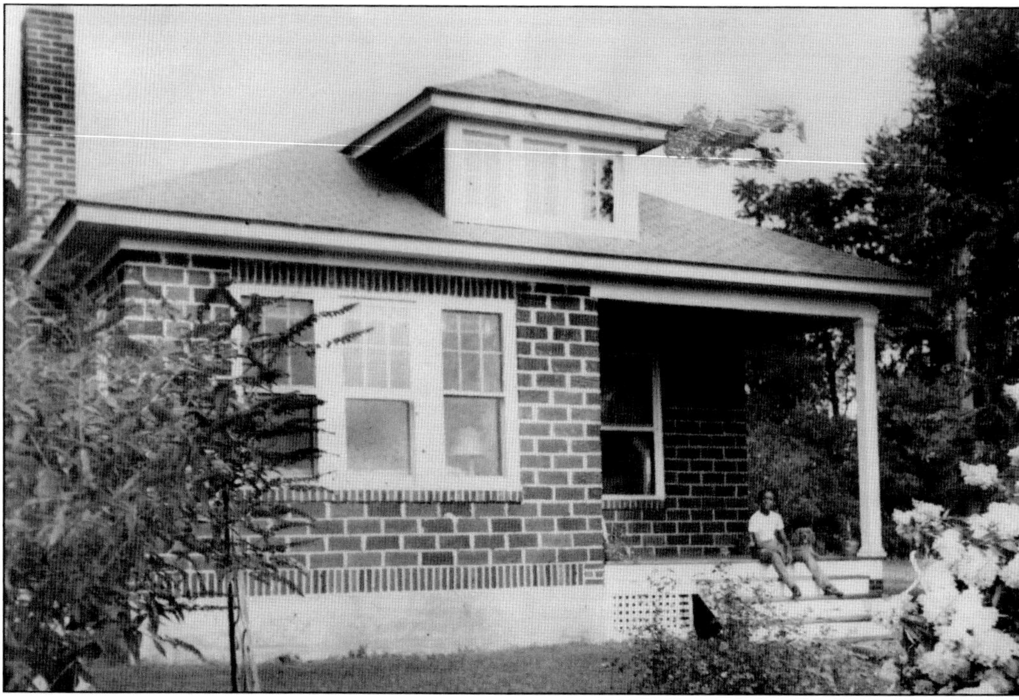

Lawrence and Gladys Lee were educators. Lawrence was a high school teacher and coach in Washington, DC, public schools. Gladys Lee held a master's degree from Columbia University in home economics and taught at Howard University and in public schools. They moved to Chantilly in 1945 and named their new dairy farm Alta Lee Farm. (Both, courtesy of the Fairfax County Public Library Photographic Archive.)

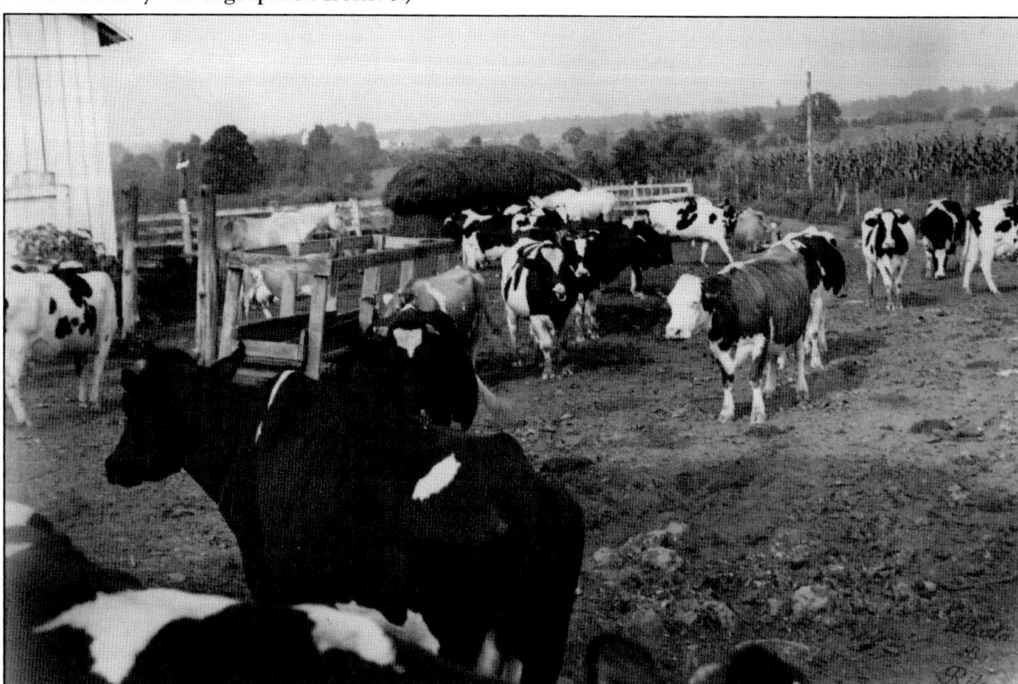

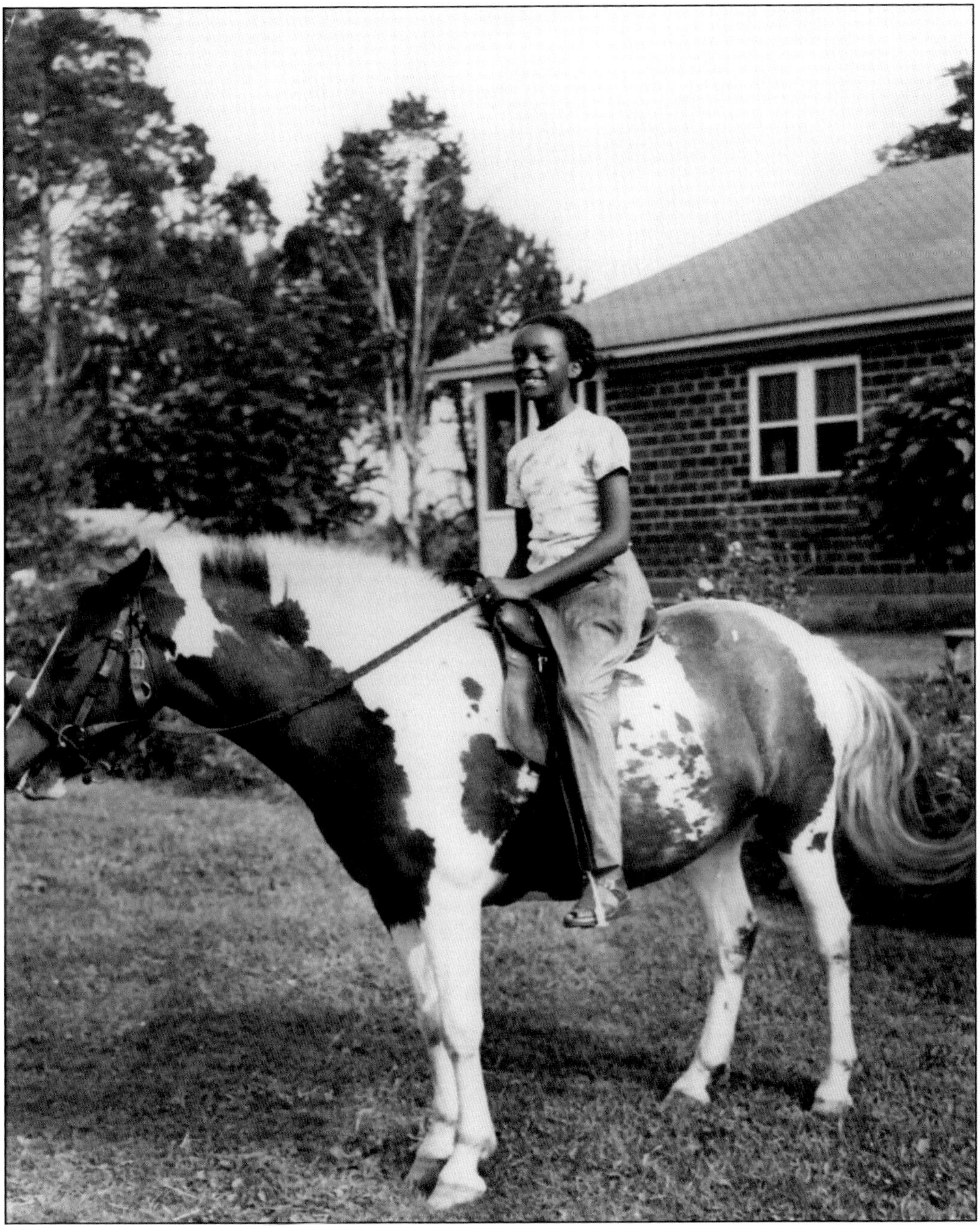

Alta Lee Newman, the daughter of Lawrence and Gladys Lee, later recalled her life on her parents' farm as one of carefree days. The Lees became dairy farmers with more than 120 acres, shipping their milk to a dairy in Washington. "Life for me was really easy. I had little work to do, so my days were filled with playing, riding my bike, or riding Star, one of the workhorses," Newman, pictured here around 1955, wrote in *Voices of Chantilly*. "Sometimes I helped Mama with the canning or freezing of fruits and vegetables from the garden." (Courtesy of the Fairfax County Public Library Photographic Archive.)

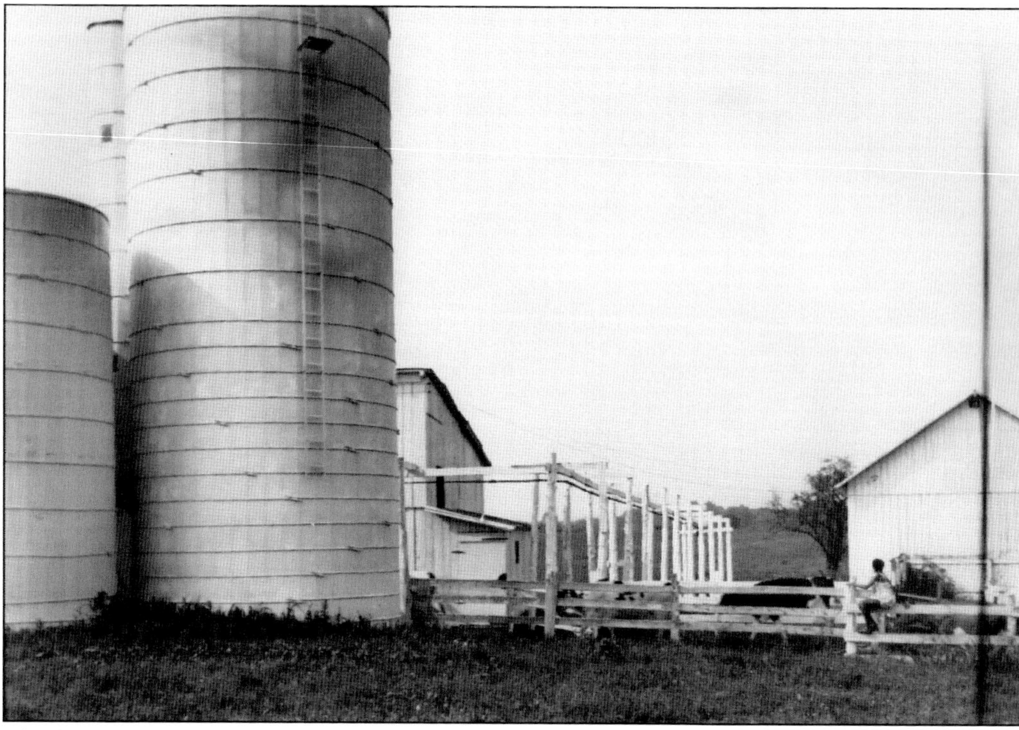

The barn and silos at Lawrence and Gladys Lee's Chantilly farm are shown here. The family also raised hogs, shown around 1955. (Both, courtesy of the Fairfax County Public Library Photographic Archive.)

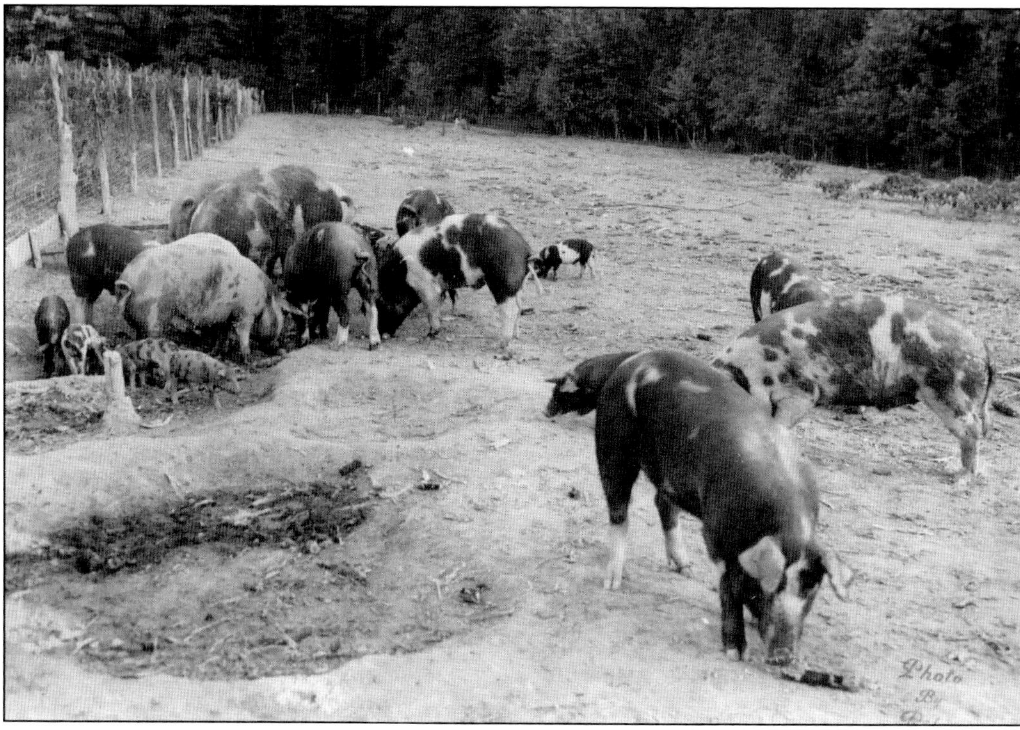

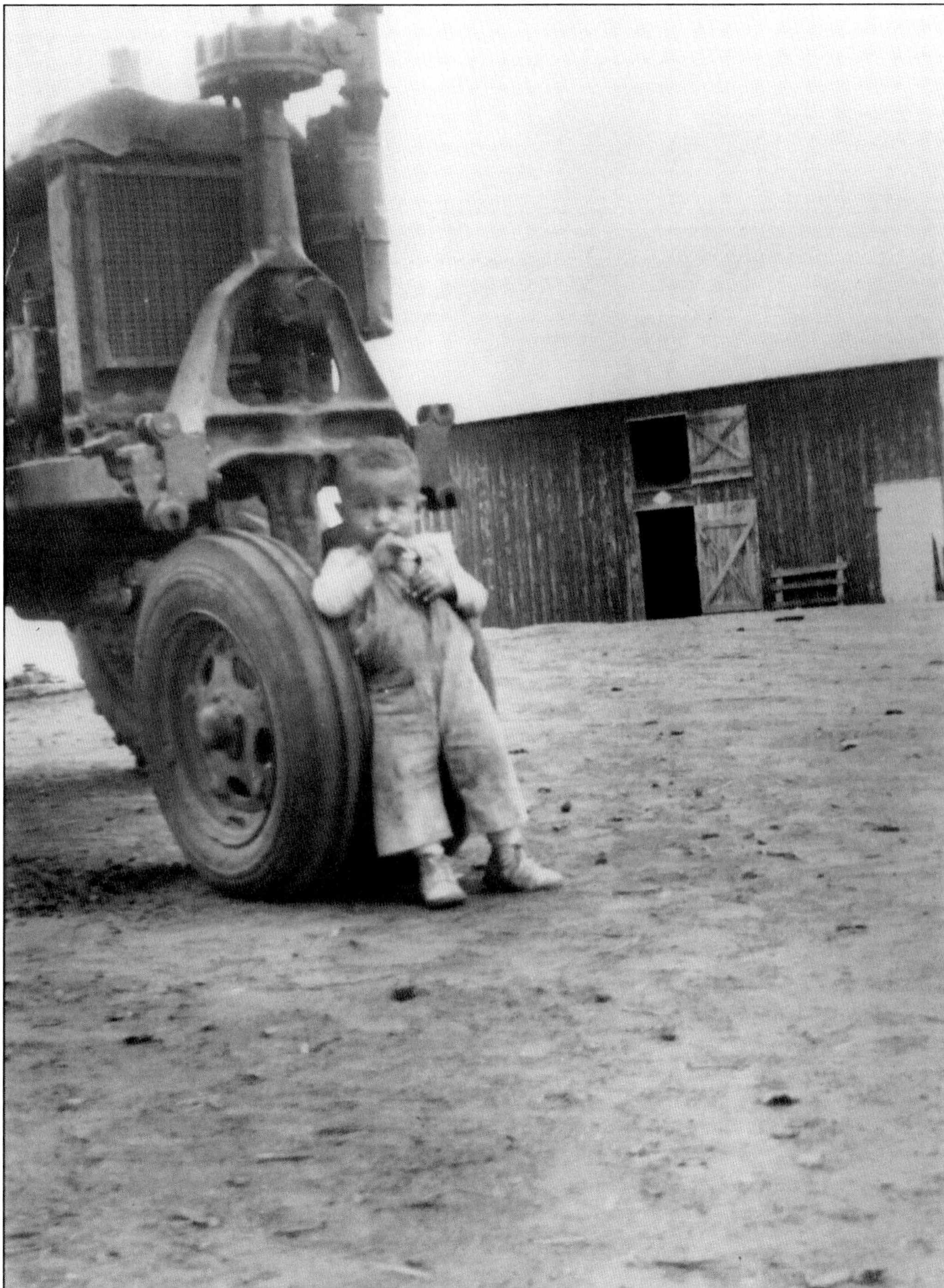

Alta Lee is leaning on the front wheel of a tractor on her parents' Chantilly farm, around 1945. (Courtesy of the Fairfax County Public Library Photographic Archive.)

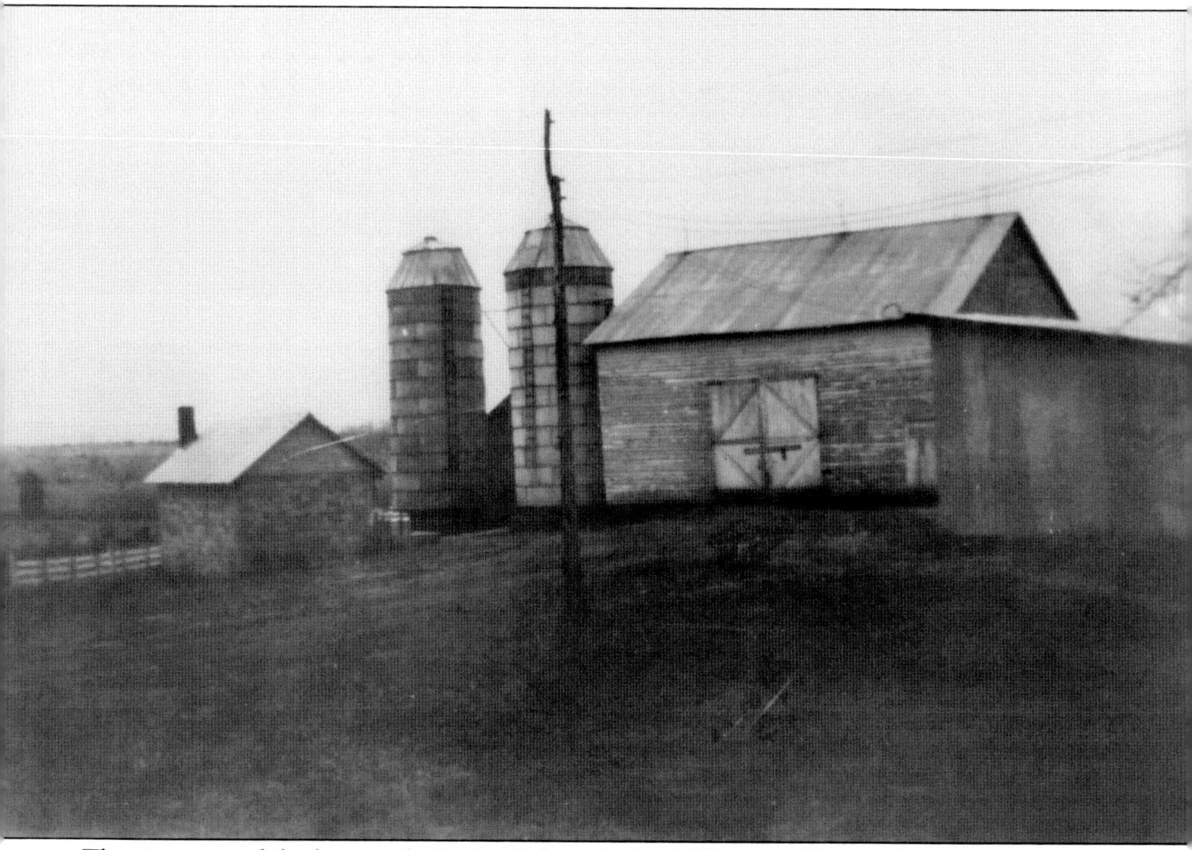

This is a view of the barn and silos in 1929 at the T.N. Woodruff Farm, which was farmed by B.L. Lowe. The farm was between Walney Road and Chantilly Road. (Courtesy of the Fairfax County Public Library Photographic Archive.)

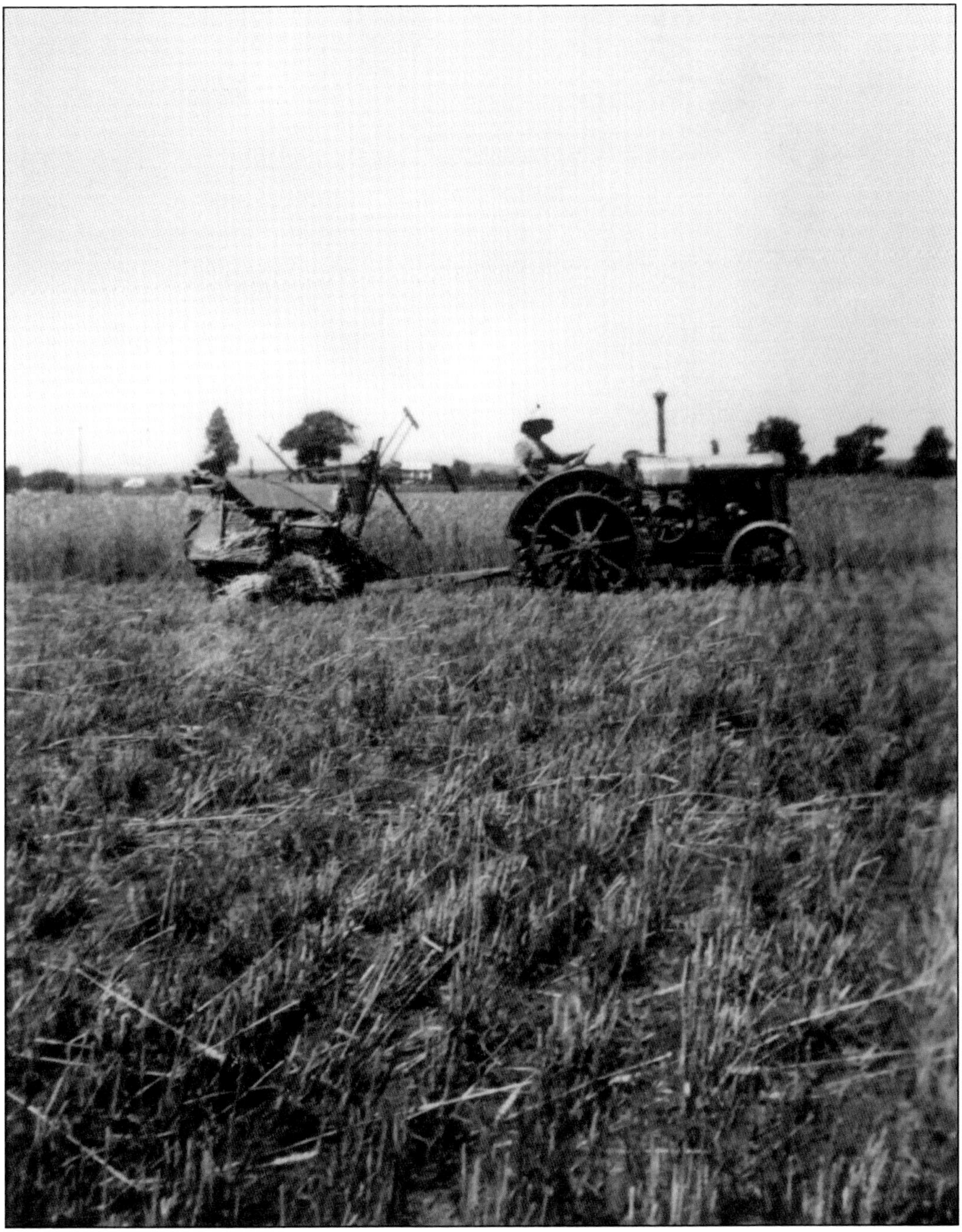

B.L. Lowe rides a tractor at the T.N. Woodruff Farm in 1933. Lowe, like other local farmers, had to deal with a labor shortage during World War II. He and many others made up for the shortage by using German prisoners of war from June to November 1945. The farmers would go to the prison on Lee Highway in Fairfax early in the morning and pay a small stipend. The prisoners returned to Fairfax at the end of the day. (Courtesy of the Fairfax County Public Library Photographic Archive.)

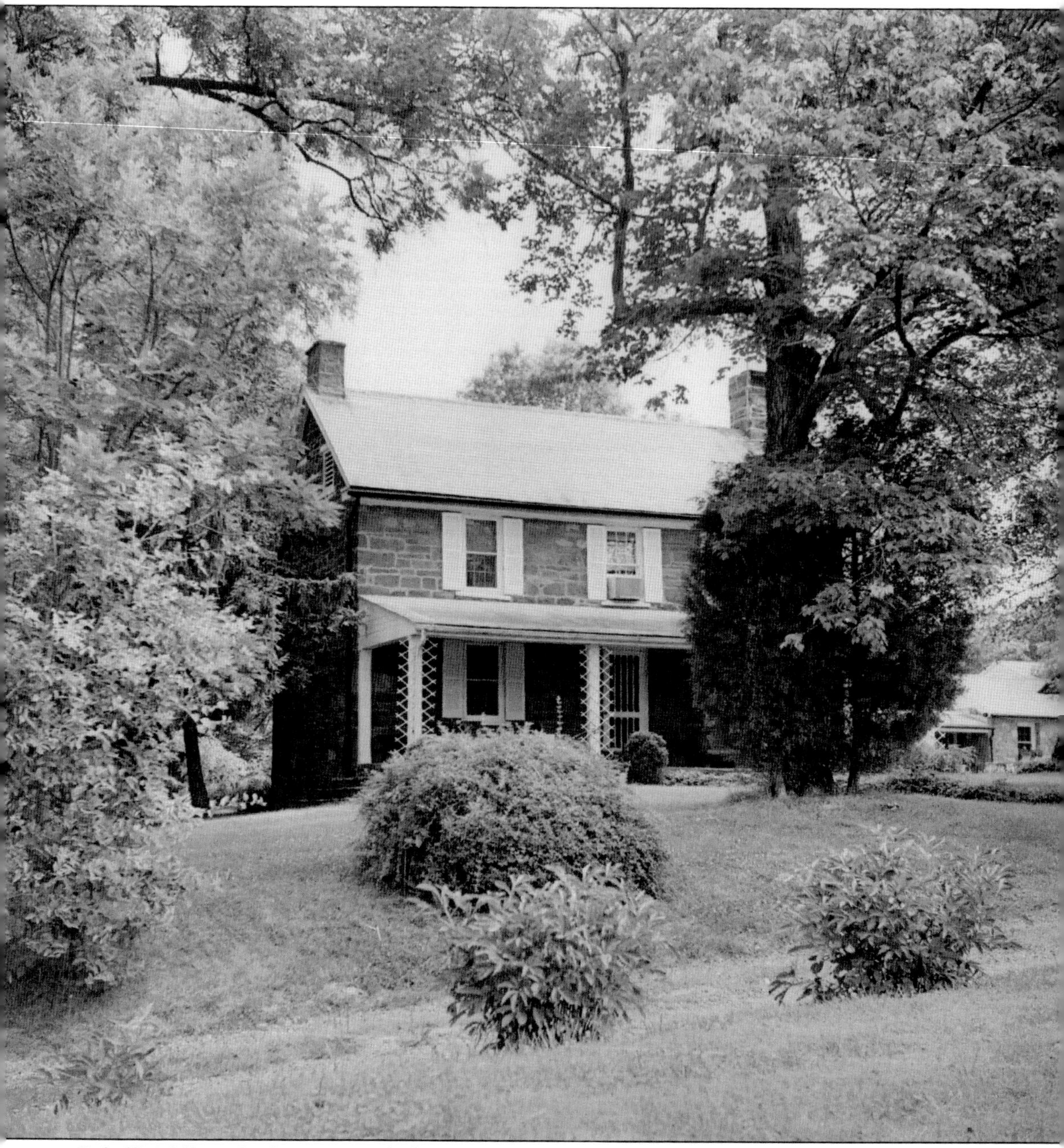

Cabell's Mill was built sometime before 1800, possibly by Willoughby Newton between 1753 and 1759. Ellanor C. Lawrence, the wife of *US News & World Report* publisher David Lawrence, bought the mill in 1944. She used it as a guesthouse. David Lawrence broadcasted from the mill on a weekly basis from 1945 to 1970. The Lawrences gave the mill, miller's house, and an extensive amount of property to the Fairfax County Park Authority upon Ellanor's death in 1971. This photograph shows the Lawrence residence, Middlegate, which was originally the miller's house. (Courtesy of the Fairfax County Public Library Photographic Archive.)

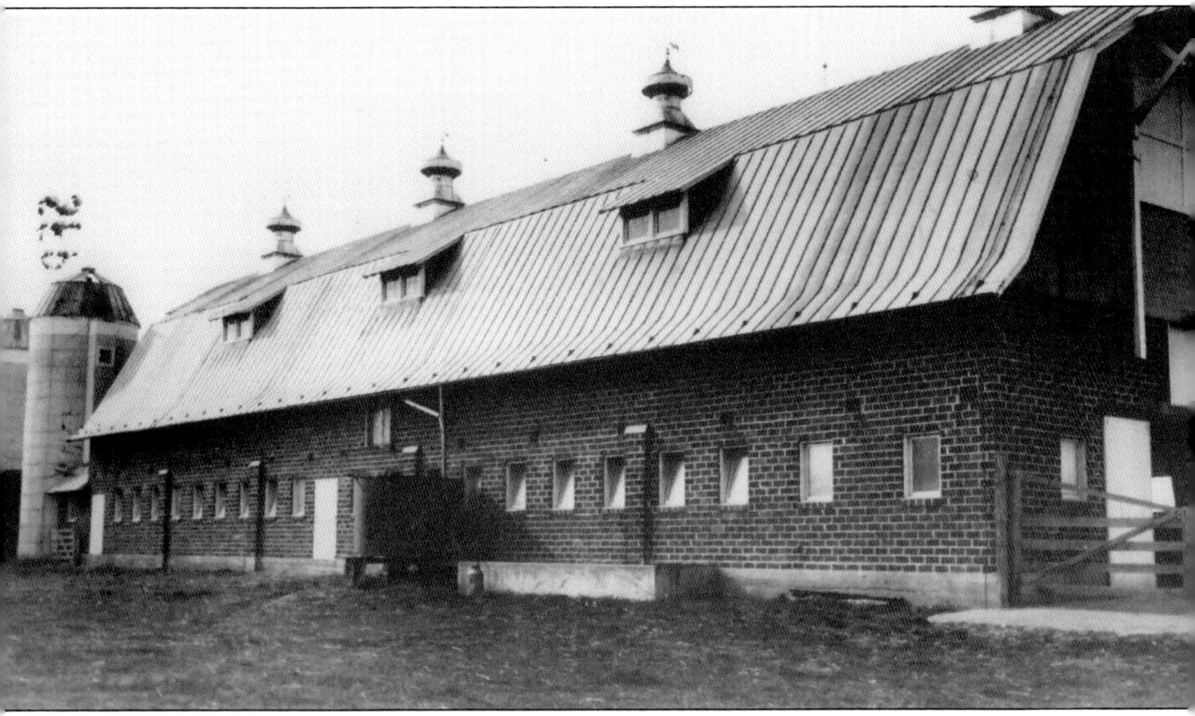

This c. 1940 photograph is of the dairy barn at "DairyLou" farm in Chantilly. Many of the local families at the time were dairy farmers. (Courtesy of the Fairfax County Public Library Photographic Archive.)

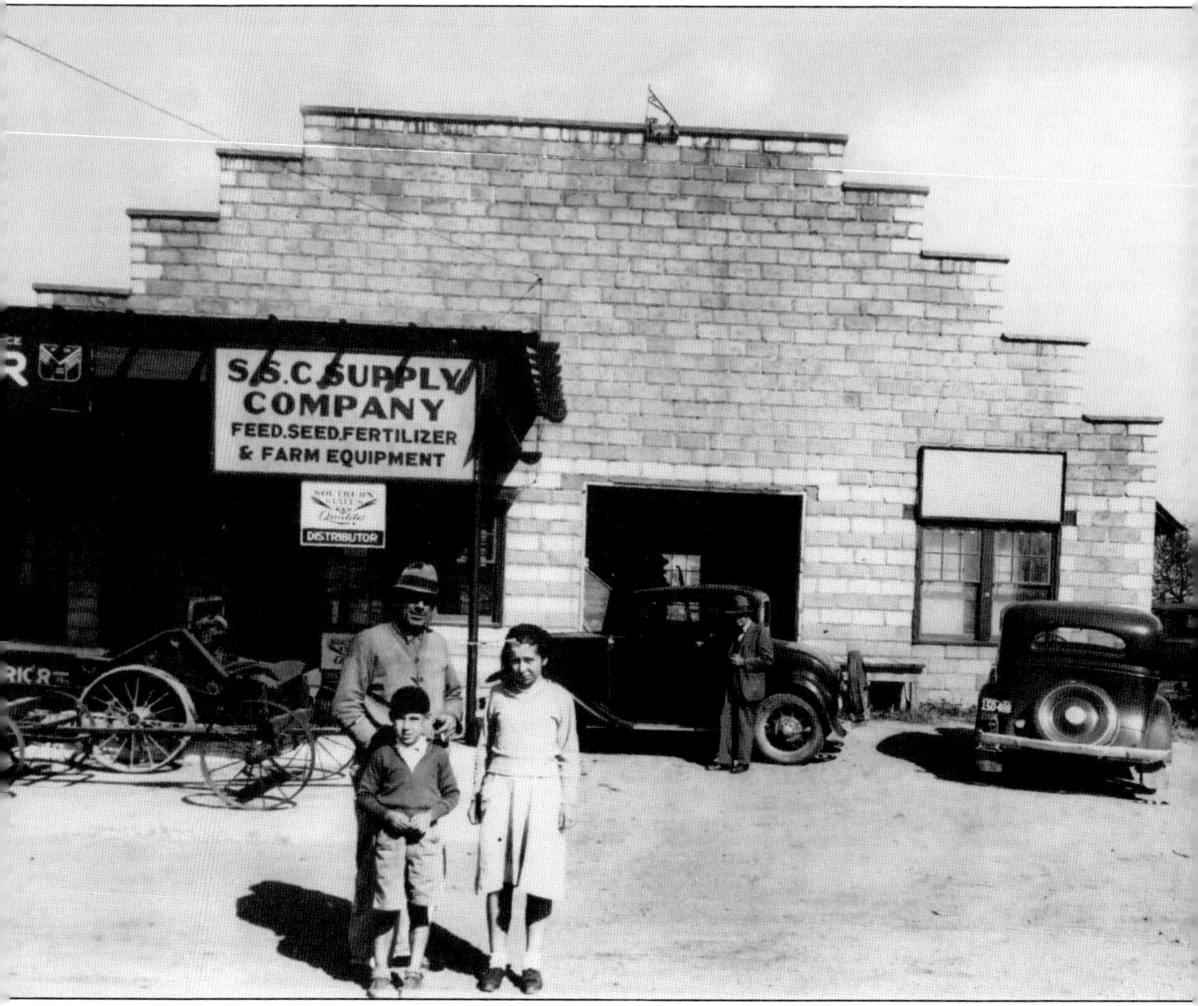

The Southern States Supply Company, on 13900 Lee-Jackson Highway, was a farm supply company. It was also the first Southern States store in Northern Virginia ("NoVa"). Dallas Page Hutchison, who ran the store, and his children Bina Ruth and Dallas Porter Hutchison are in front of the store around 1933. (Courtesy of the Fairfax County Public Library Photographic Archive.)

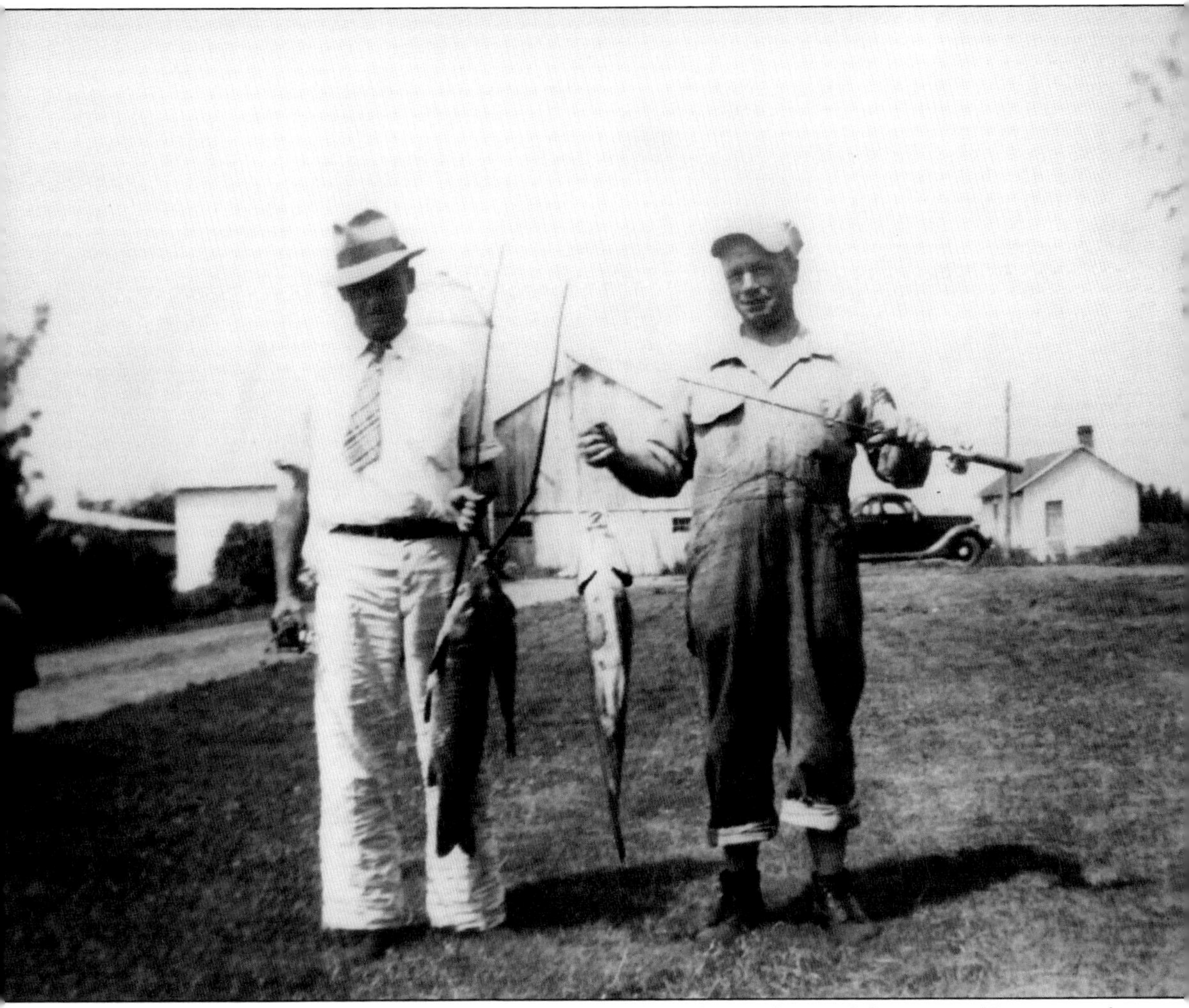

Bynum Armfield Sr. and B.L. Lowe pose with catfish and carp from a fishing trip. (Courtesy of the Fairfax County Public Library Photographic Archive.)

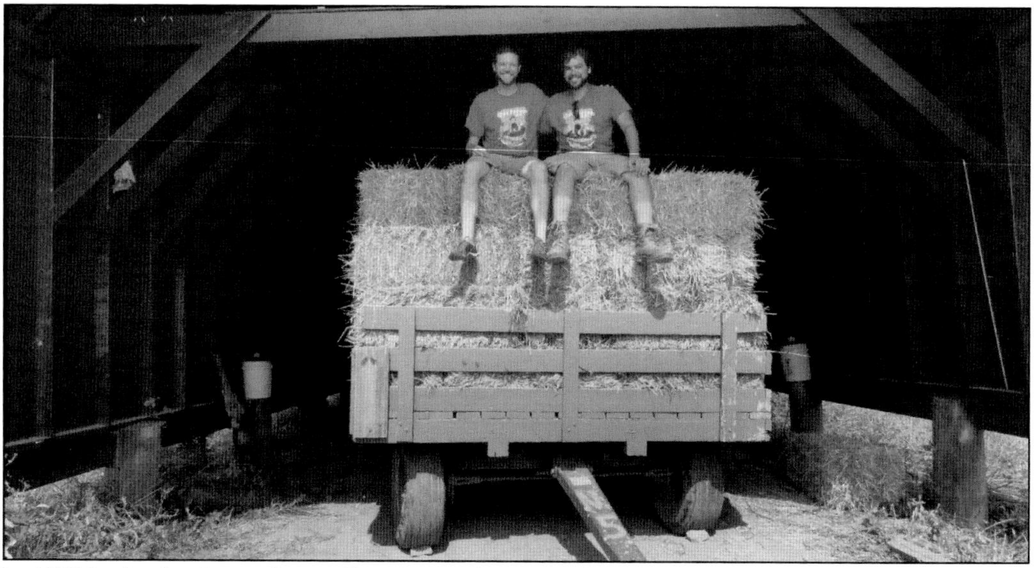

In 1979, high school sweethearts Eric Cox and Gina Richard bought 116 acres of land off Braddock Road in Centreville. Schools soon began to take classes out to the farm to pick pumpkins and go for hayrides. Then in 1983, Cox Farms held its first Fall Festival. The business is now one of the most popular fall attractions in the metropolitan area, with tens of thousands of visitors attending the Fall Festival and the haunted corn maze, "Fields of Fear," in the evenings. Eric and Gina's son Lucas Cox is pictured on the right with one of the farm workers. (Author's collection.)

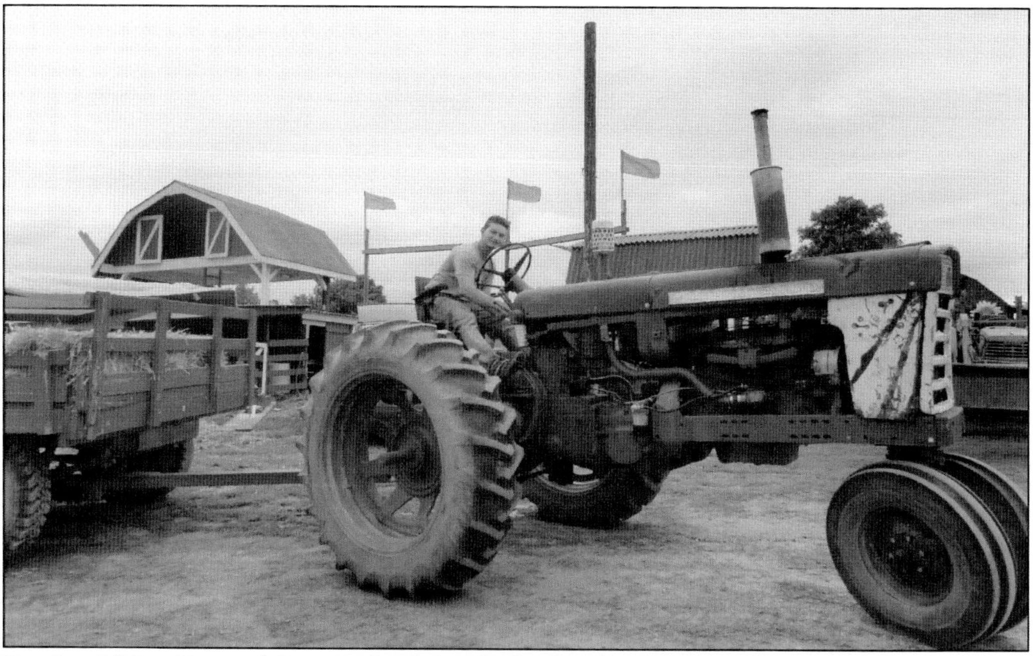

People told Eric Cox and Gina Richard that "nobody will ever travel that far out" to Centreville when the high school sweethearts purchased 116 acres of land off Braddock Road in 1979. The area had not yet experienced the explosion of growth that came in the ensuing decades. As the suburbs grew, the farm became ever more popular with tourists and locals looking to experience a taste of rural life. (Author's collection.)

Four

GROWTH

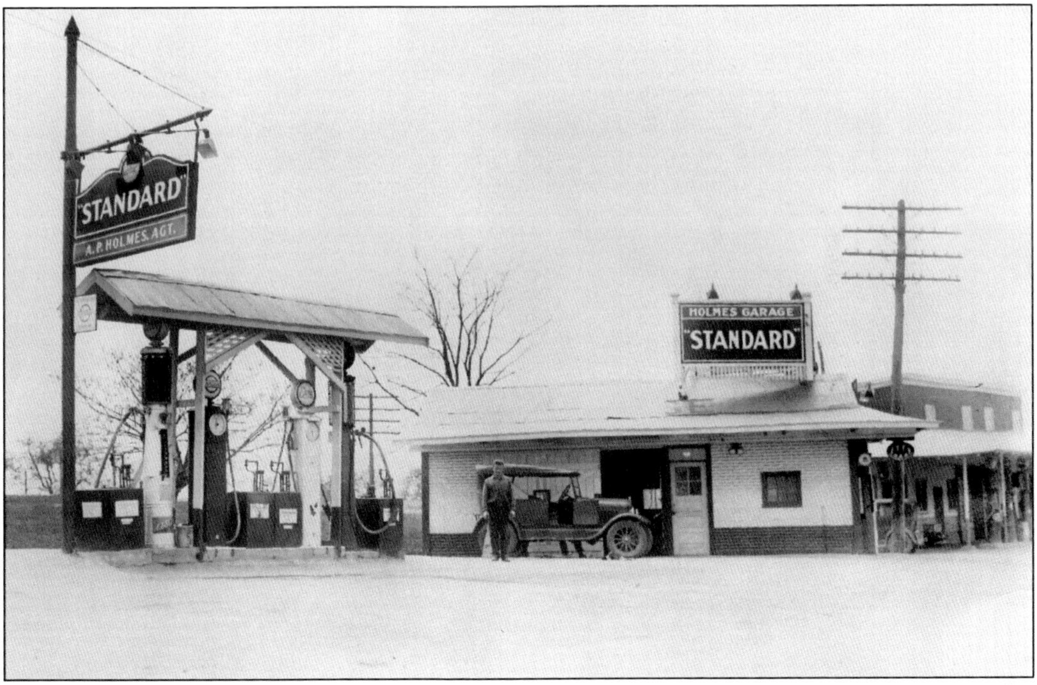

Alton P. Holmes opened a service station on Lee Highway, by Braddock Road, in Centreville. His house is pictured in the background of this photograph. The newly paved section of Lee Highway from Fairfax to Centreville opened in November 1925. Other new businesses included a general store, a filling station, a lunchroom, and tourist cabins. New subdivisions also popped up along Lee Highway, as Centreville and Chantilly became an increasingly attractive option for commuters. (Courtesy of the Fairfax County Public Library Photographic Archive.)

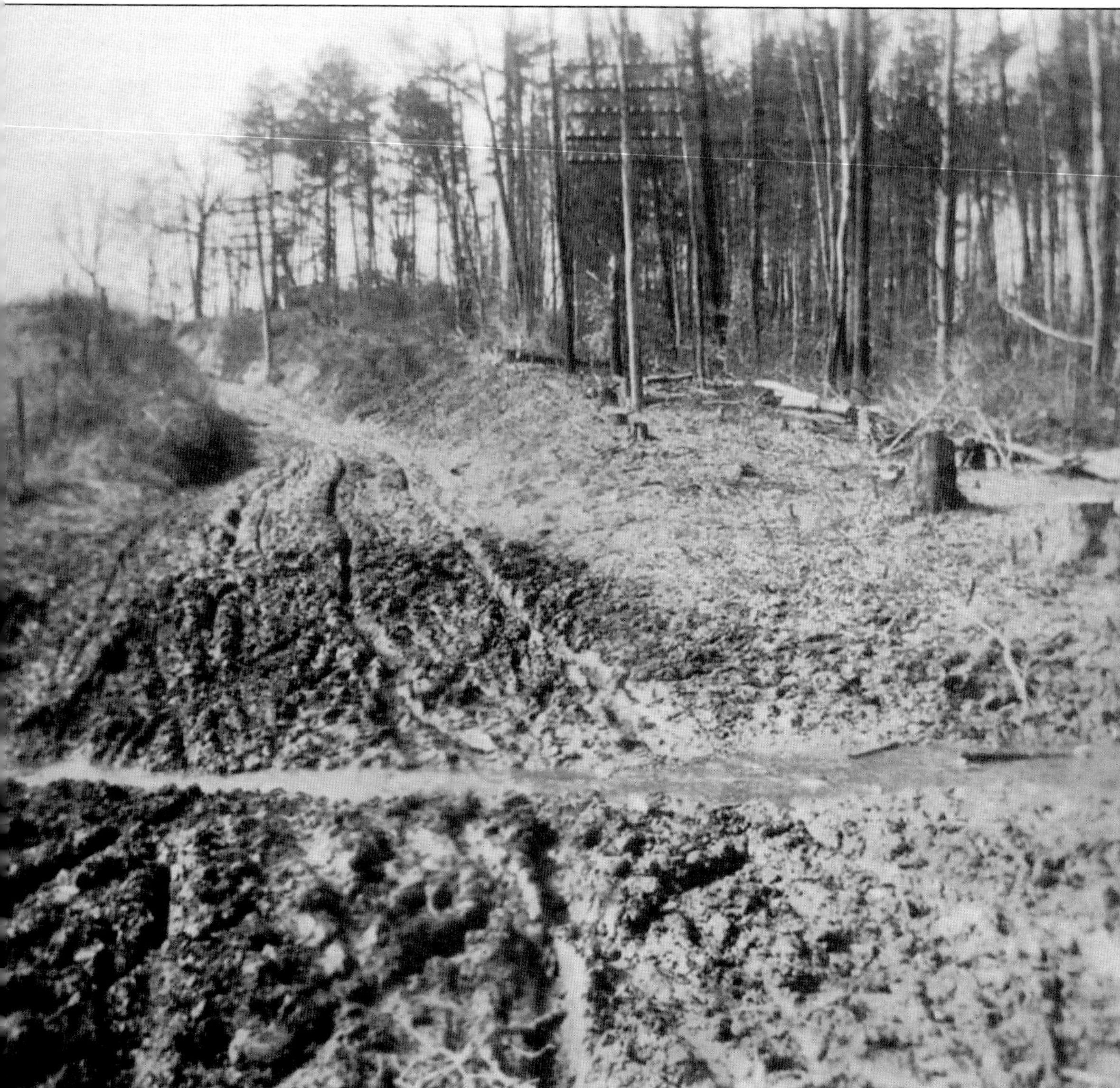

Paving is in progress in this photograph, taken at Lee Highway in Fairfax, north of Centreville. The road through Centreville, which was known as the Warrenton and Fairfax Turnpike previously, was paved in 1925 and became part of Lee Highway. Road improvements brought tourists, travelers, and commuters to Centreville—and with them, some economic improvements. (Courtesy of Lee Hubbard.)

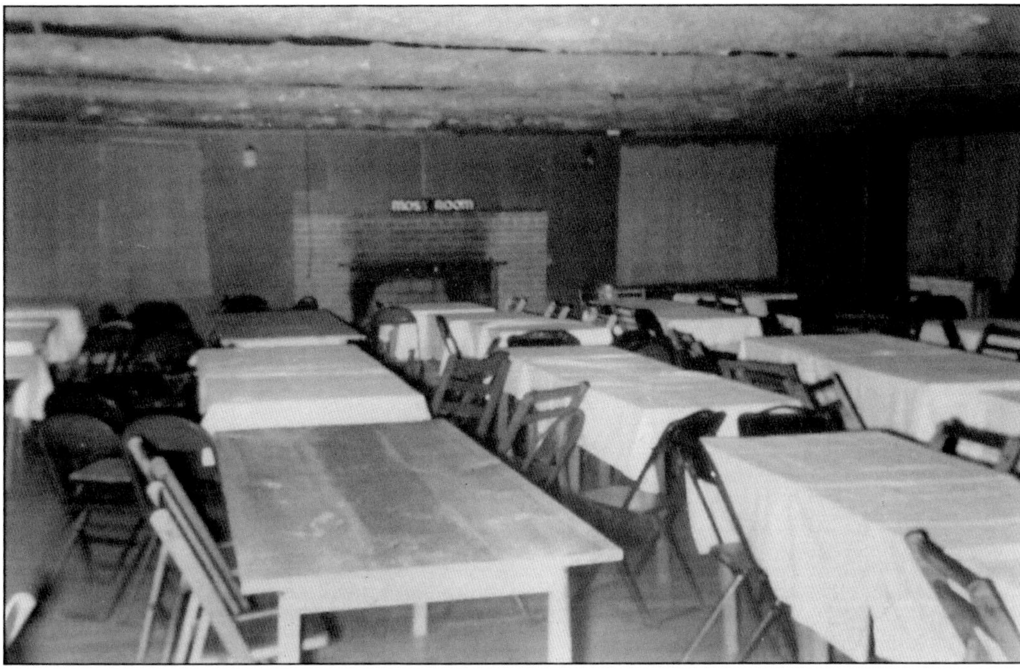

Lee Highway attracted large numbers of travelers after it was paved. Dance halls started to spring up along the road. One of them, Hunter's Lodge, thrived when it first opened around 1939. It was known for its live country music and for having an occasionally rough crowd. The lodge, which was located by the intersection of Ox Road, experience a bad fire in 1985. It eventually closed around 1986. (Both, courtesy of Lee Hubbard.)

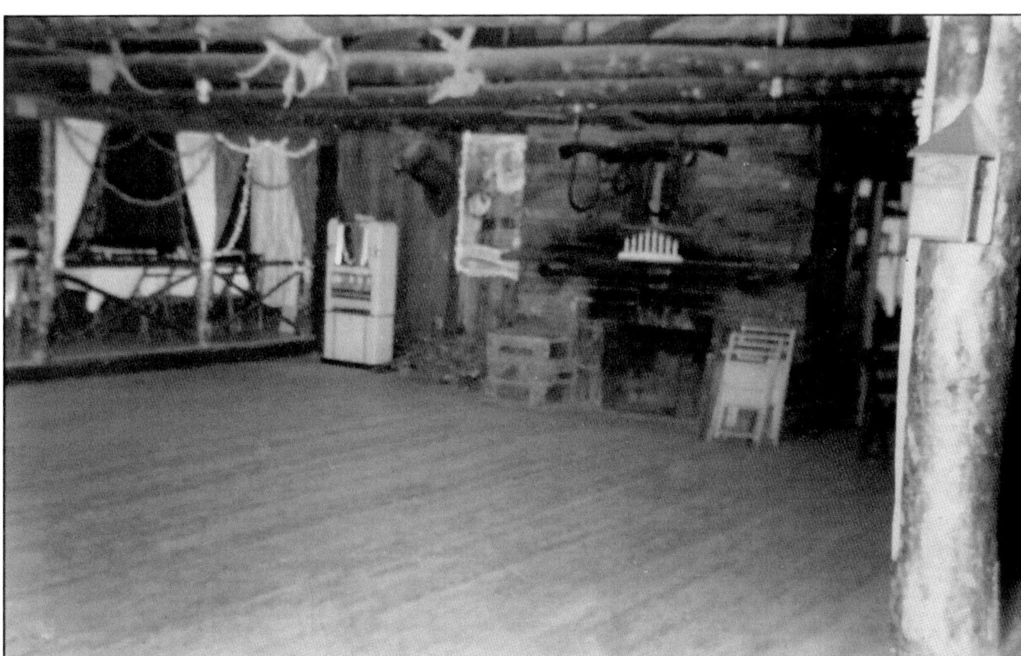

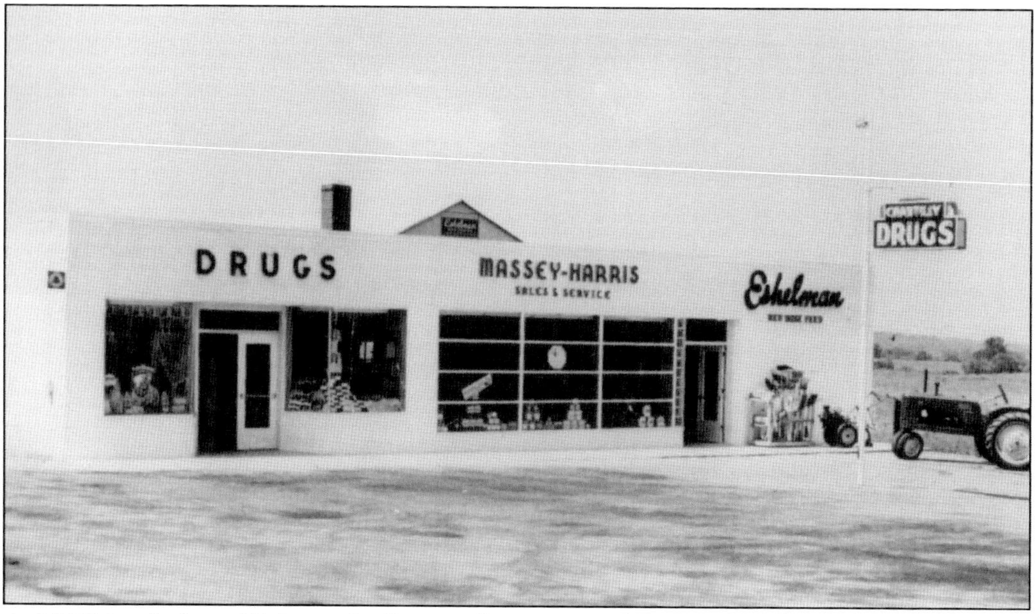

At 14019 Lee-Jackson Highway, the Bywater Drugstore and Farmers Supply Co., pictured around 1948, were opened in the 1940s by the family of Harold Douglas Smith. In 1946, the Farmers Supply Company opened, along with a drugstore. A Dr. Franklin and Nellie May Bywaters operated the drugstore. In 1965, Farmers Supply became the Smith & Sons Equipment Corporation. It eventually merged with Smith Equipment Sales in Warrenton. (Both, courtesy of the Fairfax County Public Library Photographic Archive.)

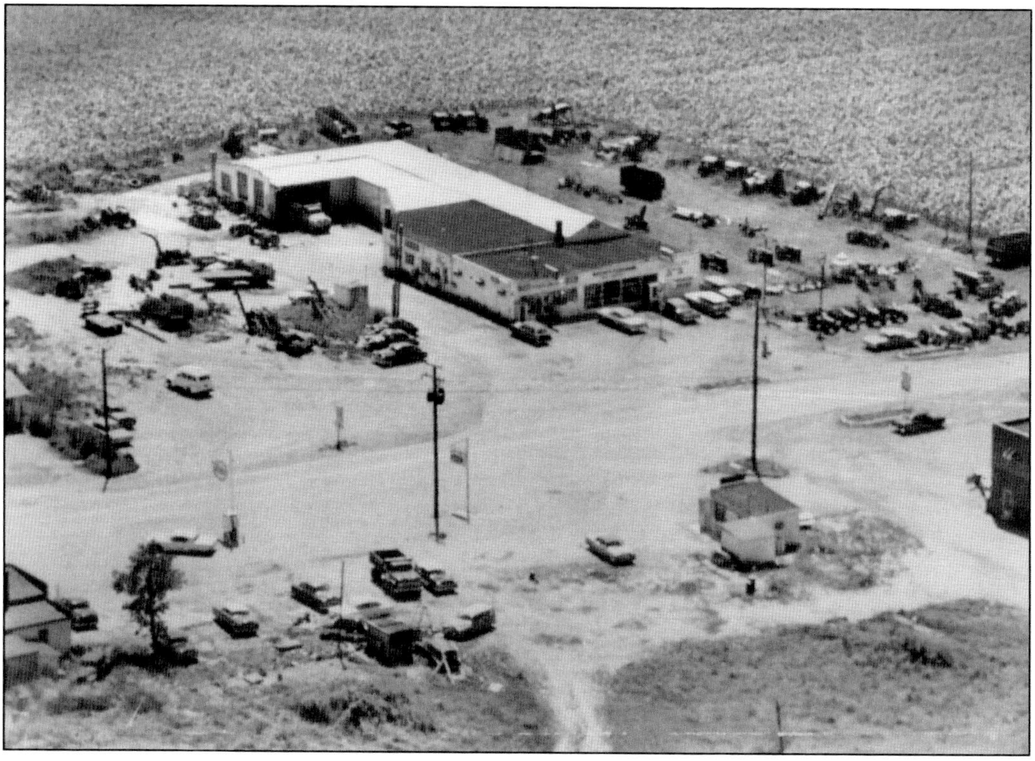

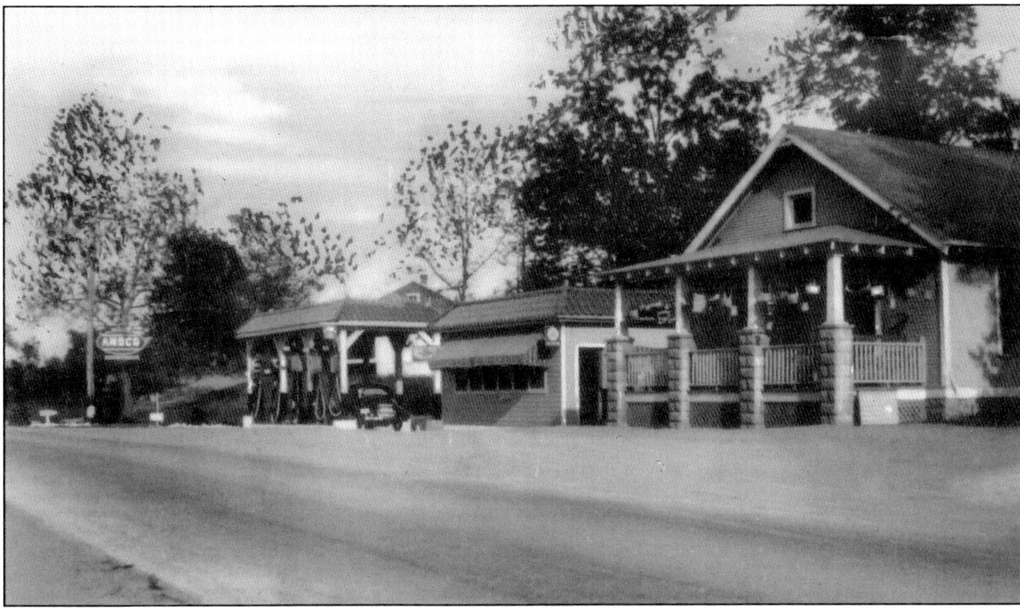

Manuel's Tourist Cabin in Fairfax and Mary Elizabeth's Tourist Cabin in Centreville (by the intersection with Braddock Road) were some of the many tourist lodgings that popped up along Lee Highway as tourism expanded, thanks to improved roads. (Both, courtesy of the Fairfax County Public Library Photographic Archive.)

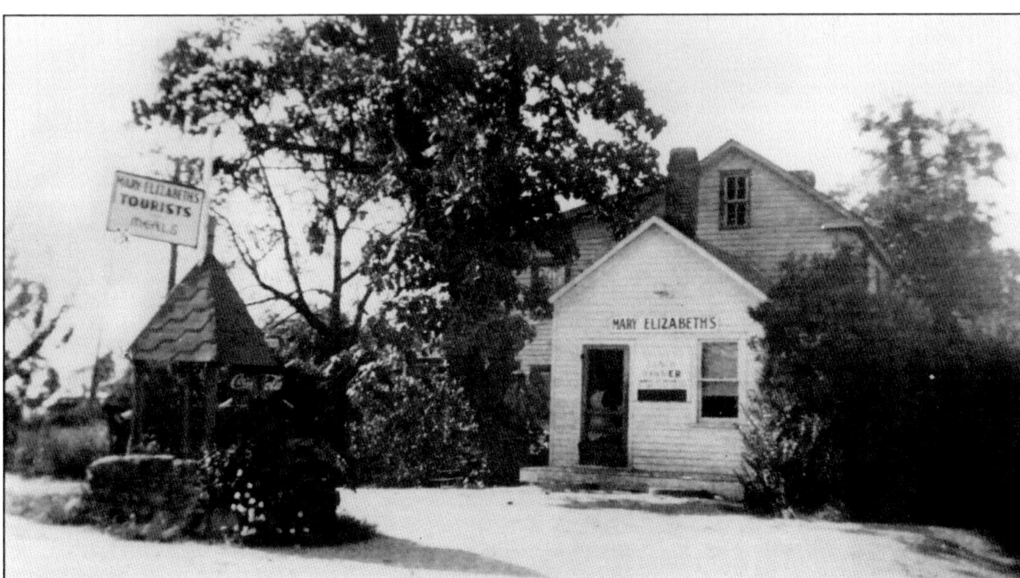

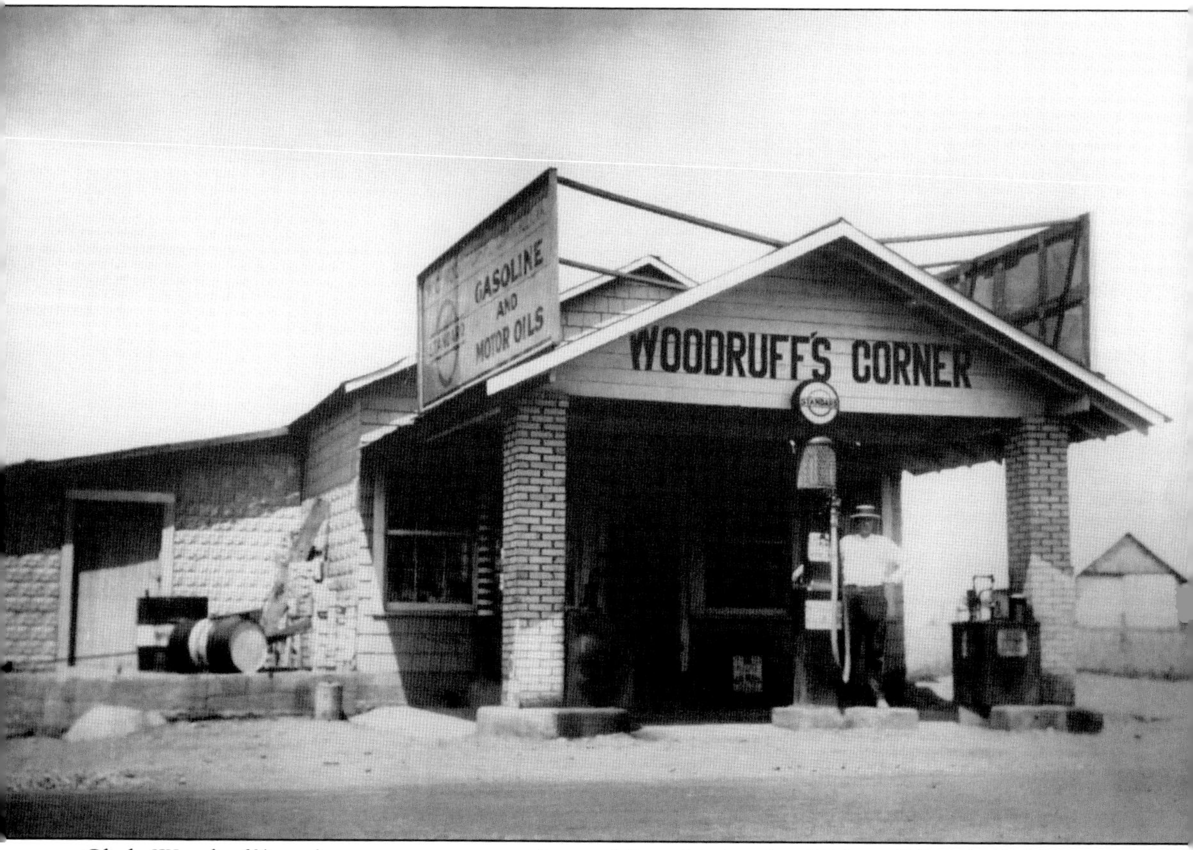

Clyde Woodruff bought a property across the road from his brother T.N. and then built a house, barn, garage, service station, general store with a lunch counter, five tourist cabins and four rental houses. The corner of Little River Turnpike (now known as Route 50) and Centreville Road (Old Route 28) became known as Woodruff's Corner. (Courtesy of the Fairfax County Public Library Photographic Archive.)

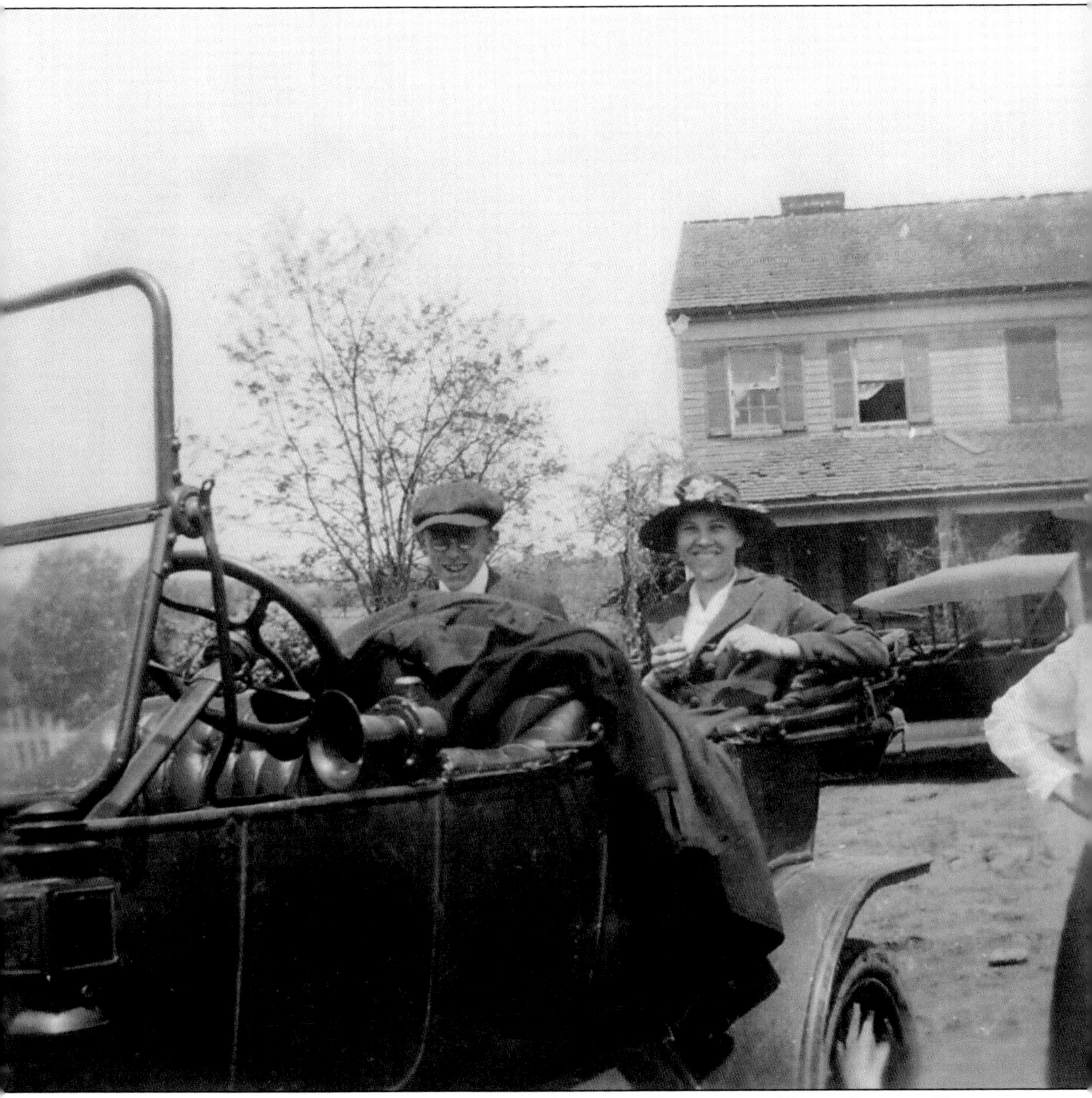

Jerome Gibson and Marie Swayze are shown here at a house, possibly in Centreville, near the Manassas Battlefield, in 1919. They married in 1927 and lived in Fairfax. (Courtesy of Lee Hubbard.)

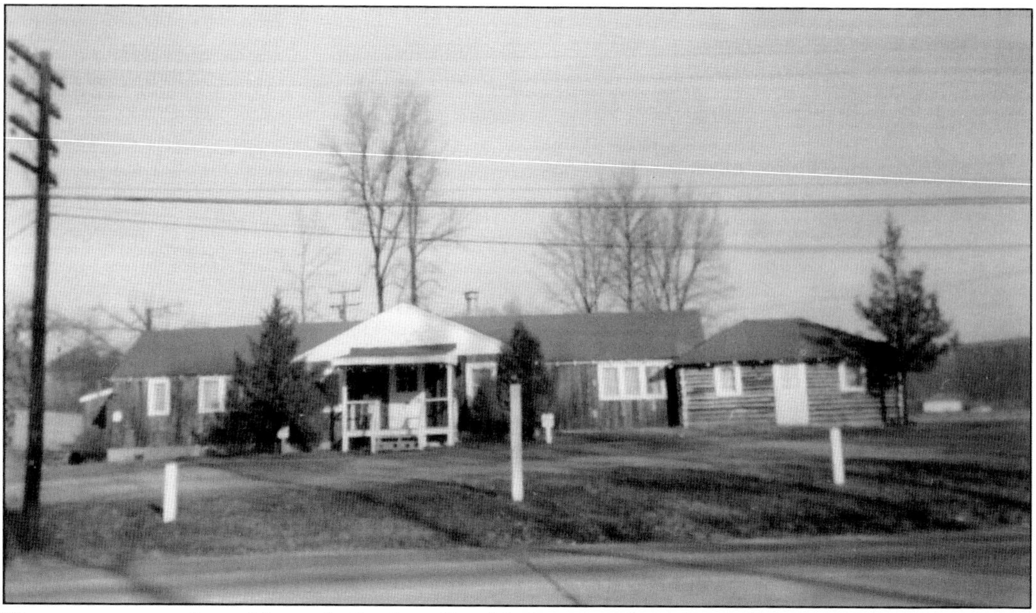

There were a number of dance halls along Lee Highway, such as the Bull Run Dance Hall, located in Centreville near the intersection of Ox Road, and Hunter's Lodge, pictured above. One band was named the Lee Highway Boys because it played at halls in the area so often. (Courtesy of Lee Hubbard.)

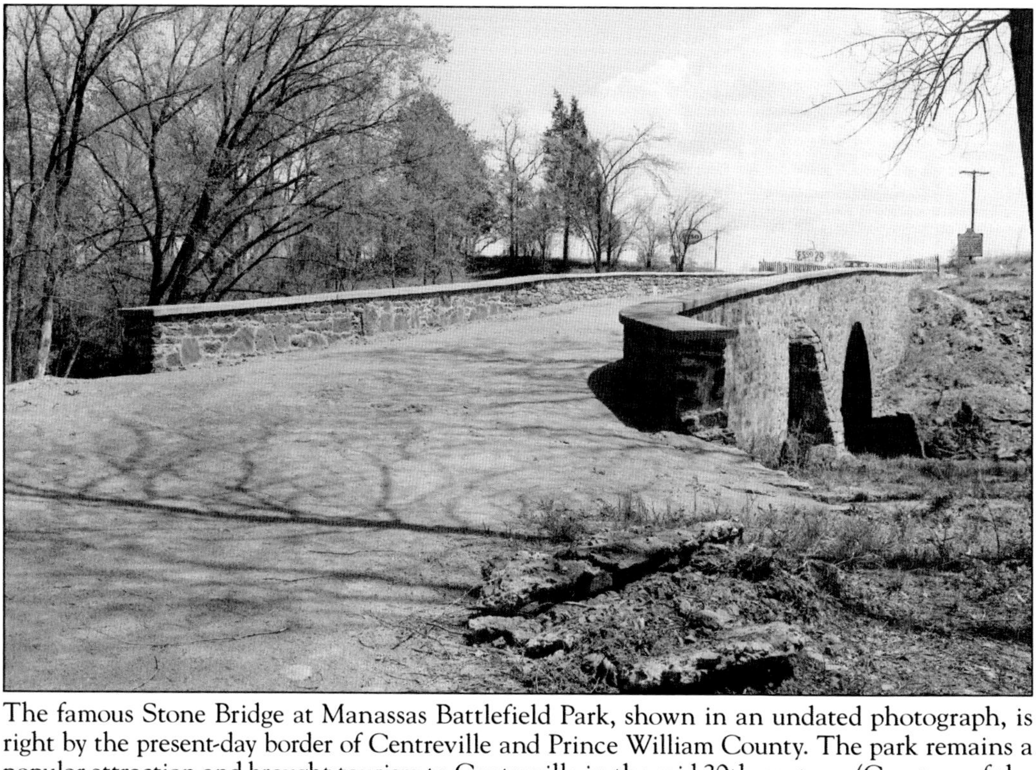

The famous Stone Bridge at Manassas Battlefield Park, shown in an undated photograph, is right by the present-day border of Centreville and Prince William County. The park remains a popular attraction and brought tourism to Centreville in the mid-20th century. (Courtesy of the Library of Congress.)

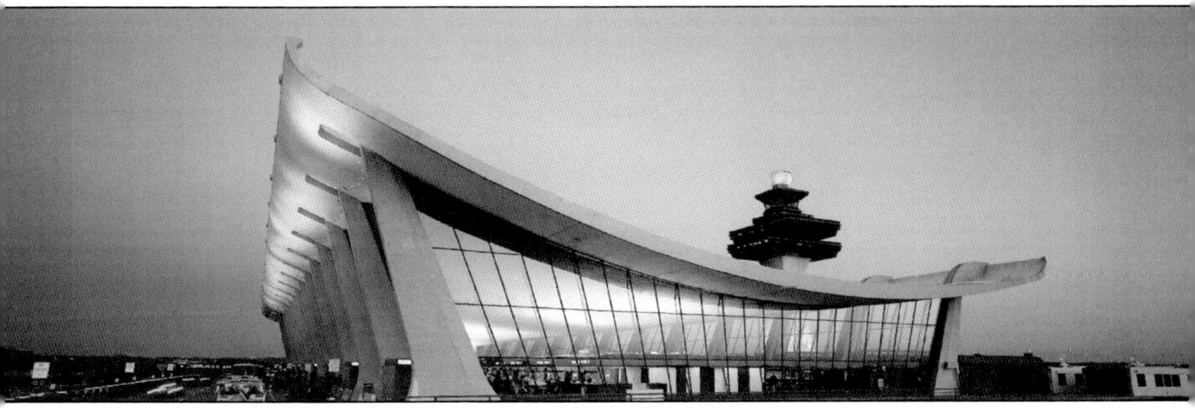

Centreville and Chantilly experienced growth with the invention of the automobile as more commuters came out to the area. Major changes were still to come in the late 1950s with the construction of Dulles International Airport. (Courtesy of the Library of Congress.)

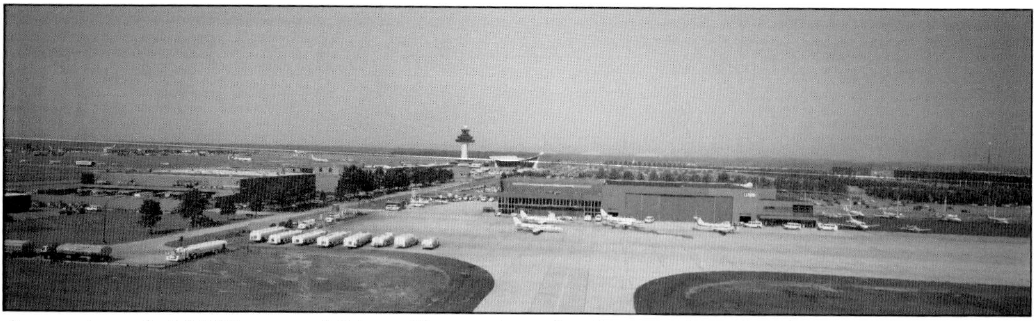

Approximately 10,000 acres of Chantilly-area farmland were selected to become the site of the new Dulles International Airport. (Courtesy of the Library of Congress.)

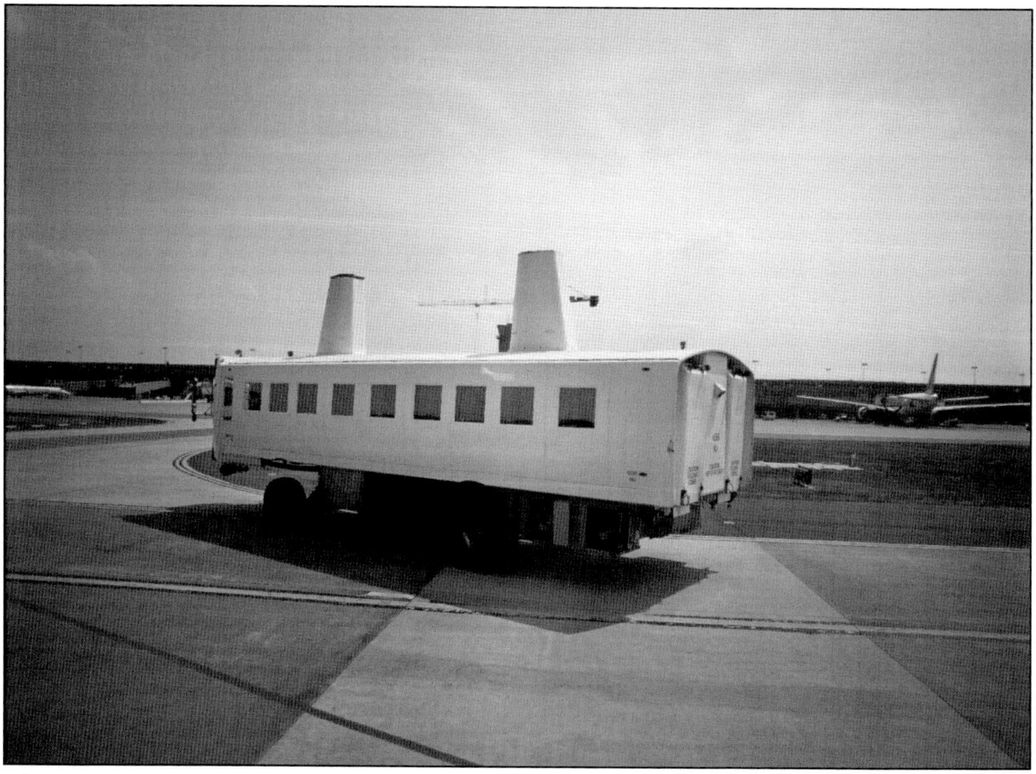

This is a mobile lounge at Dulles International Airport that locals called "people movers." The mobile lounge ferried passengers to and from the terminal at the airport. (Courtesy of the Library of Congress.)

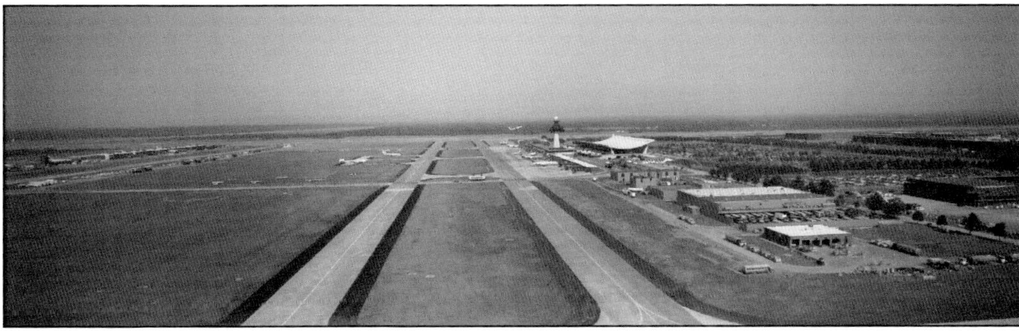

Pres. Dwight Eisenhower selected the site for Dulles International Airport in 1958. The 10,000 acres included land in both Loudoun and Fairfax Counties. Chantilly was an attractive area because of the vast amount of farmland. Pres. John F. Kennedy formally dedicated the airport on November 17, 1962. (Both, courtesy of the Library of Congress.)

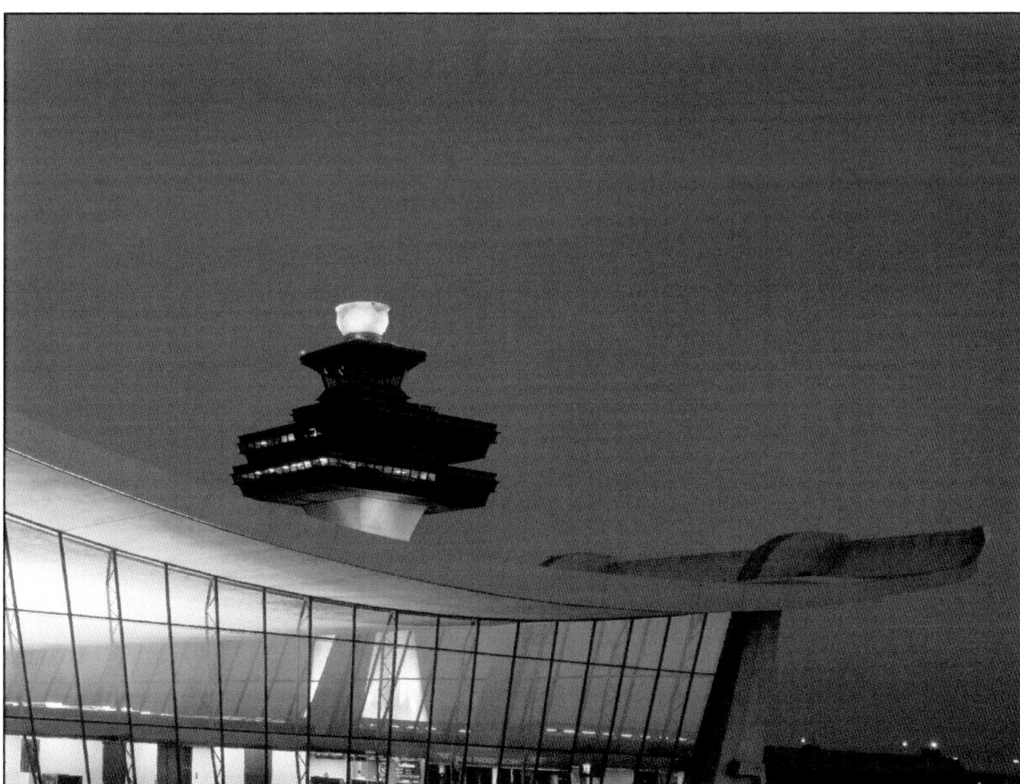

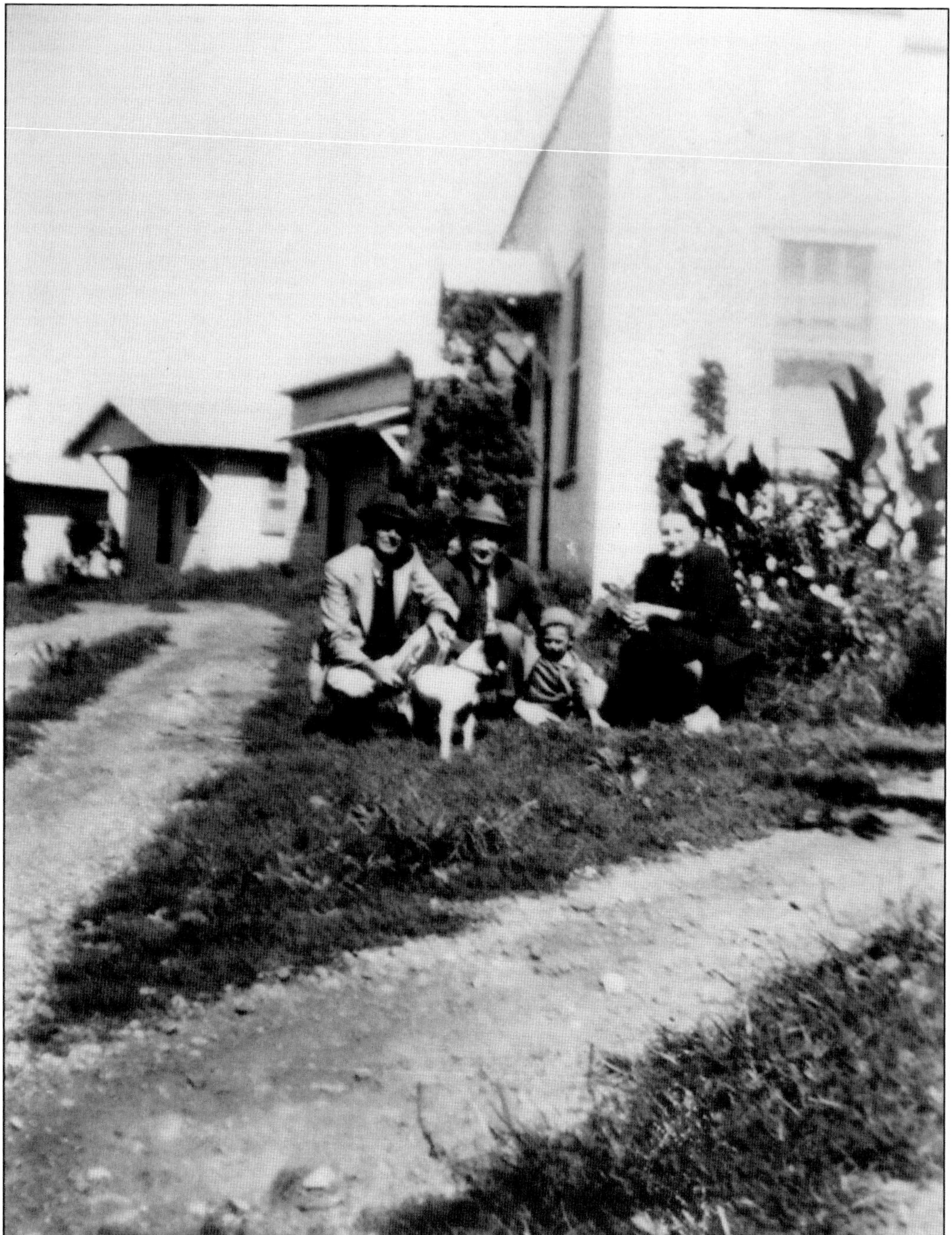

Mildred Thompson and Carlyle Thompson, realizing that there were no motels on Route 50 in the 50 miles between Winchester and Fairfax, decided to buy 28 acres from her uncle Clyde (who operated Woodruff's Corner). The motel was located at the same location as the present-day Sully Plaza. Visitors over the years included the great-great-granddaughter of Pres. Teddy Roosevelt; the governor of the Alaska territory; and Ferenc Nagy Sr., the prime minister of Hungary. (Courtesy of the Fairfax County Public Library Photographic Archive.)

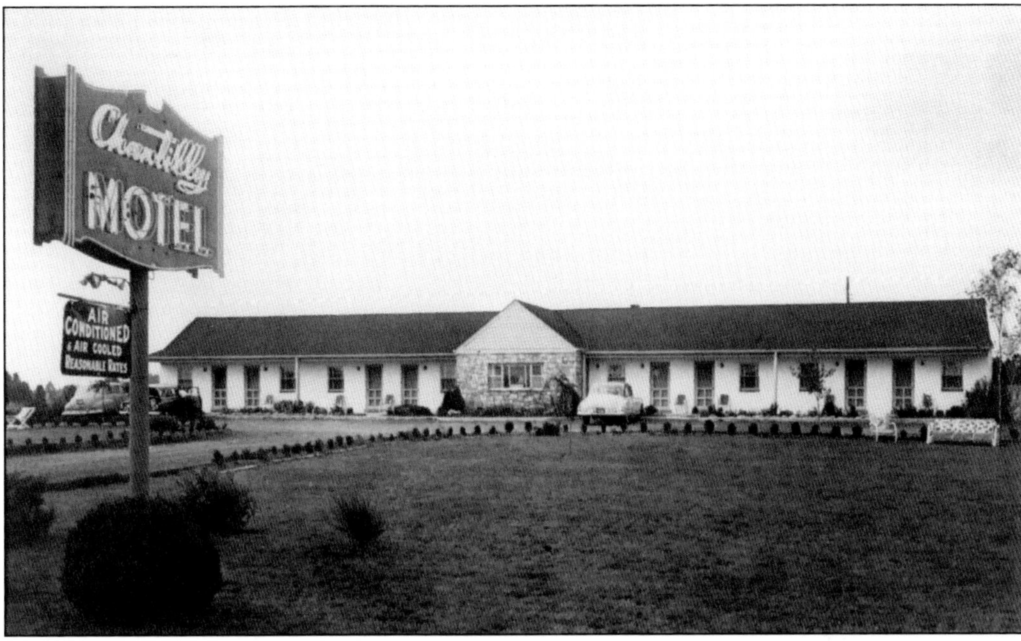

Speculators came out to Chantilly in droves to try to purchase land after news of the airport's location broke. Mildred Thompson, who ran the Chantilly Motel with her husband, recalled in *Voices of Chantilly* that they were overwhelmed with phone calls and visits offering to buy the land. "One man became so irate when we said that we were not interested in selling that he threatened to buy the land across the road and build another motel in competition with us." The motel was later demolished to make way for the airport. (Both, courtesy of Fairfax County Public Library Photographic Archive.)

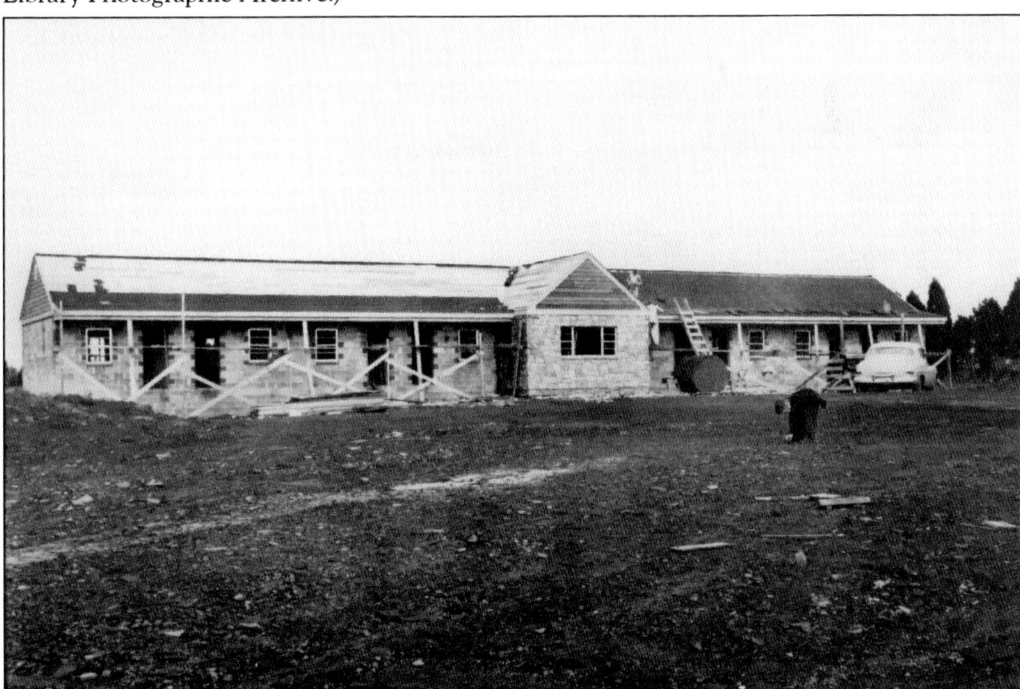

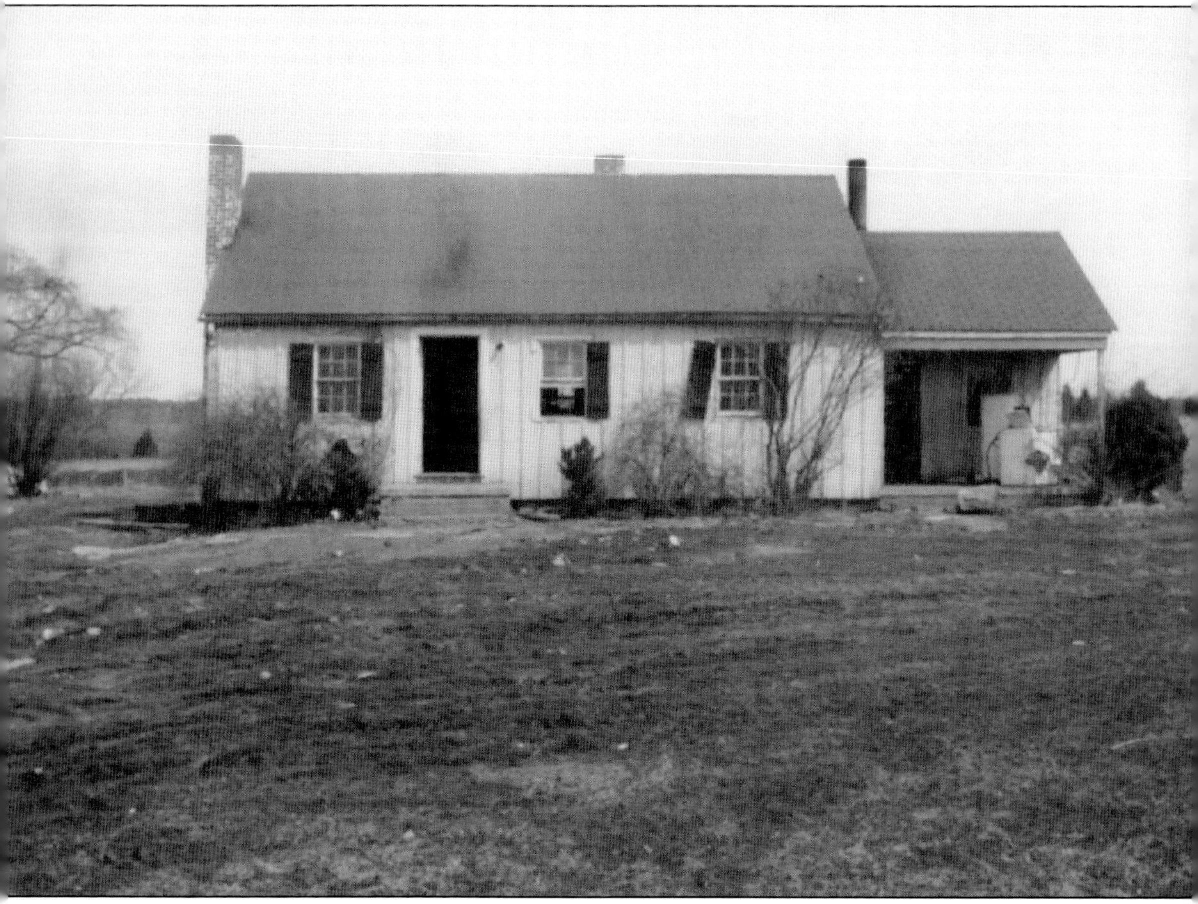

A Centreville-area, one-story house with vertical siding and a brick chimney is pictured here in 1970. (Both, courtesy of the Fairfax County Public Library Photographic Archive.)

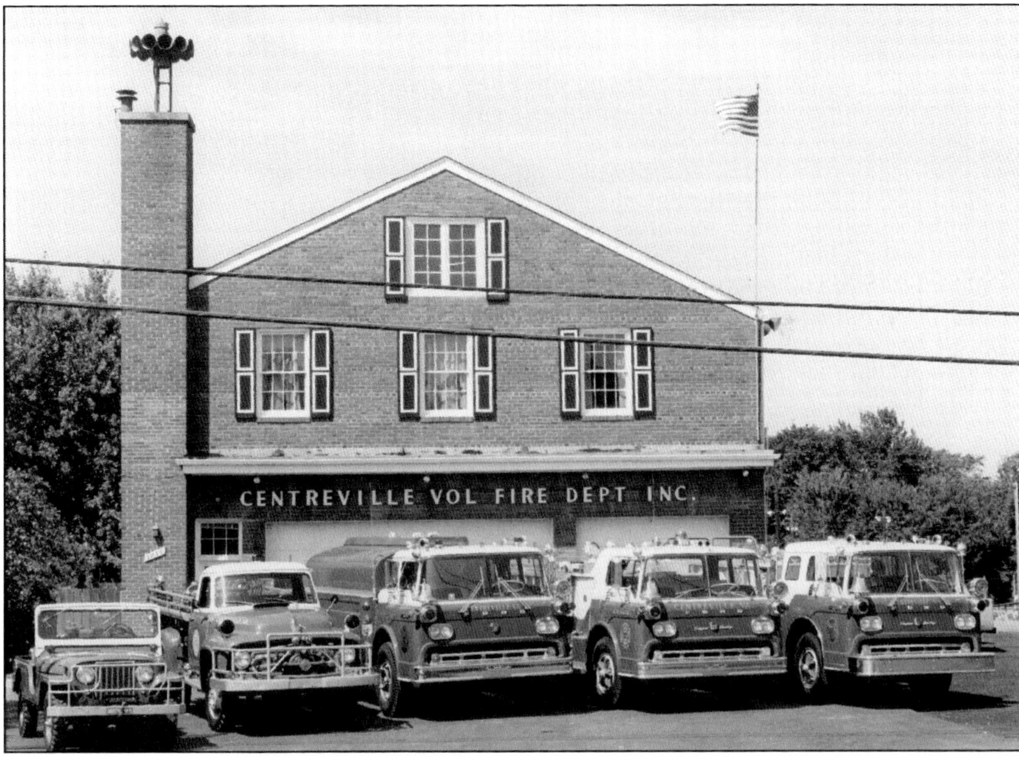

The Centreville Volunteer Fire Department Company No. 017 is shown in 1969. The photograph above shows four trucks and a jeep; below are two ambulances. (Both, courtesy Fairfax County Public Library Photographic Archive.)

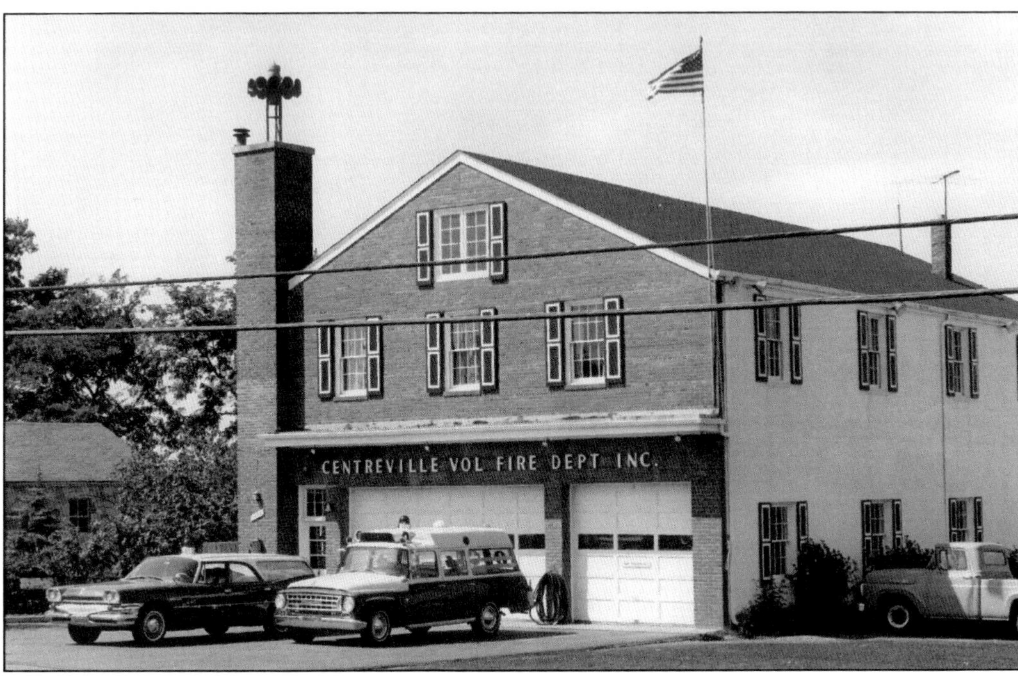

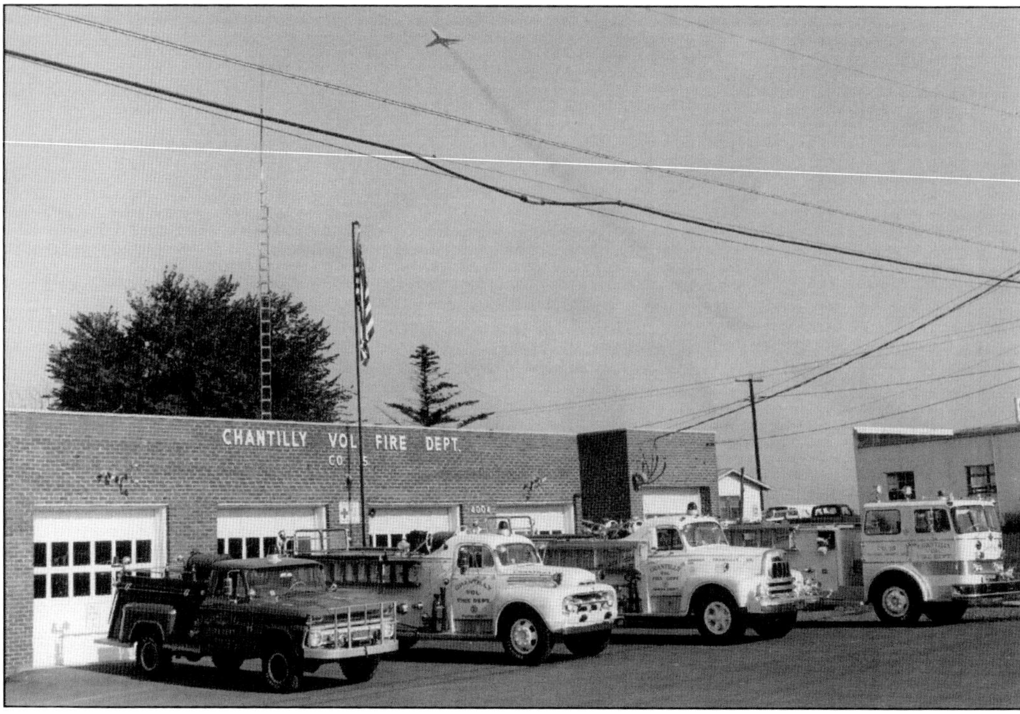

In January 1947, the Chantilly community met to organize a volunteer fire company. The family of Harold Douglas Smith donated a small lot for a firehouse. The company borrowed $5,500 from the Citizens National Bank of Herndon to construct the building and paid for the loan through suppers, dances, and "donkey basketball games." Dallas Porter Hutchison was the first paid fireman in Chantilly. The Chantilly Volunteer Fire Department Ladies Auxiliary worked to buy the new fire truck pictured above on the right. The auxiliary members put on carnivals and made food like hot dogs, hamburgers, popcorn, and cookies. (Both, courtesy of the Fairfax County Public Library Photographic Archive.)

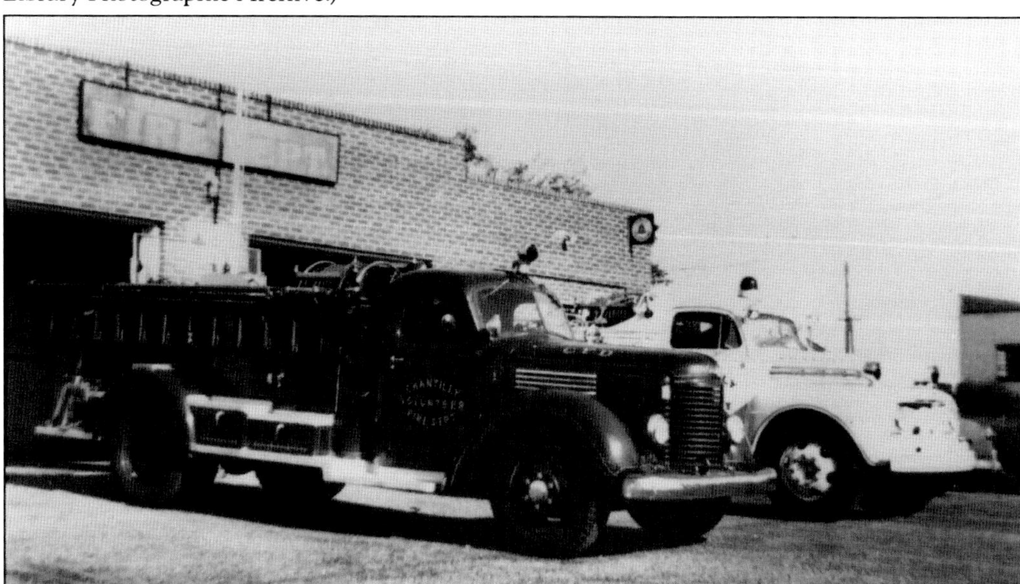

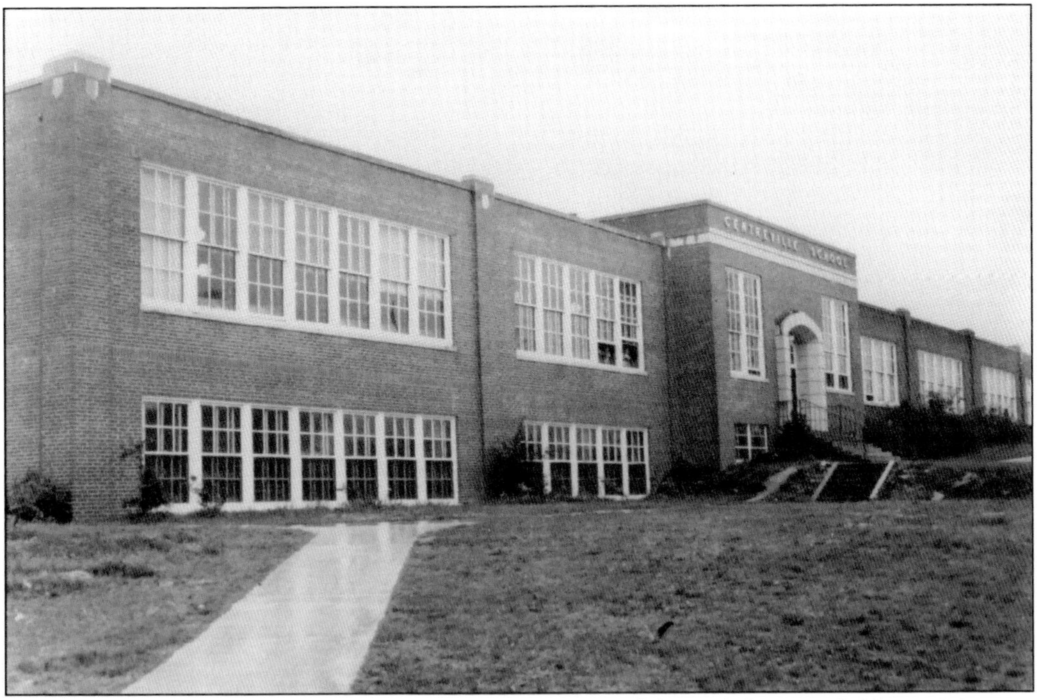

Pictured above is Centreville Elementary School in 1934, and shown below are children celebrating the school's 50th anniversary. (Both, courtesy of Centreville Elementary School.)

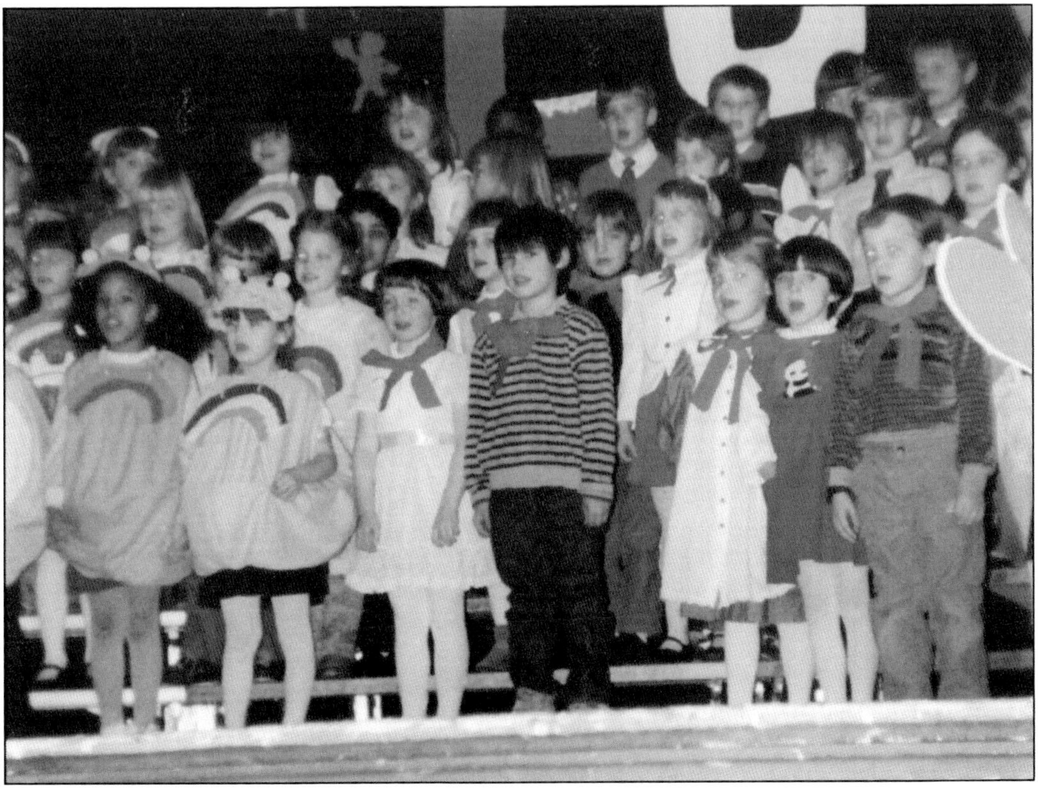

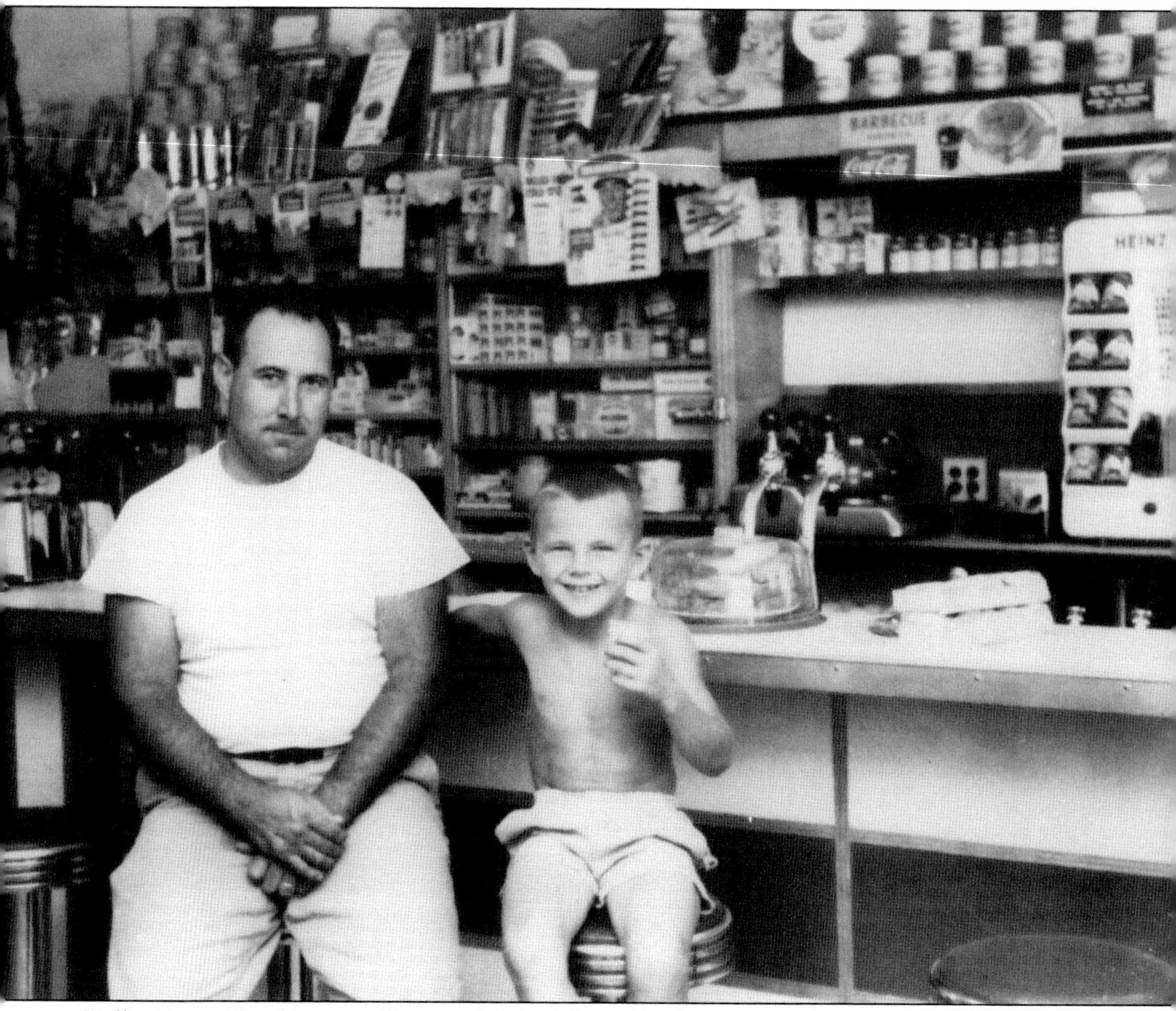

Dallas Porter Hutchison and his son Michael Page Hutchison sit at the Bywater Drugstore and Post Office lunch counter around 1958. The drugstore endured a small fire in December 1946. Shortly afterwards, the community organized a volunteer fire company. (Courtesy of the Fairfax County Public Library Photographic Archive.)

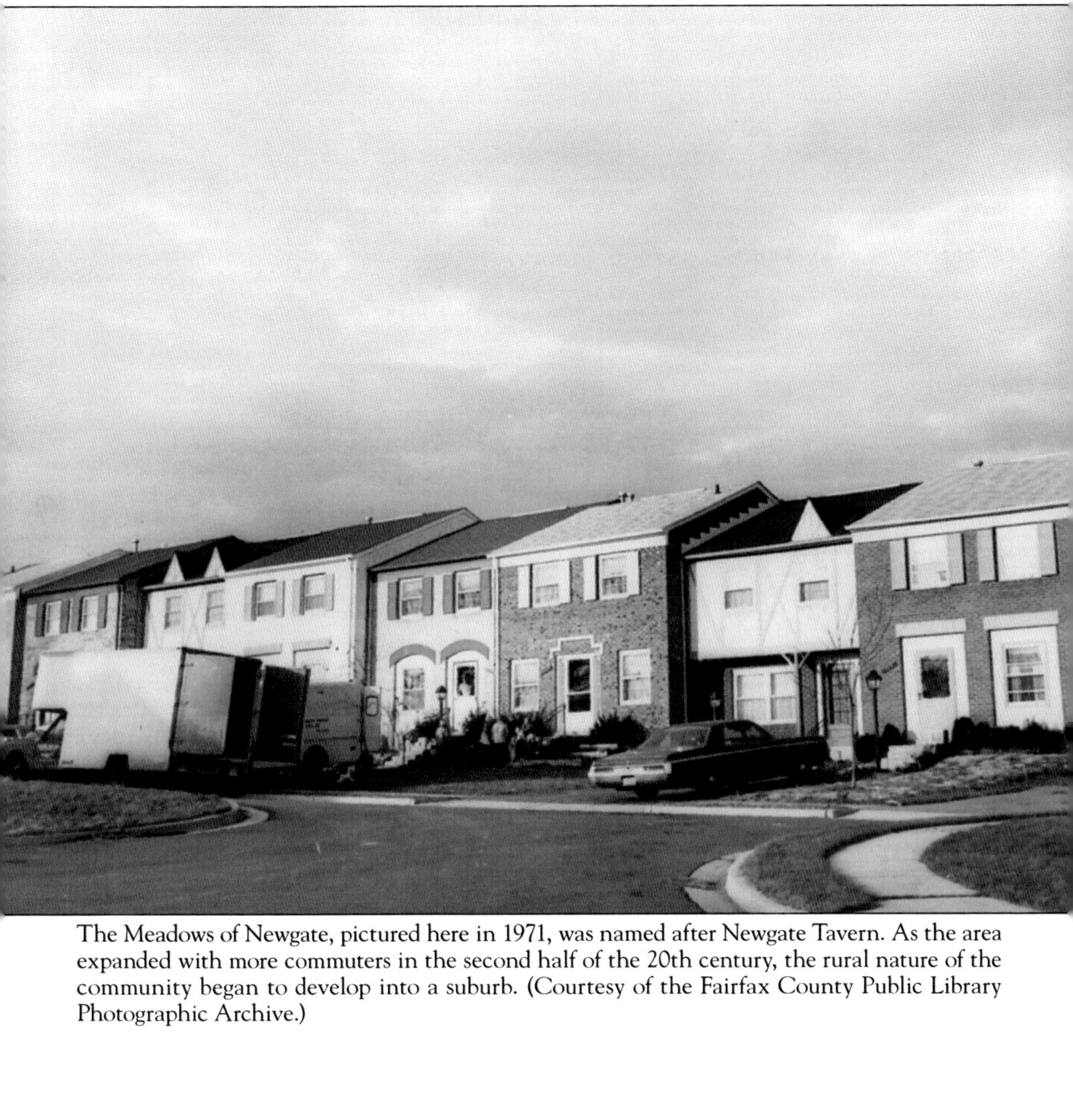

The Meadows of Newgate, pictured here in 1971, was named after Newgate Tavern. As the area expanded with more commuters in the second half of the 20th century, the rural nature of the community began to develop into a suburb. (Courtesy of the Fairfax County Public Library Photographic Archive.)

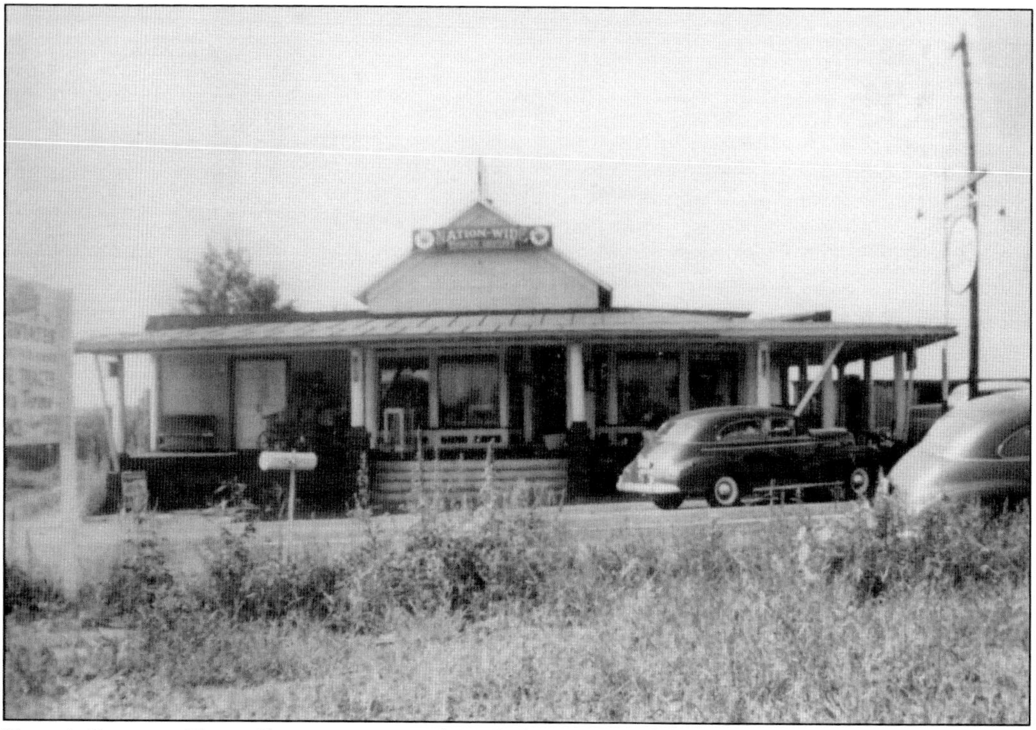

Down's Store in Chantilly is seen around 1945. (Courtesy of the Fairfax County Public Library Photographic Archive.)

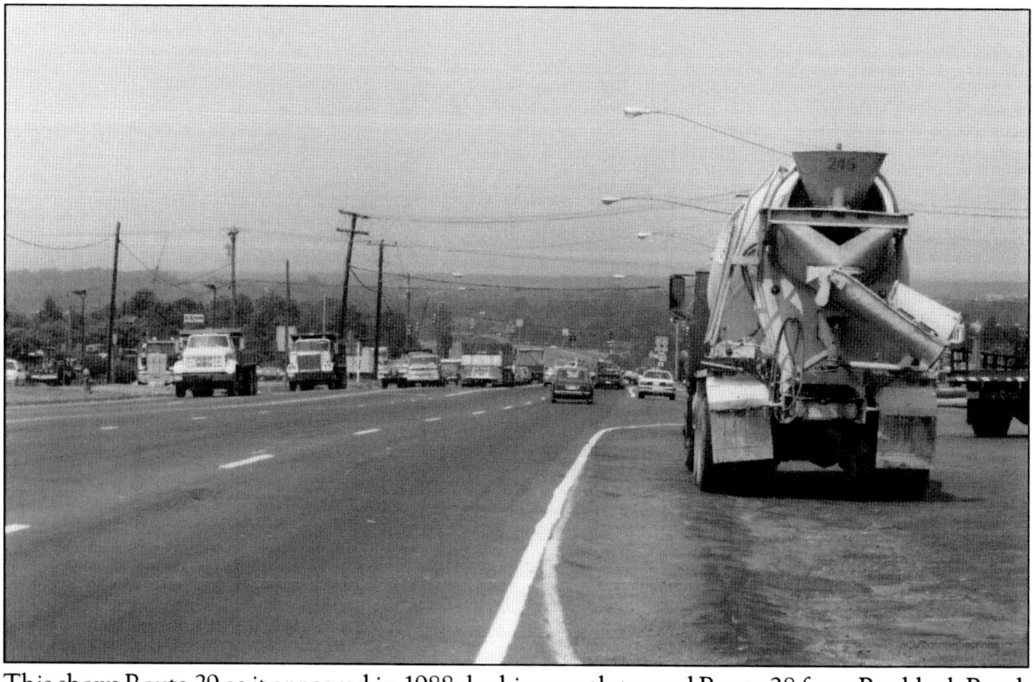

This shows Route 29 as it appeared in 1988, looking south toward Route 28 from Braddock Road. The area grew tremendously in the late 1980s and early 1990s, as more jobs came to Fairfax County. (Courtesy of the Fairfax County Public Library Photographic Archive.)

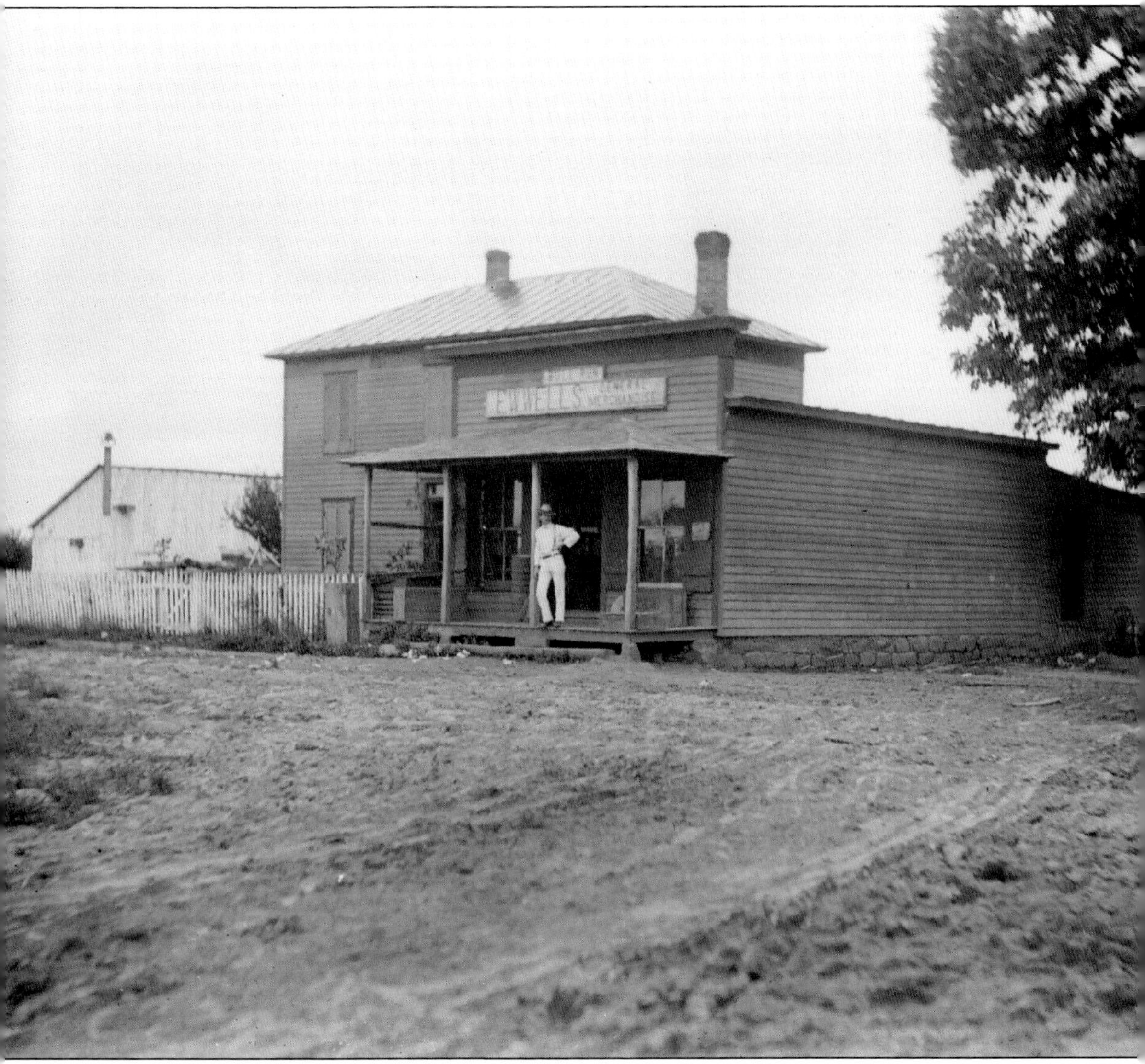

The Wells family used to run a small store (pictured here) near the present-day quarry on Lee Highway. Daisy and J.R. Wells, along with William and Henrietta Griffin, leased their land to Fairfax County for a quarry in 1928. The quarry continues operations to this day and is now known as the Luck Stone Quarry. (Courtesy of the Library of Congress.)

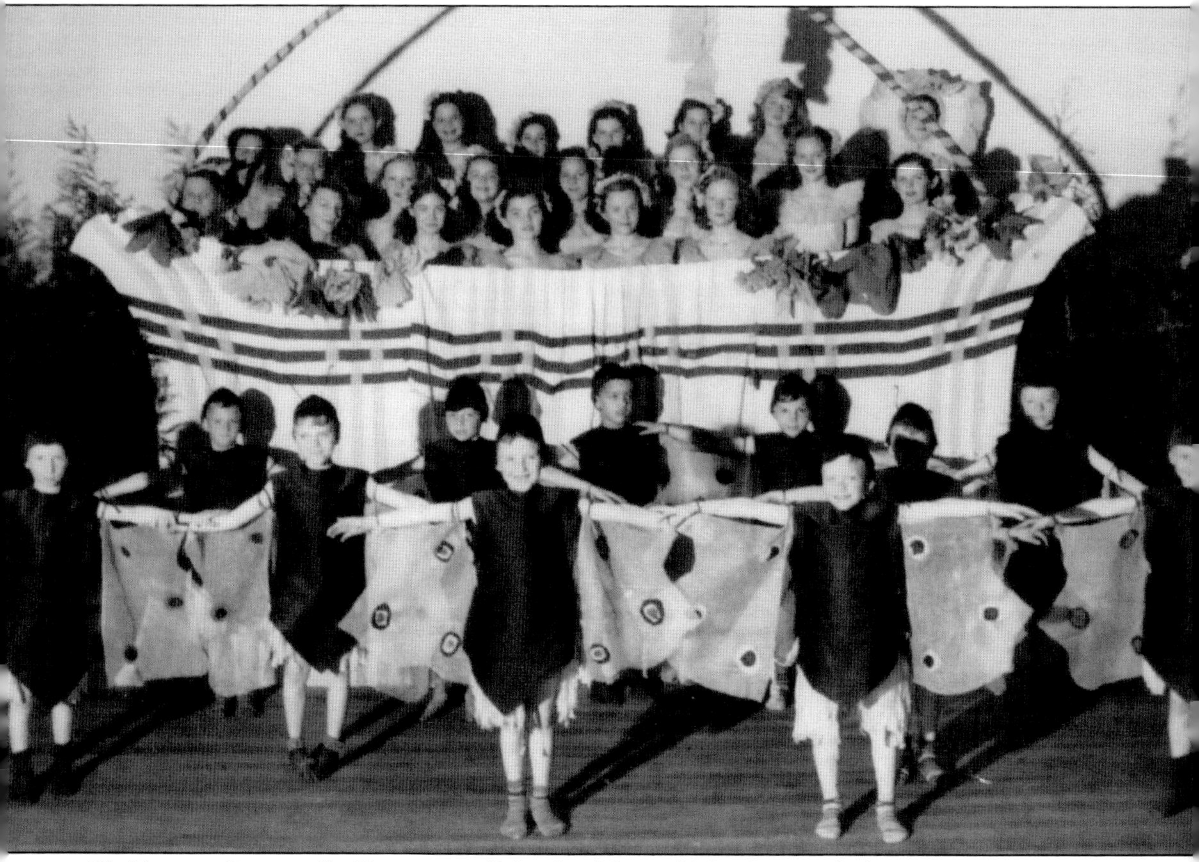

Children at Centreville Elementary School celebrated May Day with festivities in 1948. The event was a yearly tradition for the children, as with many other schools. (Courtesy of Centreville Elementary School.)

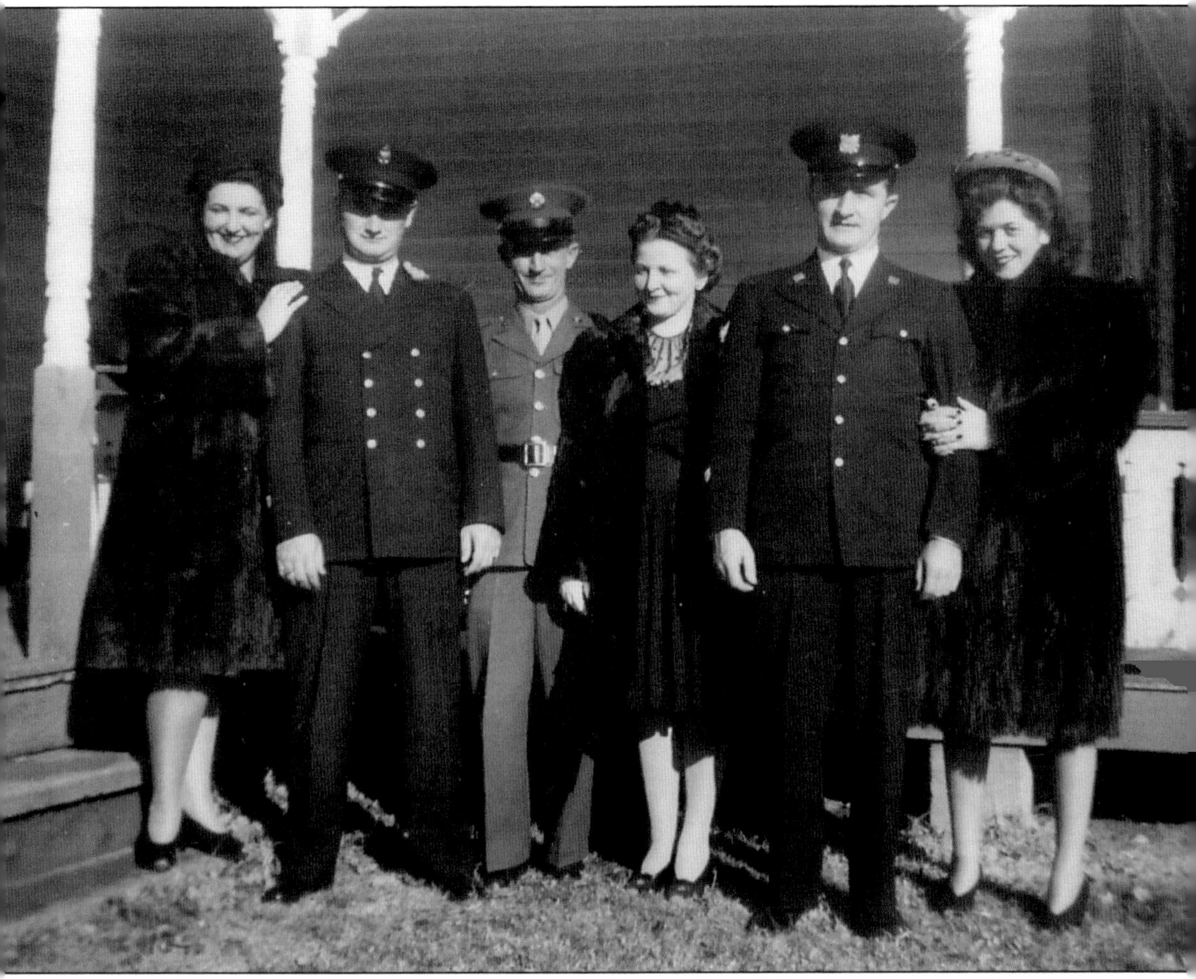

This picture was taken at the J.R. and Daisy Wells home at Bull Run in about 1942. From left to right are Ruth Wells, Murray Wells, Malcolm Wells, Iva Fairfield Wells, Grafton "Tab" Wells, and Elizabeth Hawes Wells. Malcolm and Grafton were sons of J.R. and Daisy Wells. Murray Wells was their cousin. (Courtesy of the Wells family and Lee Hubbard.)

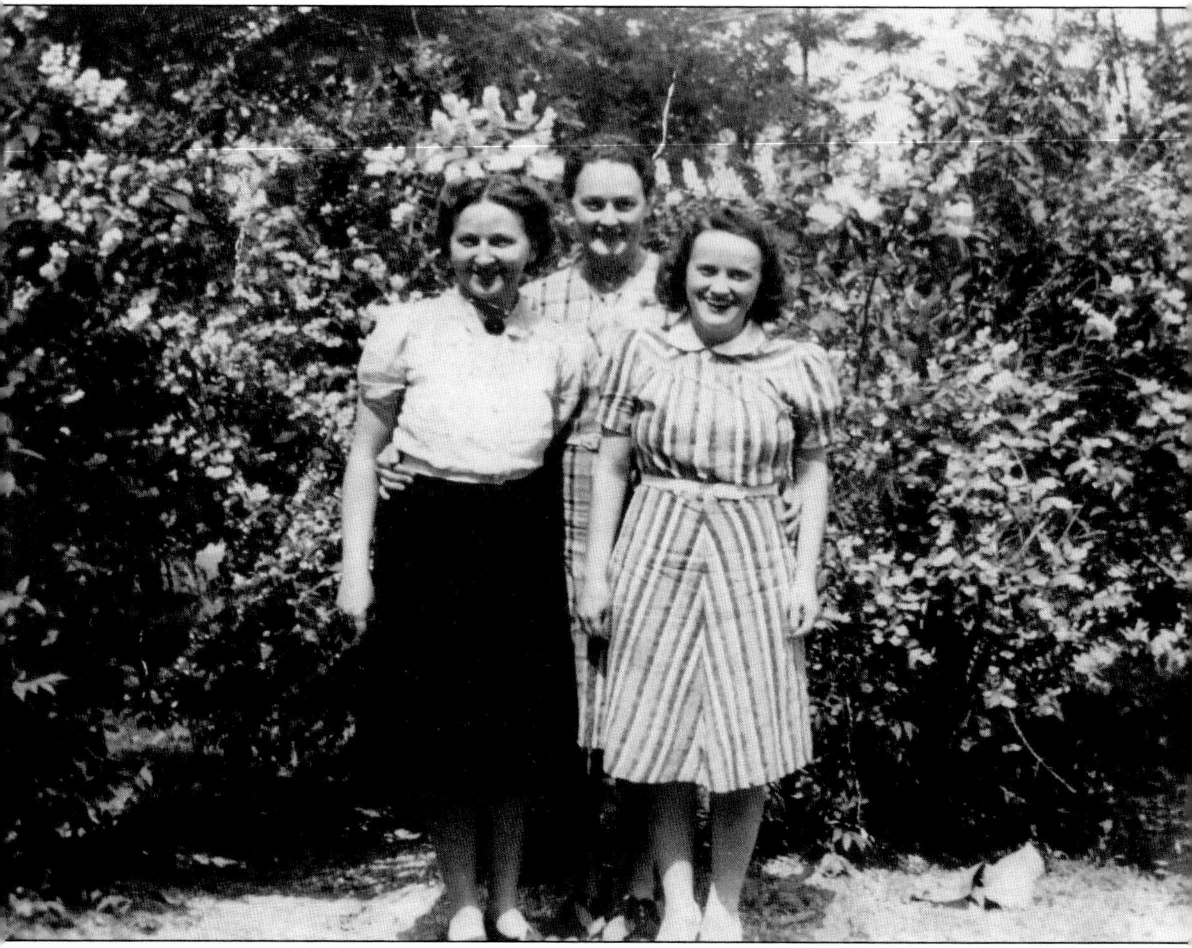

Pictured from left to right, Iva Wells, Ethel Carter, and Helen Buckley were teachers. Ethel Carter later became the supervisor for elementary education on the Fairfax County School Board. (Courtesy of the Wells family and Lee Hubbard.)

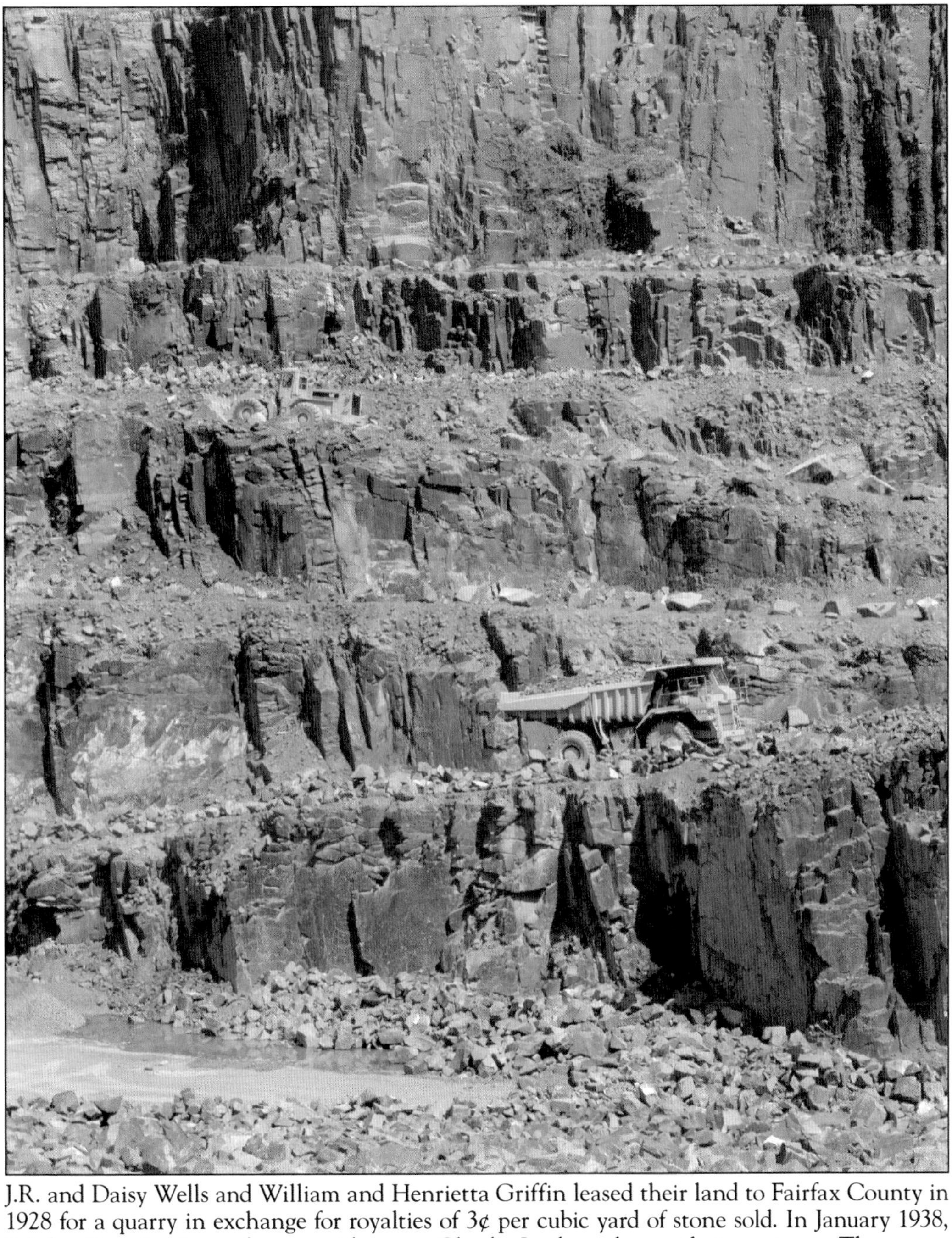

J.R. and Daisy Wells and William and Henrietta Griffin leased their land to Fairfax County in 1928 for a quarry in exchange for royalties of 3¢ per cubic yard of stone sold. In January 1938, Fairfax Quarries, Inc., whose president was Charles Luck, took over their contracts. The quarry eventually became known as Luck Stone Quarry due to the decades-long management by the Luck family. (Courtesy of the Library of Congress.)

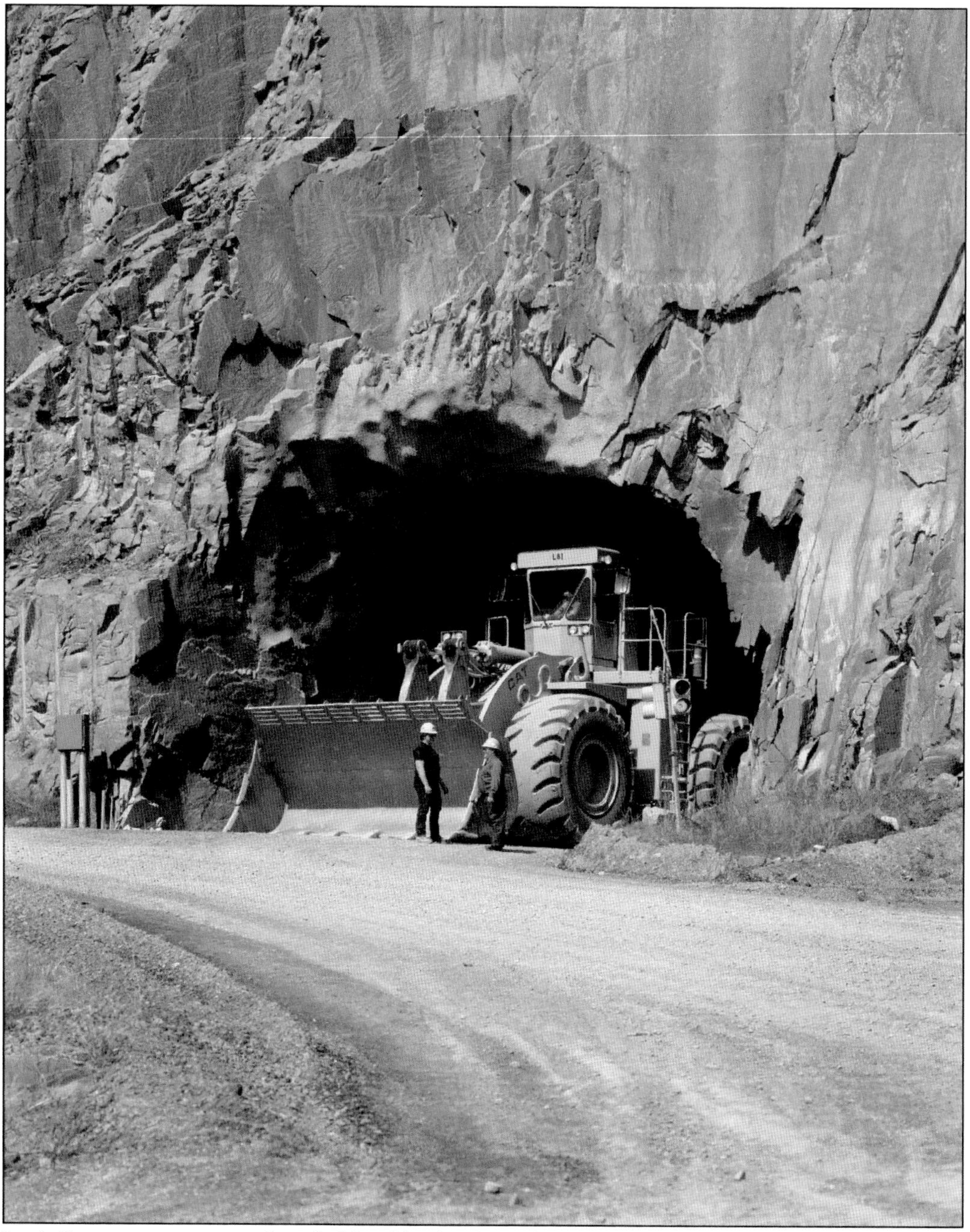

Luck Stone company was founded by Charles S. Luck Jr. as Fairfax Quarries, Inc., in 1923 and remains in operation today, under the third generation of family ownership. The company is headquartered in Richmond and operates several locations in Northern Virginia. (Courtesy of the Library of Congress.)

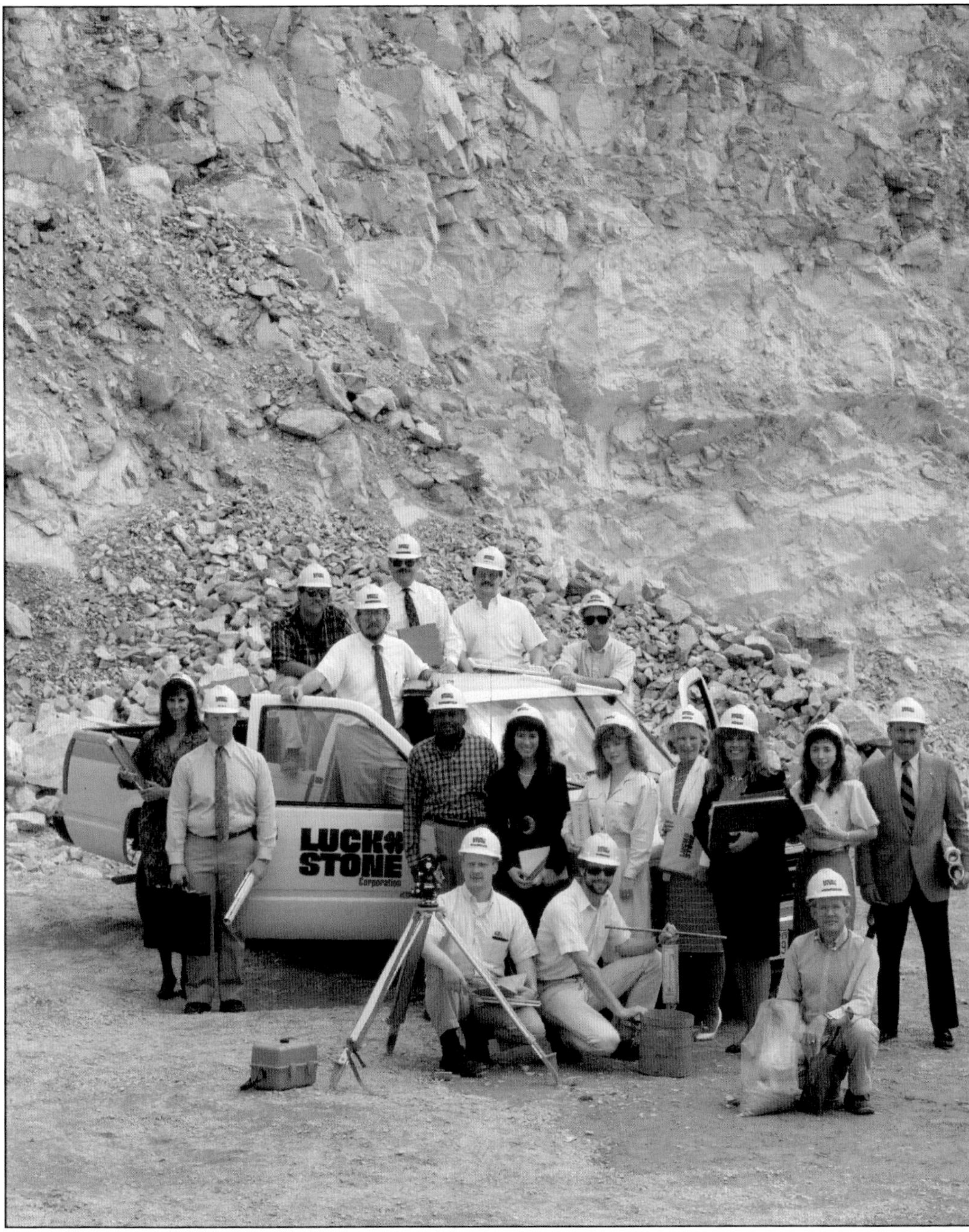

Luck Stone Quarry workers are pictured here sometime after 1980. Fairfax County sold its equipment in 1932 at a public auction, after responsibility for maintaining roads passed to the Commonwealth of Virginia. Earl W. Saum bought it for $1,287.05 and maintained the lease from the Wells family, before ownership of the quarry passed on to Fairfax Quarries. (Courtesy of the Library of Congress.)

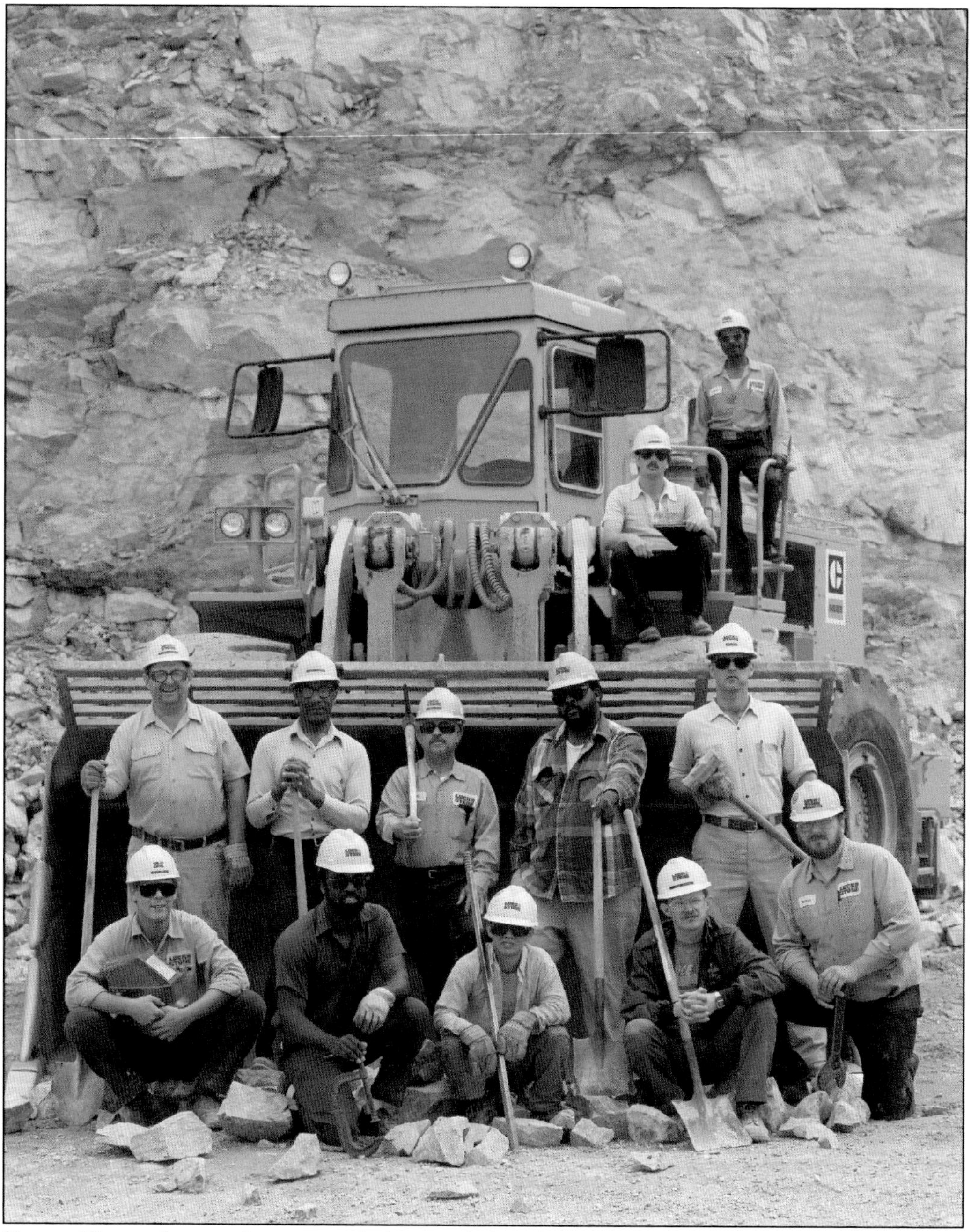

Over millions of years, the current diabase rock found in Luck Stone Quarry was formed. "This hard rock was found to be ideal as road bed material when Fairfax County was making a concerted effort to improve its muddy roads with gravel," Debbie Robison explained in her *Northern Virginia History Notes* blog. In 1928, the Fairfax County Board of Supervisors decided to open a quarry and leased the land from the Wells family, who owned it. (Courtesy of the Fairfax County Public Library Photographic Archive.)

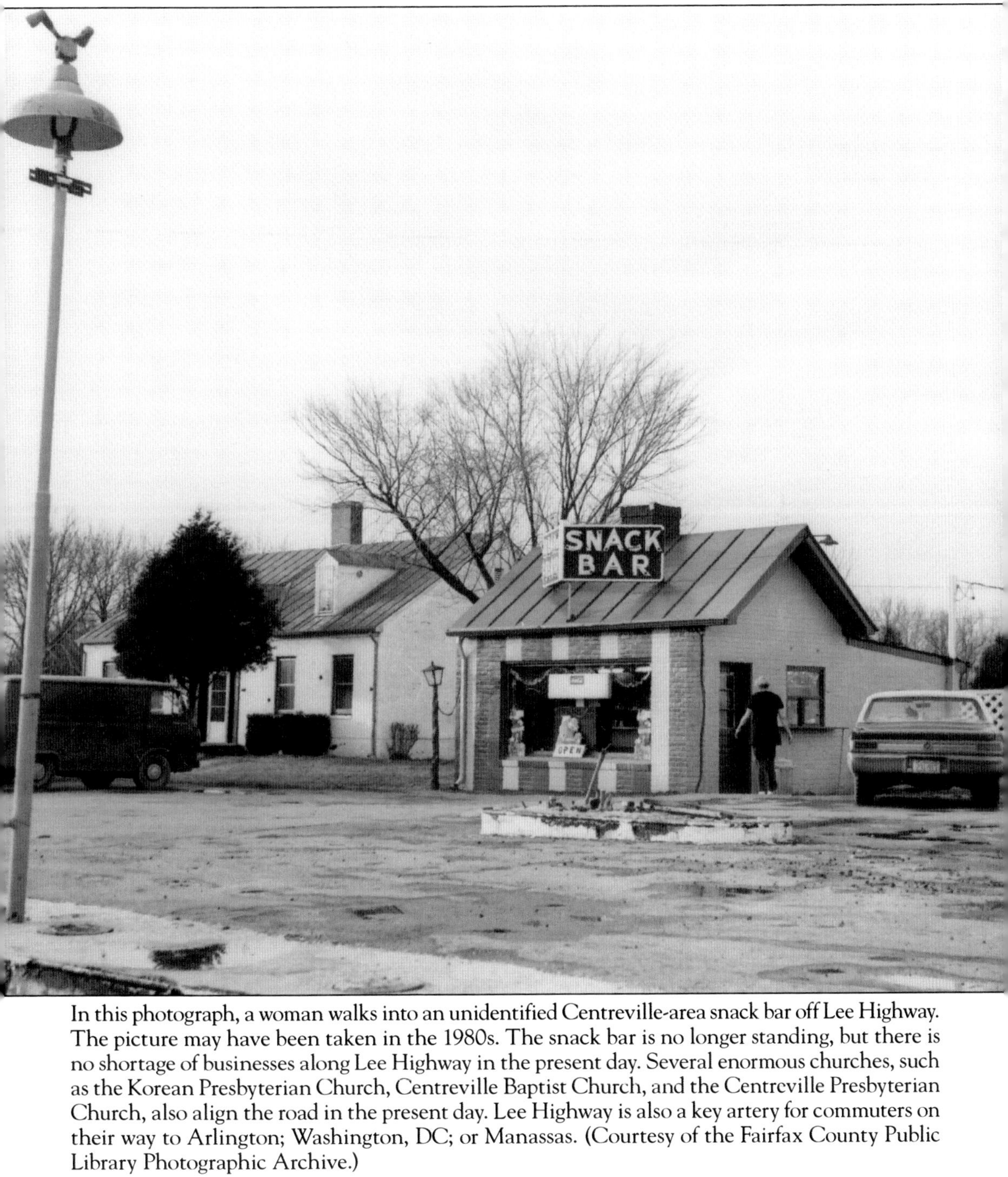

In this photograph, a woman walks into an unidentified Centreville-area snack bar off Lee Highway. The picture may have been taken in the 1980s. The snack bar is no longer standing, but there is no shortage of businesses along Lee Highway in the present day. Several enormous churches, such as the Korean Presbyterian Church, Centreville Baptist Church, and the Centreville Presbyterian Church, also align the road in the present day. Lee Highway is also a key artery for commuters on their way to Arlington; Washington, DC; or Manassas. (Courtesy of the Fairfax County Public Library Photographic Archive.)

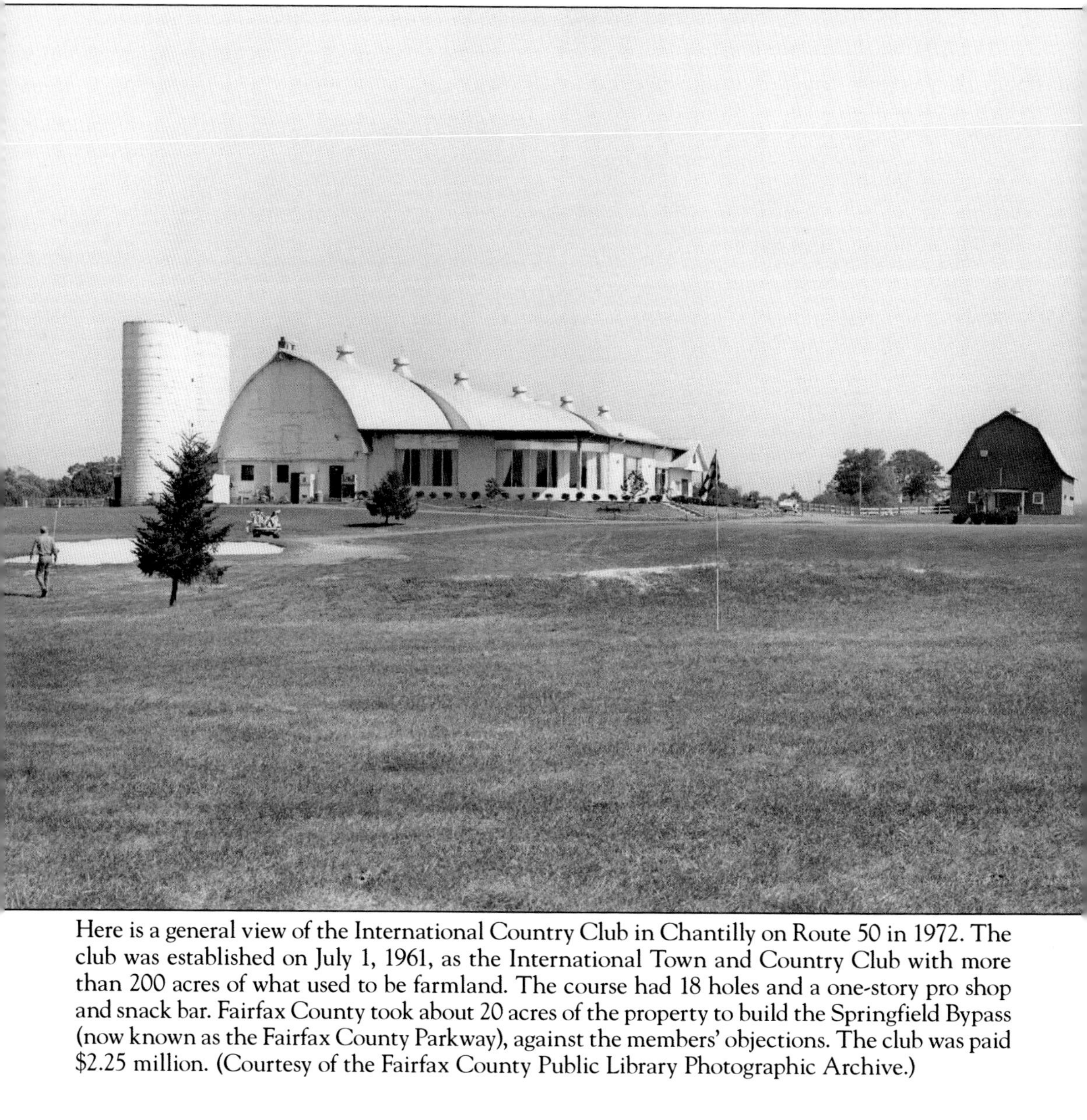

Here is a general view of the International Country Club in Chantilly on Route 50 in 1972. The club was established on July 1, 1961, as the International Town and Country Club with more than 200 acres of what used to be farmland. The course had 18 holes and a one-story pro shop and snack bar. Fairfax County took about 20 acres of the property to build the Springfield Bypass (now known as the Fairfax County Parkway), against the members' objections. The club was paid $2.25 million. (Courtesy of the Fairfax County Public Library Photographic Archive.)

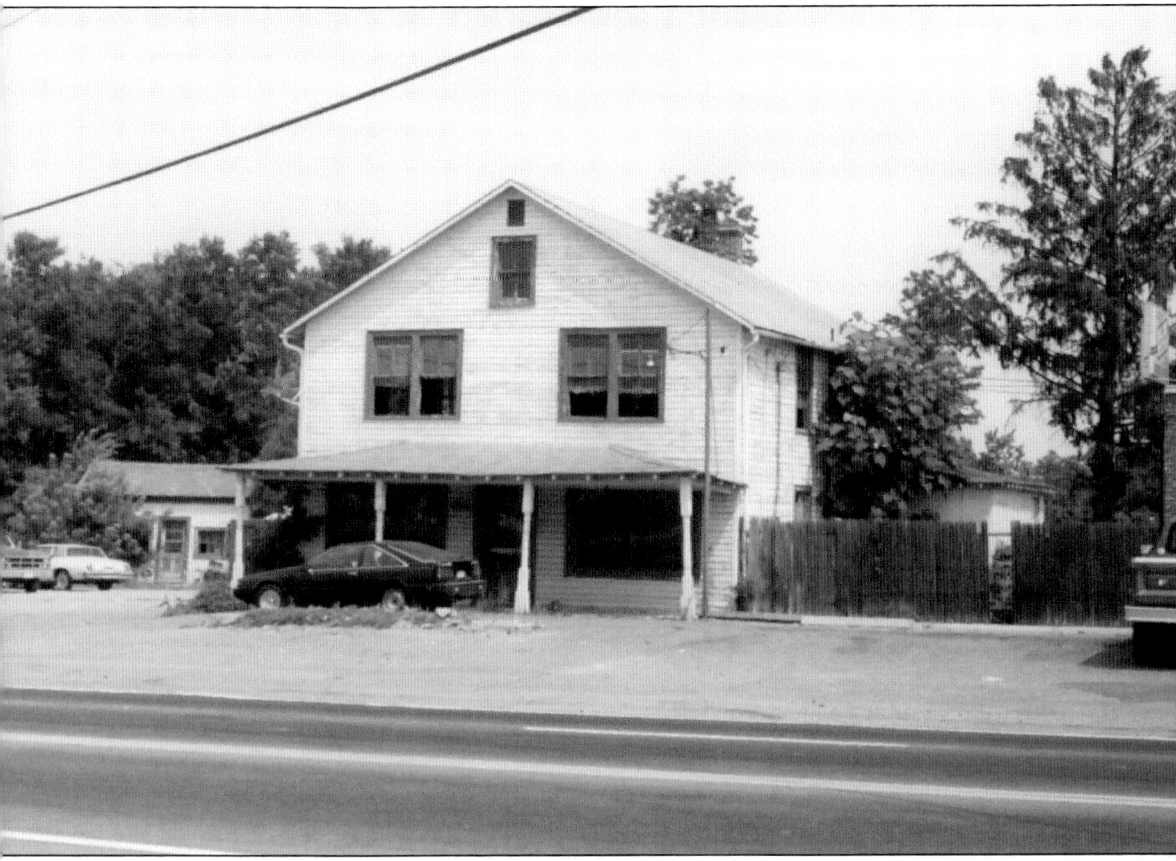

This was once Payne's General Store, one of three stores in Northern Virginia owned by Irvin Payne. The Centreville store was managed by Irvin's brother James, who lived with his family above the store. The building looks pretty beaten up in this photograph, but it has undergone substantial improvements and is now home to Jireh's Bakery Café. (Courtesy of the Fairfax County Public Library Photographic Archive.)

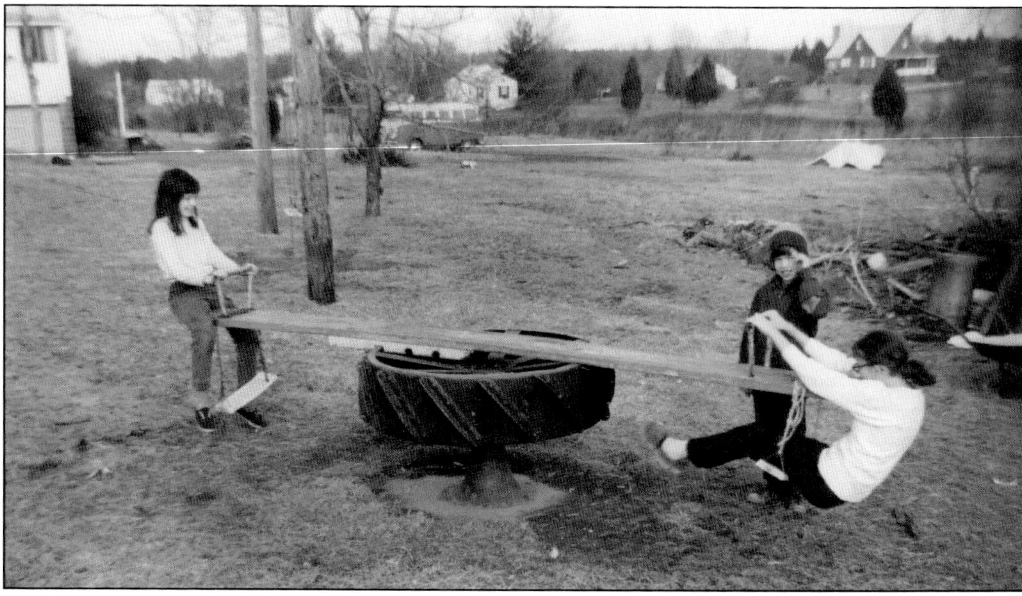

This photograph shows children playing in the 1970s in Chantilly. (Courtesy of the Fairfax County Photographic Archive.)

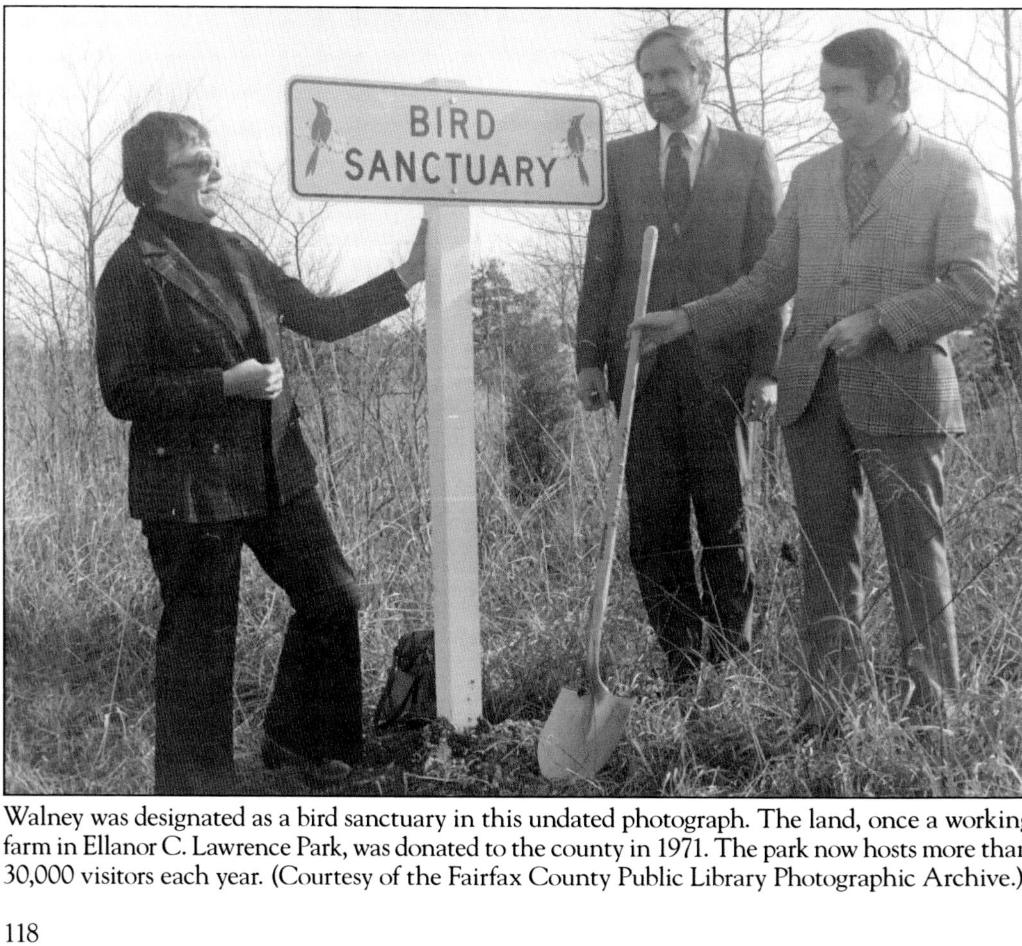

Walney was designated as a bird sanctuary in this undated photograph. The land, once a working farm in Ellanor C. Lawrence Park, was donated to the county in 1971. The park now hosts more than 30,000 visitors each year. (Courtesy of the Fairfax County Public Library Photographic Archive.)

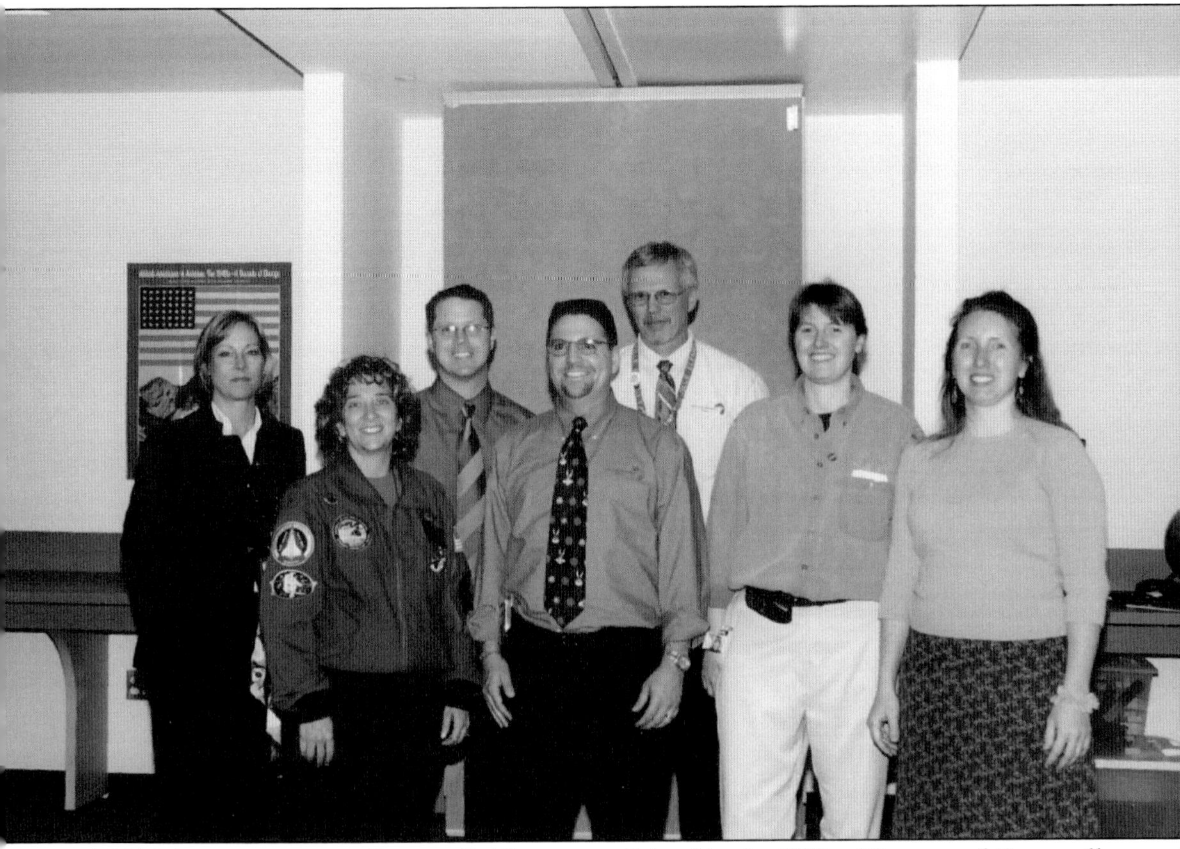

A NASA astronaut visits Centreville Elementary School in the 1980s. (Courtesy of Centreville Elementary School.)

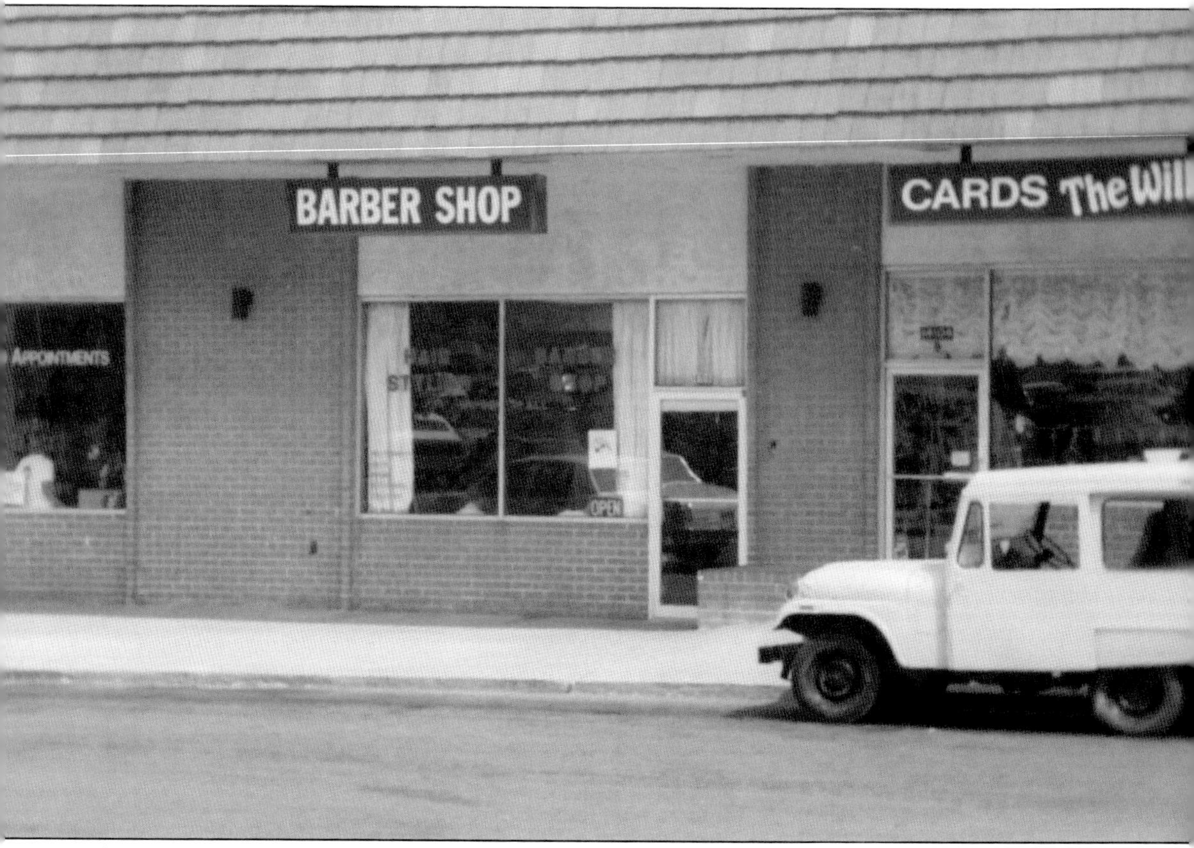

The Centreville Barbershop is pictured in this photograph. (Courtesy of the Fairfax County Public Library Photographic Archive.)

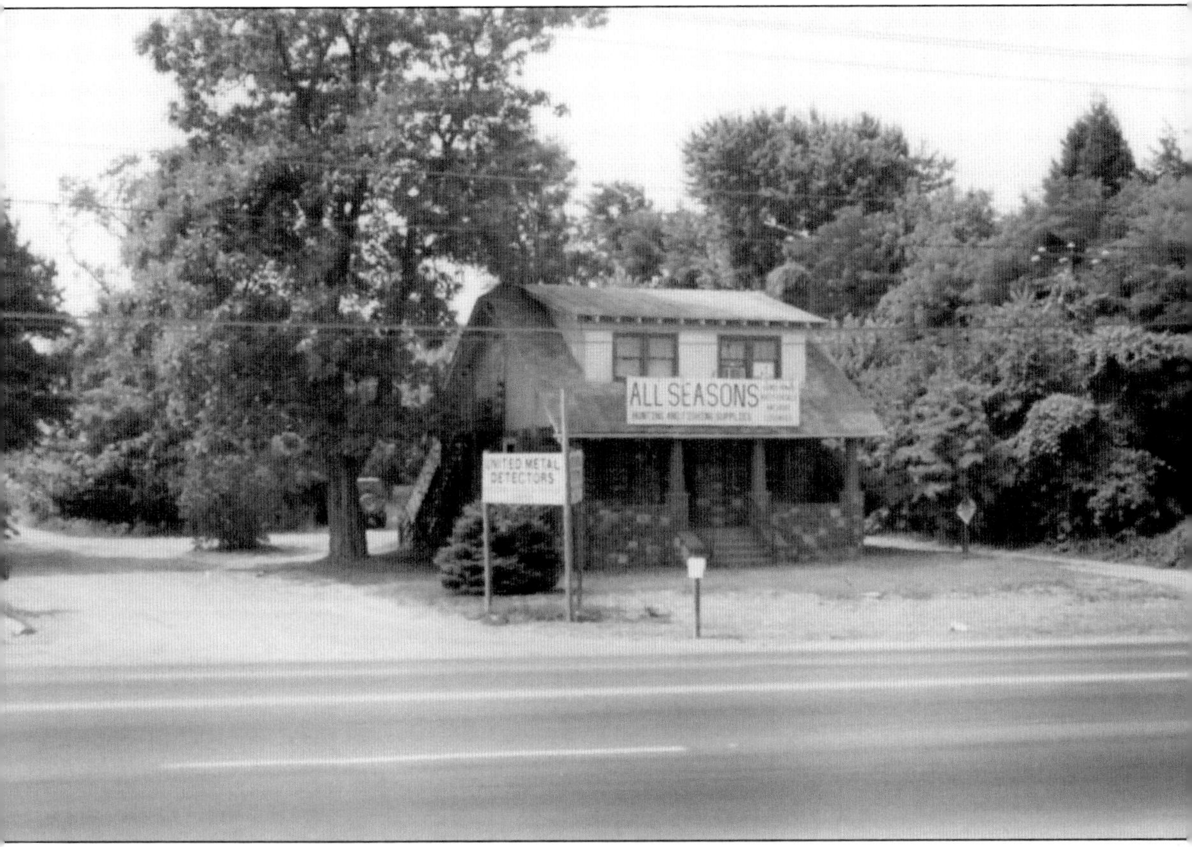

United Metal Detectors on Lee Highway is shown in this photograph from the 1980s. (Courtesy of the Fairfax County Public Library Photographic Archive.)

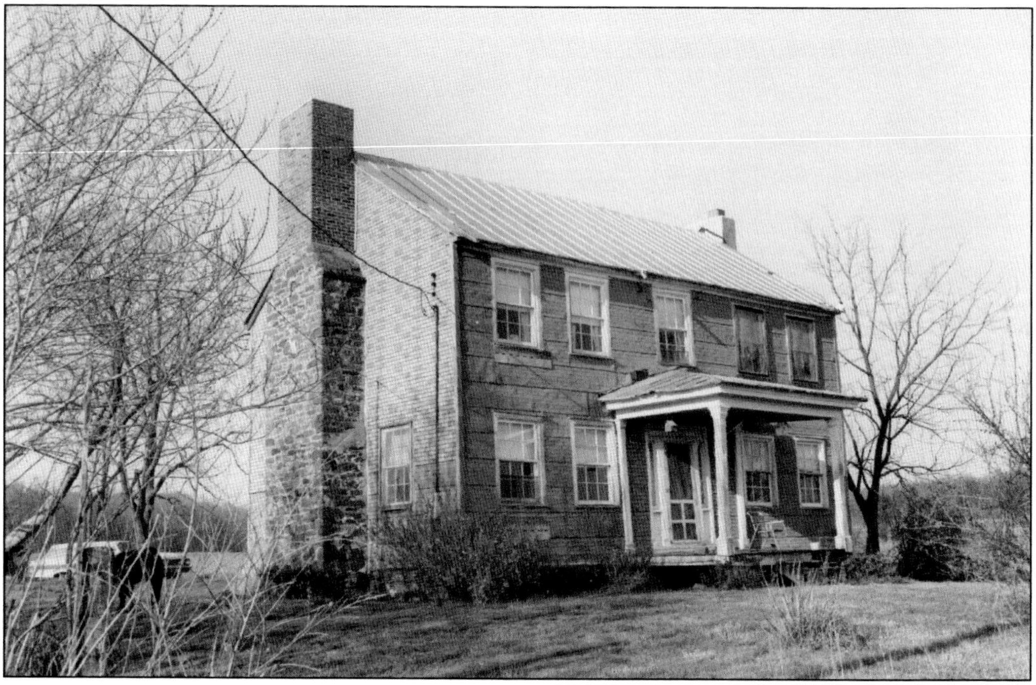

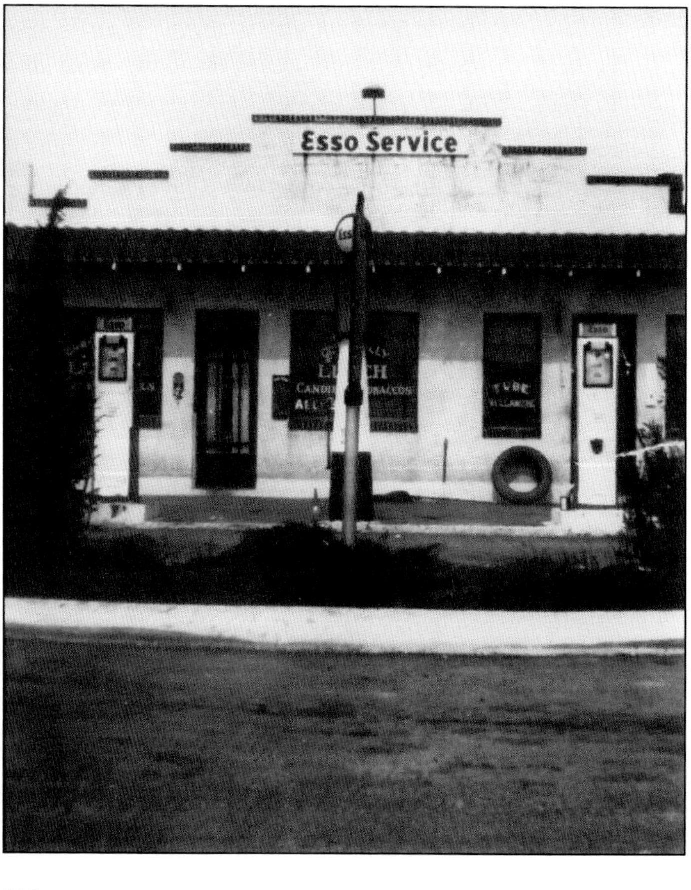

The Abner and Sam Wrenn House in Chantilly is pictured around 1973. (Courtesy of the Fairfax County Public Library Photographic Archive.)

Becker's Esso station and Jenkins Lunch Room at the 14000 block of Lee-Jackson Highway in Chantilly are seen here. (Courtesy of the Fairfax County Public Library Photographic Archive.)

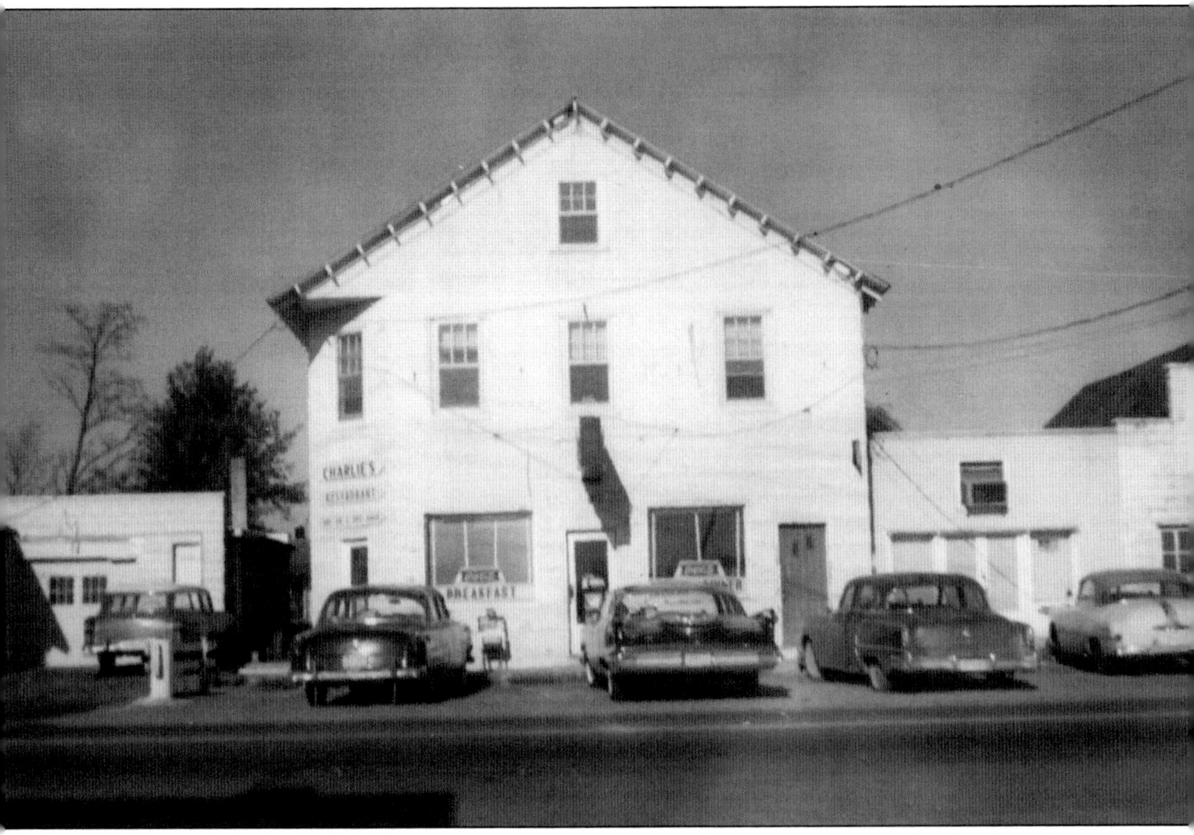

The rear of Chantilly Inn Restaurant is shown around 1961. (Courtesy of the Fairfax County Public Library Photographic Archive.)

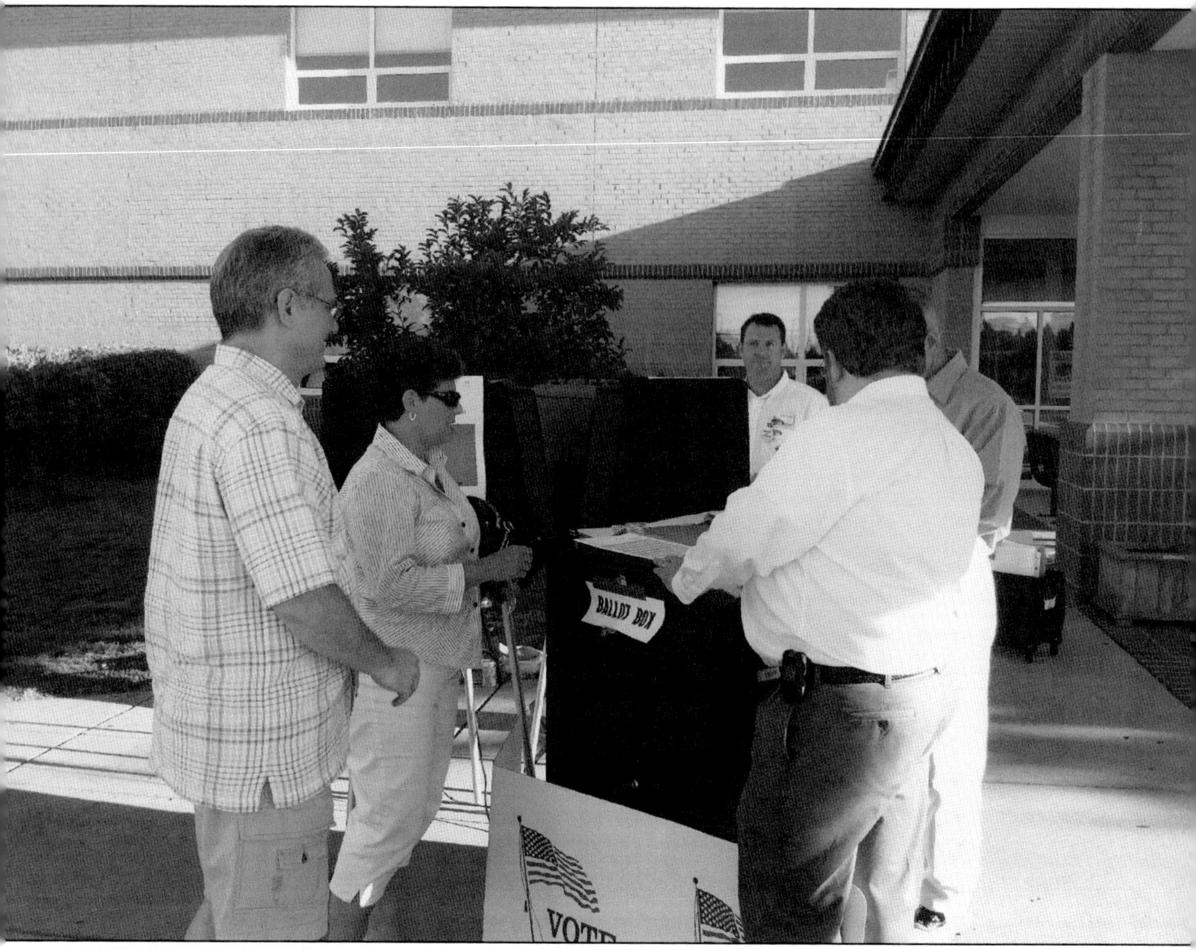

Talk about rocking the vote—after a rare, 5.9-magnitude earthquake hit Centreville on August 23, 2011, primary election day, there were fears that Bull Run Elementary School was damaged. Elected officials were forced to scoop up electronic voting machines and paper ballots and carry them outside, cords dangling. Voters cast their ballots outside, in warm, sunny weather. (Author's collection.)

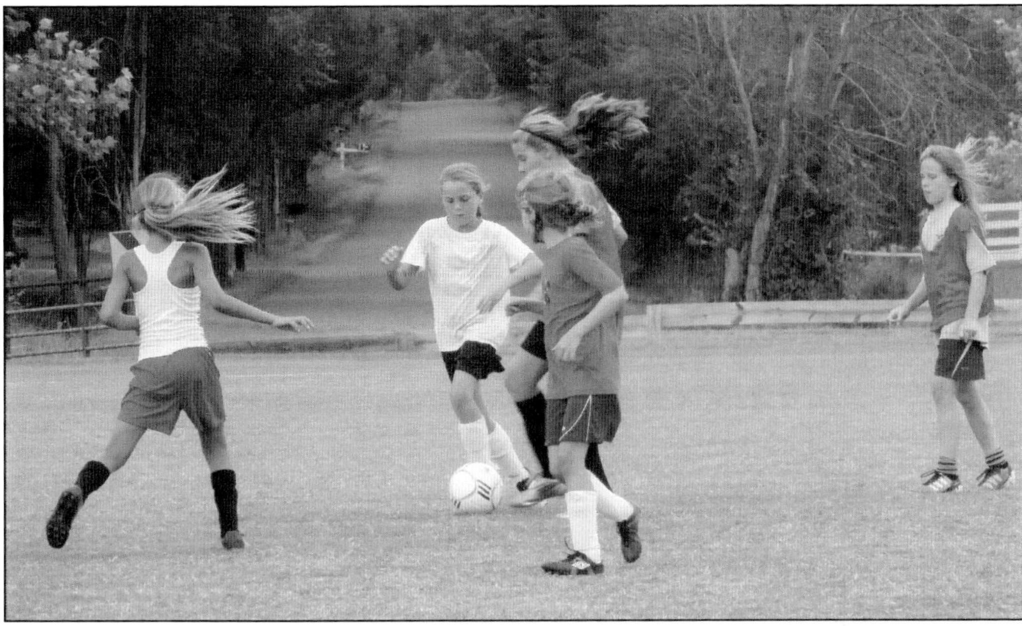

The Southwestern Youth Association was created in 1973 with a $1,500 donation from Carl Mullins, its founder. The group has since grown to serve more than 13,000 children and over 5,000 families in the Centreville and Clifton area in the present day. In 1998, the group purchased 120 acres off Bull Run Post Office Road to form a sports park—complete with hiking, horse, and cross-country trails, in addition to playing fields—that is next to Manassas National Battlefield. (Author's collection.)

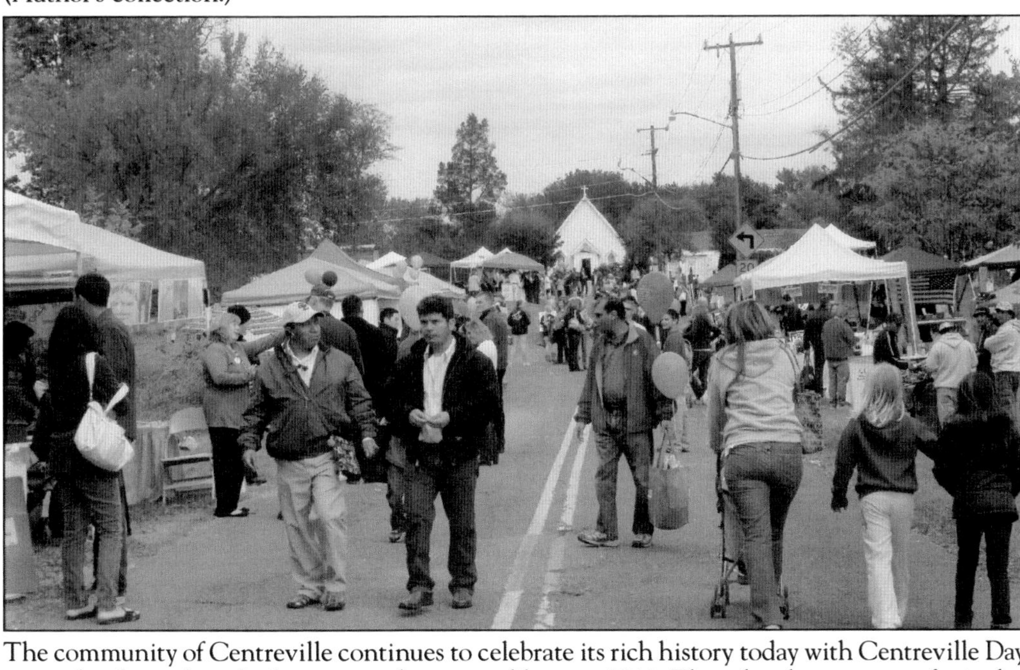

The community of Centreville continues to celebrate its rich history today with Centreville Day, a one-day festival in the historic park, pictured here in 2011. There has been a town festival of some sort almost every year in Centreville since the early 1900s. In May 2012, the first annual Chantilly Day was also instituted to much success. (Author's collection.)

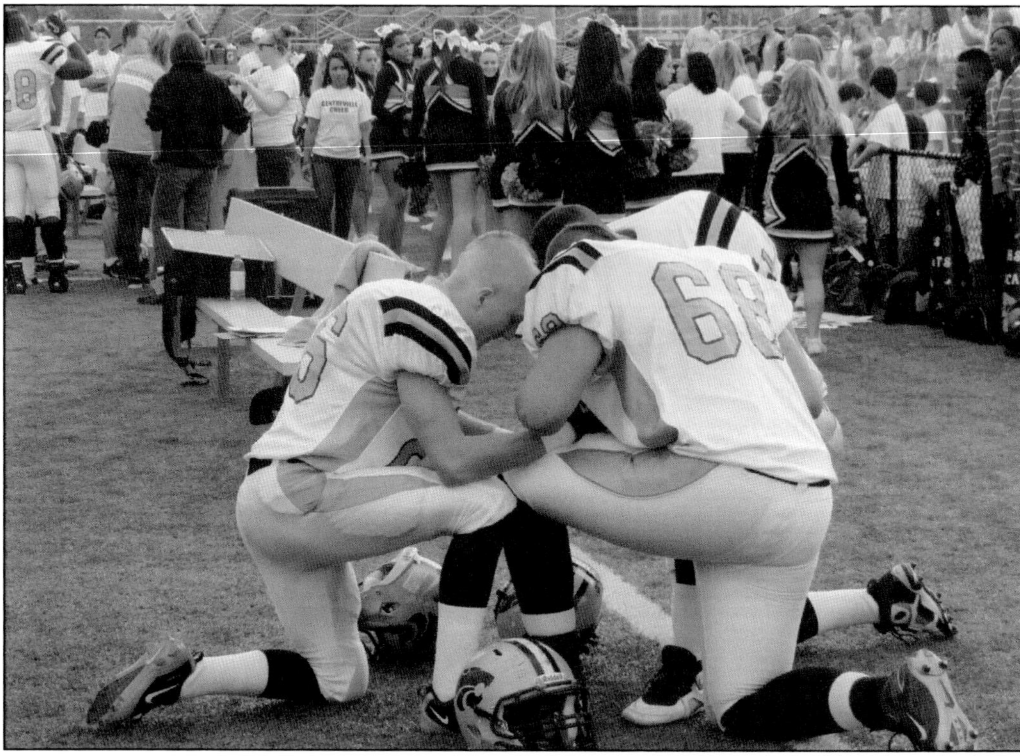

Football is the center of community life in Centreville and Chantilly during the fall season. Thousands of fans regularly show up at the Centreville and Westfield high school stadiums to cheer on their teams. The annual showdown between the Bulldogs and the Wildcats has been a center point of friendly rivalry between the two schools ever since Westfield first opened in September 2000. Many of the players on the Westfield team have grown up playing youth sports with the players on the Centreville team. Above, Wildcat players share a prayer before the game in October 2011; below, Westfield fans turn out to show their support for their team at the same game.

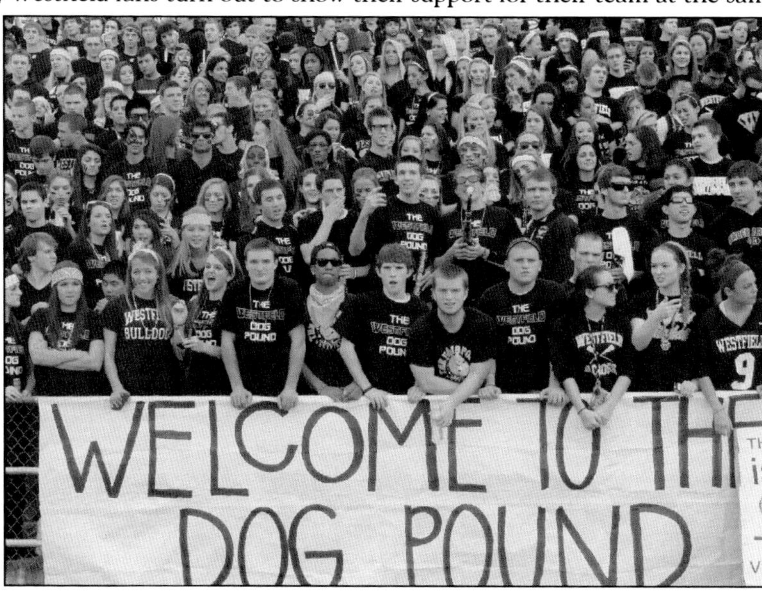

BIBLIOGRAPHY

Gamble, Robert S. *Sully: The Biography of a House*. Chantilly, VA: Sully Foundation, LTD, 1973.

Hogge, Dennis. *Mathew Brady's Manassas Photo Journal: Exploring the First Battlefield of the American Civil War in Period Images*. Centreville, VA: Old Dominion Publishers, 2011.

Mauro, Chuck. *The Civil War in Fairfax County: Civilians and Soldiers*. Charleston, SC: History Press, 2008.

Myer, Phil. "History of International Country Club, 1961–2011." www.internationalcc.com.

Smith, Eugenia B. *Centreville, Virginia: Its History and Architecture*. Fairfax, VA: Heritage Resources, 1973.

Voices of Chantilly: Recollections and Stories from 22 Long-time Residents. Floris, VA: Floris Friends, 1996.

www.fairfaxcounty.gov

www.novahistory.org